A FLORA OF NOTTINGHAMSHIRE

A FLORA

OF

NOTTINGHAMSHIRE

by

R. C. L. HOWITT

AND

B. M. HOWITT

PUBLISHED
PRIVATELY
1963

FHem

Printed by
DERRY AND SONS LIMITED
NOTTINGHAM

PREFACE

The last flora of Nottinghamshire was written in 1839 by Godfrey Howitt. He was about to emigrate to Australia and had hastily to compress his knowledge into a very small compass. Since then attempts to write a new flora have met with even less success. There have been various efforts, culminating in the writing of Professor J. W. Carr's Manuscript Flora in the first half or quarter of this century; but nothing has been published.

As this is a highly developed industrial and agricultural county, possessing little wild land, the changes in plant habitats have been enormous, and it is obviously time that a new work was undertaken. Many friends have urged us on, and we ourselves feel that our results should now be published; before they in their turn become out of date. This has necessitated leaving some of the critical genera, notably *Rubus*, underworked, but it seemed folly to delay further.

Our own records in this Flora are based on a completely new survey of the county which has extended over the past eleven years. In the course of this most enjoyable work we have visited every parish in the county, learnt about many things besides plants, and received great kindness from strangers. Our assessment of the frequency of species is based on lists of plants, both typical and rare, which we have compiled in a manuscript 'Day Book'. We have also collected a Nottinghamshire herbarium, with particular emphasis on critical species. Most woods, except some of the larger areas on the Forest, have been thoroughly worked. Old quarries, railway banks, roadsides, rough ground, dumps and other likely places have been visited.

In dealing with old records we have not had such a formidable task as some writers of county floras, the published records on Notts. are few. A difficulty has been to fit some of the older records into the structure of divisions which has been adopted, some of the old localities, i.e. Basford Scottum, lying neatly in two divisions. We have tried to adopt a common sense approach, placing the plant in the division where it would most naturally be found.

In conclusion we would like to thank all those landowners both large and small, who have most kindly allowed us to explore their property, and often taken a keen interest in our proceedings. In the whole county we have had only one refusal from an owner of any standing. We also thank the University of Nottingham for most generously allowing us to incorporate all that we required from the late Professor J. W. Carr's Manuscript Flora, and Dr. R. W. Butcher for placing his records and knowledge of the county ungrudgingly at our disposal. Besides these there are many people who have helped by identifying critical plants, looking for old records, supplying information on old botanists and on the county in general, to whom we acknowledge a great debt; G. O. Allen, the late A. G. H. Alston, the late G. M. Ash, E. B. Bangerter, R. M. Beaumont, Boots Pure Drug Co. Ltd., J. P. M. Brenan, J. Brown of Sheffield, R. K. Brummitt, J. E. Dandy, Miss U. K. Duncan, E. S. Edees, the Forestry Commission and W. V. Jackson, the Gilstrap Library, Newark, with A. Smith, J. K. Mealor and their staff, Miss E. J. Gibbons, the late R. A. Graham, Mr. and Mrs. P. C. Hall, W. O. Howarth, P. A. Kennedy, C. E. Hubbard, the Leicester Museum and Library, the Lincoln City Library and Museum and F. T. Baker, J. E. Lousley, E. Marsden Jones, R. D. Meikle, A. Melderis, R. Melville, E. Milne Redhead, the late A. E. Nelmes, the Nottingham City Library, the Nottingham Natural History Museum, the Nottinghamshire County Library, R. M. Payne, F. H. Perring, P. W. Richards, the Royal Botanic Gardens and National Herbarium Victoria, Australia, N. Y. Sandwith, J. P. Savidge, P. Sell, N. D. Simpson, W. A. Sledge, V. S. Summerhayes, H. H. Swinnerton, Sir George Taylor, the Trent Valley Bird Watchers, T. G. Tutin, D. H. Valentine, A. E. Wade, F. C. Wallace, S. M. Walters, E. F. Warburg, C. West, the late A. J. Wilmott, Miss N. Witham, D. P. Young. The boundaries of the botanical divisions are adapted from the map in the Victoria County History by courtesy of Messrs. John Bartholomew and Son Limited. Finally it is a pleasure to acknowledge the unfailing helpfulness, goodwill and patience of Mr. N. Barker and the staff of Derry and Sons Ltd.

R. C. L. HOWITT
B. M. HOWITT

Farndon 1963

CONTENTS

INTRODUCTION

Nottinghamshire

Nottinghamshire might almost be called the average English county. There are about twenty-five counties larger; twenty-five smaller; it lies in the Midlands, although in the North Midlands; its scenery is quiet, undulating and unexceptional, a gentle descent between the Pennines and the Fens. To the north lie industrial regions; west Nottinghamshire is heavily industrialised. To the South and East are the farm lands of East Anglia and the Shires, to which South east Nottinghamshire is much akin. There is nothing spectacular, no mountains or torrents, no seaboard, no natural lakes. Nevertheless there are scenes of great charm. The sweep of the Trent flowing across its wide plain towards spacious blue distances; some secluded corners of the Sherwood Forest; even the imposing modern industrial landscapes, and the homely early mills, are all memorable. All these different scenes have their typical flora, and the contrasts are perhaps more enjoyable because they are not immediately obvious.

Bounded by Leicestershire, Lincolnshire, Yorkshire and Derbyshire, the county is squashed egg shape. It is 51 miles long from Six Hills in the South to its apex at Finningley in the North, and 27 miles wide at its greatest width on a line close to Selston and Newark. Its area is 844 square miles.

The higher ground is in the west where 651 ft. is reached near Hucknall-under-Huthwaite. The levels fall gently to the east, the Carrs in the extreme north east only reaching 5 to 20 ft. Two fifths of the county is below 100 ft. The countryside is rolling, being crossed by a series of low scarps, generally running North and South. Their dip slopes are often further broken by the valleys of small streams. Across this system lies the trough of the Trent Valley.

The county is dominated by its River. Entering from Derbyshire just above its confluence with the Erewash, the Trent flows past Nottingham and north east to Newark. Here it turns sharply north and continues the length of the eastern side of the county, until reaching the boundary at Hecdyke. From ancient times it has been an important waterway. Later the development of the Nottinghamshire Coalfield and industries were given impetus by easy water transport on the Trent. There is still a large water borne traffic, particularly in petrol.

The whole of the county is drained by the River Trent, except for parts of four parishes east of Newark which fall to the Witham, and a few acres at Teversall which drain to the Don. On the East bank the Soar rises in Leicestershire and forms the county boundary until its junction with the Trent. It is a slow stream meandering through a wide valley, and may show in miniature how the Trent looked before it became polluted and its valley industrialised. The Devon, with its tributary the Smite, rise in the Belvoir hills and join the Trent at Newark. They are now very artificial streams, the firm bottom having been removed for drainage, and the level of the Devon so lowered as to impede its discharge into the Trent.

The West Bank tributaries are more numerous. The Erewash, forming the boundary with Derbyshire, and the Leen which disappears into a pipe at Nottingham, drain the industrial Permian and Coal measure region. The former is appallingly polluted, the latter only the shadow of the stream which watered the limestone marshes at Basford Scottum and Bulwell in Deering's and G. Howitt's times. The Dover Beck and the Greet are two pleasant streams rising on the junction of the Bunter and Keuper and draining the rich Keuper agricultural plateau. Other brooks, as the Wink, and the Beck at Maplebeck, drain this formation between Newark and Retford. The most far reaching system is that of the Idle and its tributaries. The Maun, Meden and Poulter all rise in the hills each side of our western boundary and flow in narrow valleys across the arid Bunter formation. Here they have been dammed to form lakes in the Dukeries. Just above Retford they unite to form the Idle, a sluggish stream, which, receiving the Ryton at Scrooby, finally discharges into the Trent at Stockwith. These 'Forest Streams' are fast flowing and have great character, the high water table in their valleys contrasting strongly with the sandy Forest soils.

The county was also served by several canals. More detail about the waterways will be found in the descriptions of the Divisions, and under Salix and Potamogeton in the body of the Flora.

CLIMATE

So small a lowland area does not have sufficient local variations of climate to affect the flora. Lying on the eastern side of England, Nottinghamshire is somewhat sheltered by the Pennines from the moderating influence of the Westerlies. The rigours of the weather are further intensified by the distance from the sea, 100 miles from the west coast, 70 from the east. The result is a relatively cold dry climate, with a large annual range of temperature, 22° for Nottingham. The mean January temperature is 38°F for the whole county; for July, 61°F in the north 62.1°F in the south. Prolonged cold spells in the early part of the year are frequent, as are cold springs, the Trent Valley in particular being subject to late frosts. Despite this there is an average of 172 days per year of westerly winds, the next in frequency being northerly, with 86 days.

The rainfall varies from 30 to 22 inches over the county. The highest rainfall is on the hills over 600 ft. round Sutton-in-Ashfield, whence amounts decrease eastwards. The Trent Valley is dry, being almost traced out by the 23 in. isohyet. The dryest places are Lowdham, Finningley and Sutton Bonington with under 22 inches. The greater part of the county receives less than 25 inches per annum. Rainfall is distributed fairly evenly throughout the year, there being rather more in the summer than the winter. April is the driest month.

GEOLOGY AND BOTANICAL DIVISIONS

The successive outcrops of rock follow a trend from north east to south west. As there is little Drift in Nottinghamshire this succession of strata reveals itself in a series of distinct bands across the county, whose soils and topography are directly determined by the underlying rock formations. This is clearly recognised by farmers and anyone who is interested in the countryside, being most obvious in the difference between 'the Forest' and 'the Clays'.

The earliest botanical writers referred to species growing 'on the Forest'. T. Jowett and G. Howitt made further steps towards the present division on a geological basis, Howitt's flora includes a geological map. The present scheme of four Divisions was laid down by Professor J. W. Carr in his article on Botany in the Victoria County History. These are: I the Coal Measures and Permian, II the Bunter Sandstones, III the Keuper Marl, IV the Lias. The Rhaetic outcrop between the Keuper and the Lias is so narrow that it does not merit separate treatment. The only criticisms that can be made of this excellent method are that the Permian and Coal Measure floras are rather diverse, and that Division III is inordinately large. The first difficulty cannot be escaped as the two outcrops are too small to be treated separately. Division III might have been sub-divided, Trent Valley, Clays east of Trent, Clays west of Trent, but the shadow of the Elders has loomed too large for the present writers to undertake this.

DIVISION I: PERMIAN AND COAL MEASURES

This is the smallest of the divisions running for 22 miles up the western boundary of the county from Nottingham to the North, and only 6 miles wide at its widest point. The area is very well watered and notable for its abundance of small streams. The tributaries of the Idle rise in the division or pass through it, the Meden at Pleasley Vale and the Millwood Brook at Cresswell Crags running through attractive small gorges where the limestone outcrops in natural cliffs. There is little Drift or Alluvium in the division, though Misk Hills have a Glacial Gravel cap, but the two solid strata are not themselves akin.

The Coal Measures outcropping on the west in a band 16 miles from Stapleford to Teversall and never more than 4 miles wide, bear more relation floristically to Division II than to the Limestone to their east. They consist of grey shales alternating with bands of sandstone and limestone and seams of coal.

Coal has been dug in this area from mediaeval times, some of the earliest pits were at Cossall and Newthorpe in the Fourteenth Century. These exploited the outcrop coal. The first pit deep enough to need a sough for drainage was sunk by Sir Henry Middleton at Wollaton. The landscape is covered with spoil heaps, in every state from the ancient ones now grassed over or wooded, to those that are still on fire. This rough grassland has produced habitats for such plants as *Lathyrus montana*, *Potentilla erecta*, *P. anglica* and *Galium saxatile*, while the damp hollows are often covered with willow and *Betula pubescens* scrub. Large waterlogged areas have formed recently where the ground has subsided after deep mining, notably in the valleys of the Leen and the Erewash, but they are of little value botanically, growing mainly *Carex nigra*, *C. ovalis* and *Glyceria* species. It is too soon to assess the results of open cast mining, but there must inevitably be a loss of species after the wholesale destruction of hedges and woodland. The whole formation is rather acid and ill drained, growing *Agrostis tenuis*, *Deschampsia flexuosa*, *Nardus stricta*, *Carex pilulifera*, *Stachys officinalis*, *Teucrium Scorodonium*, and *Digitalis*. *Equisetum sylvaticum* is a noteworthy plant occurring in several places, sometimes in large quantities. In modern times it has not been seen off this formation.

In the northern part of the county both the Upper and Lower Magnesian Limestones are present; with the Permian Marls outcropping between them, and again on the eastern edge of the formation. To the south towards Nottingham the formation thins out and only one Limestone, resting on a bed of Breccia, occurs, with a band of Marl to the east. Since the marls often outcrop on the dip slope they occupy a disproportionate area. They have been worked in many local brick pits, while Sankey's Pot Works at Bulwell send Nottinghamshire's Permian Marl into every garden and greenhouse in Britain.

The Lower Magnesian Limestone is extensively quarried. It has a magnesium carbonate content often of 40%, is highly crystalline and has been quarried at Steetley on the county boundary in blocks of two to three feet. Thoresby House is of Steetley stone, stone from Mansfield was used at Southwell Minster and from Mansfield Woodhouse at York Minster. There are quarries at Worksop and Shireoaks, and old quarries near Warsop, where the Hills and Holes area is still rich in limestone plants, despite the propinquity of the pit dump, the sewage farm and the railway. These old quarry workings, and the network of cuttings built for the railways which serve the pits, form a refuge for lime loving plants, which would otherwise have been lost as the old pastures were built over or ploughed up. *Arabis hirsuta*, *Helianthemum Chamaecistus*, *Geranium Columbinum*, *Campanula glomerata*, *Blackstonia*, *Gentiana amarella*, *Origanum*,

Orchis pyramidalis, *Ophrys apifera* and *Ophrys insectifera*, *Habenaria conopsea* and *Carex distans* can still be found in a few places.

There are some patches of bog near the limestone streams with *Galium uliginosum*, *Valeriana dioica*, *Oenanthe Lachenalii*, *Anagallis tenella* and *Carex lepidocarpa*. *Parnassia* is still found in two places; *Schoenus nigricans*, *Orchis incarnata*, *Carex dioica* and *Littorella* in one.

The woodland has a rich flora, *Tilia cordata*, *Sorbus torminalis*, *Sorbus Aria* and *Prunus Padus* are some of the more unusual trees. Under them grow *Geum rivale*, *Campanula latifolia*, *Lathraea*, *Polygonatum multiflorum*, *Carex strigosa*, *Melica uniflora* and *M. nutans*, *Scolopendrium*, *Polystichum aculeatum*, and *Equisetum maximum*. *Allium ursinium* is often offensively dominant. *Ribes alpinum*, *Campanula Trachelium* and *Iris foetidissima* are only native in this division.

A group of plants with a principally western distribution in the county occur on both the Coal Measures and Permian. The most noticeable of these is the holly which is definitely native in Division I and the west of Division II. Rough pastures which would turn to thorn scrub elsewhere, quickly sprout small holly bushes, and it is common in the hedges. *Cardamine amara*, *Scirpus sylvaticus* and *Cystopteris fragilis* are plants which decrease eastward and are rare or unknown in Division IV and Lincolnshire.

DIVISION II: BUNTER SANDSTONE

Division II consists of a large area of dry rolling Forest country which though scenically beautiful has little botanical diversity. The alluvium of the valleys and the small patches of Glacial Drift produce a gravelly soil which is not very different from the Bunter Sandstone on which they rest, and the patches of Boulder Clay are too minute to influence the flora. Only in the fenny Carrland which lies in the northern part of the Idle Valley is there any striking change in the plant life.

The Bunter outcrop in Nottinghamshire is 40 miles by 7 or 8 miles wide, and consists of the two lower divisions only, the Lower Mottled Sandstones and the Bunter Pebble Beds.

The Lower Mottled Sandstones, outcropping on the west of the formation, overlie the Permian for the greater part of their length. They consist of fine sands with a little marl and angular pebbles, and are much quarried for moulding sand. The disturbed ground round the sandpits makes an excellent habitat for such sand land annuals as *Eriophila verna*, *Cerastium semidecandrum*, *Anthriscus neglecta*, *Hypochaeris glabra*, *Myosotis hispida*, *M. versicolor*, *Aira caryophyllea* and *A. praecox*.

The Pebble Beds contain more sand and fewer pebbles than in some counties. The Sandstone is solid enough to form natural bluffs, but can be crumbled in the hand and is not a building stone. Around Nottingham it is yellowish, becoming red further north. There is a noticeable escarpment throughout its length rising to over 600 ft. at Robin Hood Hills near Mansfield, and terminating in Nottingham Castle Rock, which stands imposingly 133 ft. above the Trent Valley. The scarp then runs west through Bramcote and Stapleford Hills to the Derbyshire border.

The Sherwood Forest anciently covered a large part of this division. At the Perambulation of 1300 it ran 20 miles north from Nottingham and was about 8 miles wide, an area of 100,000 acres or about one fifth of the Shire. These bounds continued almost unchanged until the break up of the Royal Forest at the end of the sixteenth century. At the Dissolution the lands of the Abbeys and Priories which surrounded the Forest, mostly sited on the spring line at the edge of the Bunter, were granted to lay proprietors. These holdings were increased by grants from the royal domains in ensuing years, and the great families of 'the Dukeries' increased in power. Now the Forest is again changing, before the inexorable encroachments of the collieries and death duties. Of the five great houses, Thoresby and Osberton alone are lived in. Welbeck is a military academy, though the estate remains in private hands; Newstead has been given to Nottingham Corporation, who keep it as a museum and pleasure ground. Clumber House is destroyed, and the Park administered by the National Trust. Rufford is fragmented, the ruinous house a practice ground for the Civil Defence.

The Sherwood Forest has also become the stronghold of the Forestry Commission, who at present control about 15,000 acres west of the Trent (this includes land in other botanical divisions). They started operations in the county in 1925 and at first planted considerable areas of heathland and some marginal agricultural land. Since the last war most planting has been on devastated woodland sites. The natural vegetation is oak and birch with a ground cover of bracken and wild hyacinth. Open heathland is dominated by *Calluna*, *Erica*, and *Deschampsia flexuosa*. Sherwood oak was once famous, and used both as building timber and for ships. Although at the Survey of 1609 many trees were already past their prime, there was still Welbeck oak for the rebuilding of St. Paul's. This old oakwood was increased by the Eighteenth Century landscape plantings, which also included sweet chestnut and beech. Now the falling water table and atmospheric pollution have made the Forest unfit for oak. Both the Commission and private owners are planting large areas of conifers, though there are considerable stands of beech and red oak.

Monotropa is an interesting inhabitant of the oak and beechwood, but in general there is little vegetation except on the rides. These have similar flora to the open heath and park land, with *Viola ericetorum*,

Hypericum humifusum, Ulex Gallii, U. nanus, Trifolium striatum, Vaccinium Myrtillus, Veronica officinalis, Carex pilulifera, C. Pairaei, Sieglingia and *Nardus* growing among the heather and grass communities. *Lycopodium clavatum* has been re-found recently in two localities. Many of the annuals found on the Lower Sandstone are here also, but generally this is a less open community. At Welbeck and in the west a few of the 'strong woodland' species, like the primrose, appear. Mistletoe is frequent in thorn, lime and other trees.

The Forest soils are mainly acid, though more calcareous patches occur, growing *Viola hirta, Leontodon hispidus, Carlina vulgaris* and *Brachypodium pinnatum.* One of the most interesting of these communities is at Barrow Hills near Everton. Here and in other places in the north *Viola lepida* is found. Some of the now extinct plants of Nottingham Castle Rock and Larkdale, *Silene nutans, Helianthemum, Hippocrepis comosa,* also indicate a more calcareous formation.

The whole formation is extremely porous. Springs rise at the junction of the Bunter with adjoining formations, but there are practically no streams rising within the division. The Idle tributaries cross it from south west to north east. Their valleys formerly contained areas of acid bog but are now very much drier. *Ranunculus hederaceus, Genista anglica, Potentilla palustris, Juncus squarrosus,* and *Eriophorum angustifolium* can still be found. Beside the rivers are wet woods dominated by alder and *Salix fragilis* and now increasingly planted with poplar. These have an interesting flora, including *Corydalis claviculata, Viola palustris, Chrysosplenium oppositifolium, C. alternifolium, Salix pentandra, Carex paniculata, C. curta,* and *Blechnum spicant.*

The natural dryness of the higher ground has been increased by the coal pits, which pump much water to waste. The formation is also a natural reservoir for the surrounding towns, Nottingham, Lincoln, Mansfield, Newark and many smaller places draw all or part of their water from wells in the Bunter. The water table is falling and some streams have vanished even in the last ten years. This and the present craze for land drainage accounts for part of the list of extinct Nottinghamshire plants, *Thelypteris palustris, T. cristata, Drosera rotundifolia, Vaccinium Oxycoccos, Empetrum nigrum,* have vanished since G. Howitt's time, some since J. W. Carr wrote the Victoria County History.

The Carrs. The small area of Carr, or fen land, in the north is one of the most interesting parts of the county. The Isle of Axholme and Hatfield Chase, of which the Nottinghamshire Carrlands form the southern fringe, are a low lying district south of the Humber and west of the Trent in many ways similar to the Fens. Comparatively little modern research has been done here—an opening for one of the local universities. The land does not often reach 20 feet above sea level, falling as low as 5 ft. It is drained by the rivers Idle, Torne,

Went and Don, which originally formed an interlacing pattern of meres and watercourses flowing through reed beds and marsh. Their beds are now above the level of the drained Carr lands, whose waters must therefore be artificially pumped away.

The Idle is a Nottinghamshire river and for a few miles the Torne enters the county. Some authorities consider that the Bycarrs Dyke from Idle Stop to the Trent at Stockwith, which now carries the whole of the Idle waters, was of Roman construction. The main pattern of drainage was laid down in the Seventeenth Century by Vermuyden, who worked on Hatfield Chase before his venture on the Bedford Levels. He dammed the Idle at Idle Stop, cutting off its circuitous links with the southern arm of the Don and carrying the waters in a straight course north to Dirtness and then east to the Trent at Althorpe. The old course can still be traced in the county and parish boundaries. The results were as usual patchy, with improvements to some land and new inundations on others. Piecemeal improvements continued until recently. Now the area north of the Idle is drained by a scheme inaugurated by the Trent Catchment Board. It is served by the new pumping station at Keadby. Scaftworth, Everton, Gringley, Misterton and Walkeringham Carrs, south of the Idle were formerly drained by the Mother Drain, running parallel to the river and discharging through Misterton Soss (Sluice) to the Trent at Stockwith. The steam engines which replaced the original windmill used five tons of coal each per day. These waters now pass into the Idle through the modern pumps at Gringley Carr. The architecture of the Victorian pumping stations in the Isle is admirable.

The Carrs lie partly in division II and partly in III. The peat cover is rather thin, and the soil poor over the Bunter but richer over the marls. Only those parishes downstream of Bawtry are truly carrland, but a band of peat borders the Idle upstream to Retford and some of the typical species occur on it. The soils are acid to neutral, PH readings of from 5.5 to 7+ have been obtained. The more acid soils occur north of the Idle, becoming less so over the Keuper in Misterton Carr. Water from the drains has given a reading of 7 at Gringley Carr. Sizeable bog oaks are still recovered from the peat.

West Stockwith and part of Misterton parish lie on the richer warp lands which border the Trent. The typical fenland crops of red beet, celery, potatoes, etc. are grown here. Warping has not been practised for about sixty years.

Viola stagnina was discovered at Misterton by the Rev. Thomas Owston in 1840. Mrs. Sandwith found it at Misson where she also discovered *Lathyrus palustris* in 1909. To within the last ten years the meadows at Misson have remained rough mowing grass with *Sium latifolium*, *Valeriana dioica*, *Lysimachia vulgaris*, *Cirsium dissectum*, *Juncus subnodulosus*, *Calamagrostis canescens* and *Glyceria maxima*. Now they have mostly been ploughed and re-seeded, and the *Viola* is lost, but the other plants can still be found along hedge and drain sides. The Carrs south of the Idle are arable land intersected by drains. The drains each side of the river have many interesting species, *Myriophyllum verticillatum*, *Samolus*, *Hottonia*, *Hydrocharis*, *Alisma ranunculoides*, *A. lanceolata*, many *Potamogeton* species, *Eleocharis acicularis*, *Scirpus fluitans*, and other plants which are more widespread. *Viola lepida*, *Arnoseris* and *Apera Spica-venti* are interesting species of the light sands which surround the Carrs.

DIVISION III: KEUPER WATERSTONES and MARLS

The Keuper countryside presents a great contrast to the last two divisions. While the Permian is highly industrialised and the Bunter a mixture of Forest and coal pits, in division III we have a rich red agricultural country with pleasant villages, brick built from the local clay. Newark is a growing centre but still a typical market town, with fine buildings round its thriving market square. Retford is smaller and even more of a country town, though the Great North Road, despite the bypass, still wrecks its peace. The Trent Valley from Nottingham to Newark is rather built up. It is being further disfigured, here and in the unspoiled north, by almost contiguous mammoth power stations, surrounded by smog and birds' nests of pylons. In contrast the ' nodding donkeys ' pumping oil round Eakring are not offensive, though the clearings and roadways made in the woods let in light and nettles, destroying the woodland plants. East of the Trent round Gotham, Cropwell Bishop and Newark rich gypsum deposits which are quarried for plaster, occur in the Marls. Gypsum has been dug all over the division in the past. It was used ornamentally for effigies and pillars, and most old houses have upper rooms floored with plaster laid on reeds.

This is the largest division, covering half the county. The escarpment runs from Nottingham to Misterton reaching a height of 508 feet, and a large portion of the formation lies south and east of the Trent. The Keuper Waterstones outcrop on the west, in a belt from one half to two miles broad, and also in the valleys of some of the streams, notably the Greet and Dover Beck. They are flaggy sandstones with bands of marl and sometimes form quite conspicuous hills, as at Edingley, Bothamsall and Kirton. The soil is clayey but rather lighter than the Keuper Marl, and supports a more heathy vegetation including such species as *Potentilla erecta*, *Carex pilulifera*, and *Nardus stricta*. The woods, often on the scarp slopes, are well watered mixed woodland, chiefly oak and ash with birch and *Tilia cordata*. They are full of ferns, including large colonies of *Polystichum setiferum* and *P. aculeatum*, *Dryopteris Borreri* and sometimes *Thelypteris Oreopteris*. *Chrysosplenium oppositifolium* and *Allium ursinium* are common, *Geum rivale* and *Epipactis Helleborine* occur.

The Waterstones pass almost imperceptibly into the Marls. These form a pretty countryside of small hills and valleys each side of the

Trent flood plain, which (except for a small excursion on to the Bunter at Wilford) is entirely contained by this formation. Though weathering to a stiff red soil the Keuper Marl is not strictly a clay but a calcareous silt. It contains bands of sandstone, which being resistant are responsible for the relief, crowning the principal scarp and the slopes of smaller valleys. They are known locally as skerry, and have been quarried for building, particularly near Tuxford. The skerries of the west are dolomitic and dress well. Many of the churches are built of them, and all the villages have walls if not houses of the typical grey stone. Around Kelham and the Trent Valley there is a more sandy, brownish stone, which is less calcareous, rougher and more intractable for building. The scarp slopes of the marl have an attractive calcicole flora. *Viola hirta*, *Genista tinctoria*, *Trifolium medium*, *Scabiosa Columbaria*, *Cirsium acaule*, *Clinopodium vulgare*, *Brachypodium pinnatum* and *Bromus erectus* are typical species, while *Helianthemum Chamaecistus*, *Lotus tenuis*, *Blackstonia*, *Gentiana amarella*, *Orchis pyramidalis* and *Ophrys apifera* can still be found. The old gypsum pits form a good habitat for many of these species. *Cynoglossum officinale* often occurs near gypsum workings. The marls to the south and east of the Trent are more featureless in all ways than those to the west. The skerry outcrops are less numerous and the country therefore flatter. Much of the marl is covered by the alluvium of the Devon and Smite, and of Bunny and Gotham Moors, and in other parts there is some remnant of glacial drift which destroys the character of the marl. Trent Hills, forming the boundary of the Trent Valley from Stoke to East Bridgford, are interesting. The woods contain many of the typical clay woodland plants and are the last known habitat for *Gagea*. There are also interesting species at Clifton Grove, opposite Nottingham. Nearby the peats of the Fairham Brook supported a delightful flora, *Viola canina var montana*, *Valeriana dioica*, *Spiraea Filipendula*, *Lychnis Flos cuculi*, *Orchis Morio*, *Carex demissa*, *Ophioglossum vulgatum* were some of the plants of these flowery meadows. They are now a council estate.

Though not containing Forest country like division II the Keuper is well wooded. These moist clay woods are some of the botanical highlights of the county. They are mixed woodland, often oak with hazel coppice, though the Forestry Commission are planting much beech in the woods they are re-habilitating. *Sorbus torminalis* and *Salix Caprea* are frequent, with Aspen and Birch on the lighter soils. The different woods vary greatly, often having a characteristic dominant plant, as *Anemone Nemorosa*, *Asperula*, *Sanicula*, or *Mercuralis perennis*. *Ranunculus auricomus*, *Vicia sylvatica* (this division only) *Dipsacus pilosus*, *Campanula latifolia*, *Myosotis sylvatica*, *Lamium Galeobdolon*, *Epipactis Helleborine*, *Orchis mascula*, *Platanthera chlorantha*, *Paris*, *Allium ursinium*, *Carex remota*, *C. pallescens*,

C. pendula (abundant in some woods) *C. strigosa*, *Bromus giganteus*, *B. asper* and *Poa nemoralis* are some of the species of this flora.

An unusual feature of this division is the number of miniature gorges, known as Dumbles, carved out by small streams in the soft marls. The stream runs on a skerry bed with small waterfalls at intervals and the steep wooded banks are as much as fifteen feet high. These unexpected, and often rather impenetrable, clefts between the ploughed lands afford a home for many woodland species, especially ferns. Several dissect the plateau between Nottingham and Southwell. In many parts of the division the Dumbles run through larger woods, as at Bevercotes Park.

On the Keuper plateau south east of the Trent, the woods are dull, containing chiefly elms and rooks. The ground flora at the best is campion, at the worst elder.

The Trent Valley. From the Derbyshire boundary to Newark the Trent flows north east over a flood plain about two miles wide and bounded by low marl hills. The valley is floored with gravel, the riverside villages being built on low gravel terraces which raise them above the floods. At Muskham Bridge the marl floor of the valley is 23 to 26 ft. below the gravel and alluvium. The soils vary locally but there seems little difference botanically between the Old and New River Gravels. These light soils grow sand-loving plants which do not occur in other parts of the division. *Erophila verna*, *Cerastium arvense*, *Medicago arabica*, *Trifolium subterraneum*, *T. striatum* are typical of the gravel banks and pastures, and *Montia* and *Trifolium fragiferum* grow in damper hollows. Many of the old Trent-side pastures are however markedly calcareous and grow species such as *Viola hirta*, *Ononis spinosa*, *Spiraea Filipendula* and *Scabiosa Columbaria*, which are not very different from those found on the marl. *Campanula glomerata* and *Orchis ustulata* were found here in the past. The Spring and Autumn crocuses, most famous of the meadow plants, are now nearly extinct, though there is still a fine field of Autumn Crocus between Nottingham and Newark.

The valley contains many low lying hollows, pools and marshes, some of which are old ox-bows of the river. Here may be found *Thalictrum flavum*, many *Batrachian Ranunculi*, *Rorippa amphibium*, *Oenanthe fistulosa*, *O. aquatica*, *Veronica catenata*, *Stachys palustris*, *Butomus*, both species of *Typha*, *Glyceria maxima*. Many of these wet places were planted as willow holts in the past. Ballast pits by the railways support a similar flora, but the larger gravel pits which have been excavated in the past twenty years are still incompletely colonised. *Ranunculus* species, *Myriophyllum spicatum*, *Polygonum amphibium*, *Potamogeton crispus*, *P. natans* and *P. pectinatus* are appearing in the water, with *Sparganium*, *Typha* and Willows round the edge. *Juncus compressus* often colonises the disturbed ground. By the Trent side grow *Rorippa islandica*, *Impatiens glandulifera*, (*I. capense* occasionally occurs in willow holts), *Sparganium*, *Acorus*, and *Scirpus lacustris*. There is also an interesting group of ruderal plants, some aliens, which grow on the river banks, towing paths or on arable land close by. These include *Barbarea stricta, Brassica campestre, Archangelica, Artemisia Absinthum, Chenopodium ficifolium.*

Downstream from Newark the river swings north, and below Clifton becomes the county boundary. The valley widens out and the influence of the tides is felt up to Cromwell Lock, six miles north of Newark. The meadows of the tidal stretch, known as ings, are highly prized grazing land. The soil is finer silt than the gravels above Newark and the calicole species do not occur. The flora of the damp hollows is similar to that of the upper valley with the addition of *Rumex maritimus* and *R. palustris* (which also occur sporadically higher up the valley), *Scirpus Tabernaemontani* and the pretty inland form of *Scirpus maritimus* with its loose panicle. The dominant plants of the mud banks are *Ranunculus repens* and *Rorippa sylvestris. Aster Tripolium* has been found at Stockwith and Saundby.

The Soar Valley is very similar to that of the Trent, perhaps a little damper. Narrow alluvial tracts also border the Devon, Smite, Greet and Dover Beck.

North of Newark, between the River and the county boundary lies an extremely interesting patch of sand land. These very light sands and gravels were laid down when the Trent flowed through the Lincoln Gap, and extend over the lower lying parts of the Keuper and the Lias. On the western slopes of the gravel terraces and of the clay ridges facing the River, are patches of even lighter Blown Sand. Their origin is somewhat debated, but the sand is generally considered to have been wind borne in post glacial times off the mud flats of the valley, or of the Lake then formed by the Trent waters. Where any attempt at cultivation is made the sand is blown into the bottom of the hedges, some is still in natural sand dunes as at Spalford warrens. *Deschampsia flexuosa* and *Carex arenaria* (which occurs nowhere else in the county) are often dominant, with *Polytrichum juniperinum. Festuca eu-ovina* var *glauca* is confined to this formation. Over the whole area of light land many interesting sandland plants occur, *Teesdalia, Vicia Lathyroides, Potentilla argentea, Hypochaeris glabra, Vaccinium Myrtillus, Erica, Myosotis collina, M. versicolor, Echium vulgare, Convallaria* grow on the heaths and in the woods; some of the species find a congenial home in abandoned fields. The farming is precarious; *Centaurea cyanus, Chrysanthemum segetum* and other weeds still linger, while *Centaurea solstitialis, Solanum sarrachoides* and *Panicum Crus Galli* are introduced with carrot seed. There is a high water table, *Potentilla palustris, Lysimachia vulgaris, Myrica, Hydrocharis, Carex rostrata* and *Blechnum* still occur.

DIVISION IV: LOWER LIAS

The Lower Lias is the only member of the Jurassic system which occurs in Nottinghamshire. It forms a small division lying to the south and east of the Keuper, next to the Leicestershire and Lincolnshire boundaries. Two considerable outliers cap Leake and Gotham Hills. The formation consists of dark blue shales in which occur bands of flaggy limestone. These have been used for building both houses and churches and are sometimes called Bennington Bluestone. They are quarried for lime at Staunton, and at larger works at Barnstone, where *Cirsium acaule*, *Picris Hieraciodes* and similar species occur. The Lias weathers to a very sticky blue clay of a calcareous nature. Typical species are, *Spiraea Filipendula*, *Sison Amomum*, *Pastinaca sativa*, *Daucus Carota*, *Carlina*, *Picris Echiodes*, *Senecio erucifolius*, *Bartsia Odontites* and *Bromus erectus*. There is an interesting group of cornfield weeds, some of which only grow in this division but they are now becoming very rare through the use of sprays, *Silene noctiflora*, *Carum segetum*, *Scandix*, *Galium tricorne*, *Valerianella dentata*, *Specularia hybrida*, *Linaria Elatine*, *L. spuria*, *Lithospermum arvense* and *Galeopsis vulgaris*. *Cirsium eriophorum* and *Falcaria* are two of the rare plants of this division.

West of the Fosse Road a large part of the Lias outcrop is covered by Boulder Clay, the only considerable sheet in the county. This, known as the Nottinghamshire Wolds, is the edge of the sheet of Boulder Clay covering the Eastern Counties. It is rolling country with wide views and, like the rest of the Lias, traversed by many green verged lanes. The flora is in the main similar to the rest of the division, as the tough stony clay is derived from the Lias, Oolite and Chalk. On Clipstone and Cotgrave Wolds however, there is a sandier Drift, and such plants as *Calluna*, *Gnaphalium sylvaticum*, *Hypericum humifusum*, and *Viola ericetorum* occur within a few yards of *Gentiana amarella* and *Ophrys apifera* growing on the limestone outcrop. Around Rempstone there is another very interesting area where the Drift is derived from the Bunter and crossed by the calcareous Sheepwash Brook. In the cornfields are *Matricaria Chamomilla*, *Chrysanthemum segetum* and other weeds of light land, while by the stream in the Old Church Yard is one of the few good marsh communities of this part, growing *Galium uliginosum*, *Valeriana dioica*, *Eleocharis pauciflora*, *Carex rostrata*, and *C. lepidocarpa*.

The division is in general very short of water. If it was not for the Grantham Canal there would be practically no habitats for waterside plants, but it does produce *Oenanthe Lachenalii*, *Butomus*, *Carex Pseudo-cyperus* and the usual canal side species. There is also one field round a pond at Granby where *Veronica catenata*, *Polygonum amphibium*, *Juncus compressus*, *Potamogeton densus* and *Zannichellia* give some idea of what the flora might have been like before modern drainage and deepening of the rivers. Unfortunately the nineteenth century botanists never got down here.

The countryside is still unspoiled and rural so therefore lacks the abundance of ruderal species that grow in the rest of the county—*Lepidium Draba*, *Tanacetum*, *Erigeron canadense*, *Senecio viscosus*,

Artemisia Absinthum and similar plants, are absent or rare. The whole question of plants that do not grow on the Lias is intriguing. Apart from the ruderals and water loving species, (a glance through the list of *Carices* will show what is meant), there are several species whose absence is not so easily accounted for. Most noticeable are the woodland plants. The division is well wooded but the woods are rather dry and the canopy often elm. Such species as *Anemone, Adoxa, Viburnum opulus, Lonicera Periclymenum, Asperula, Veronica montana, Lamium Galeobdolon* and *Millium*, which are common in I and III and often in the damper valleys of division II, are rare or missing on the Lias. *Euonymus, Allium vineale* and *Carex spicata* are further absentees. Sanicle is one of the more frequent woodland plants and *Orchis mascula, Daphne Laureola, Mercuralis perennis*, and *Campanula latifolia* occur.

The Lias outcrop north and east of Newark is covered except for the scarps with the light gravels laid down by the ancient Trent, which have been described in Division III. There are also patches of Glacial Gravel which are difficult to distinguish from the Old River Gravels. Roughly, the River Gravels occupy the lower land and the Glacial Gravels cap the hills. Light, low-lying, ill-drained and remote, this has always been an interesting area botanically. Langford Moor and the adjacent Stapleford Moor in Lincolnshire were ancient areas of heath on the River Gravels and used to grow *Radiola, Drosera rotundifolia, Gentiana Pneumonanthe*, and *Narthecium. Viola ericetorum, Hypericum humifusum, Peplis*, Heathers, *Potamogeton polygonifolius, Juncus squarrosus, Carex binervis, Molinia* and *Nardus* still persist, although the moors have been afforested since the last century. In 1926 *Tillaea muscosa* was found on the rides by Miss Bacon (Mrs. Foggitt) when staying in Newark. The light soils continue on Turf Moor, Brough, and into Barnby and Coddington parishes to the south, where interesting plants may be found on the Newark Golf Course.

The sandy area around Wigsley, Thorney, Harby and Broadholme is similar to the adjoining part of Division III. Here is the only existing station for *Melampyrum pratense. Rhamnus Frangula, Apium inundatum, Samolus Valerandi* and *Hottonia* can be found in or near the drains.

REFERENCES:

Victoria County History of Nottinghamshire Vols. I and II, 1906.

Sheet Memoirs of the Geological Survey, Nos. 70 (old series); 83, 1888: 113, 1911: 142, 1909: 126.

H. H. Swinnerton: Nottinghamshire, Cambridge County, Geographies 1910.

Archdeacon Stonehouse: History and Topography of the Isle of Axeholme 1830.

J. Bramley: Sir Cornelius Vermuyden, Trans. Thoroton Soc. 1931.

M. W. Barley: Lincolnshire and the Fens 1952.

Nottinghamshire. Land Utilisation Survey 1944.

J. W. Carr (ed.), A contribution to the Geology and natural History of Nottinghamshire 1893.

NOTTINGHAMSHIRE BOTANISTS

Botany in Nottinghamshire was well studied in earlier times. Deering's *Catalogus Stirpium* is among the more ancient local floras, and John Ray was a visitor to the county; but since the middle of the last century botanical publication has fallen under a blight.

The earliest references to Nottinghamshire plants are in William How's *Phytologia Britannica* 1650. He records three plants from localities provided by a Mr. Stonehouse, vicar of Darfield near Barnsley. Two more are added by Christopher Merrett in his *Pinax* of 1666, on the authority of T. Willisell who visited the county about this time. Willisell was also a correspondent of Ray and was the first person to record *Silene nutans* on Nottingham Castle. The great John Ray himself had occasion to visit Nottinghamshire as the guest of his friend Sir Francis Willoughby at Wollaton Hall. He records several species in his correspondence and botanical works.

The next major contribution was the publication in 1738 of Deering's *Catalogus Stirpium* . . . . . or *Catalogue of Plants naturally growing* . . . . . *about Nottingham*. Charles Deering M.D. was born in Saxony, probably in 1695. He graduated in physics at Leyden, and after practising at Bedford, London and Rochester settled in Nottingham in 1736 and remained there till his death from gout in 1749. He was buried in St. Peter's Churchyard. As a doctor he was considerably in advance of his time and "not endowed with that degree of prudence and equanimity of temper which is so necessary to the practice of physic". His practice was correspondingly meagre, though he had at first been successful. His *Catalogus* is a scholarly work giving the scientific name of the plant according to Ray's *Synopsis*, followed by synonyms from Gerard, Parkinson, etc., the English name, and a note on the habitat and medicinal or culinary use of the plant. He lists some 840 Phanerogamic and Cryptogamic plants of which a few are garden species. His localities can usually still be traced, though the plants have long vanished under the streets of Nottingham. Dr. Deering also wrote an *Historical Account of the Town of Nottingham* published in 1751, in which he adds a few species not remarked in the *Catalogus*.

Most of the lists of plants published in various works during the rest of the eighteenth century are taken from Deering. Richard Pulteney of Leicester contributed Nottinghamshire plants to Gough's *Camden* of 1789, and also mentions some species in *Phil. Trans.* 1759 and in his contribution to Nichol's *History of Leicestershire*. Another Leicestershire botanist, the Rev. George Crabbe, chaplain to the Duke of Rutland at Belvoir, also records from South Nottinghamshire.

Thomas Ordoyno, a nurseryman of Newark, published his *Flora Nottinghamiensis* in 1807. He worked in collaboration with the Rev. J. T. Becher of Southwell. Ordoyno's work does not quite reach the high standard of Deering's. One feels that of the three major floras his contains the most records open to doubt. The main body of the work is nevertheless perfectly reliable and most interesting in giving a picture of a different part of the county from Deering, or from his successors Howitt and Jowett, who were based on Nottingham and the Forest.

Thomas Jowett was born in 1801 at Colwick, the son of the steward to the Musters family. He also was a doctor, and practised in Nottingham till 1831 when ill health made him retire to Morton. When only twenty five he published in the *Nottingham Journal* under the name of Il Rosajo a series of *Botanical Calendars*, or *Notices of native Plants of the County of Nottinghamshire arranged according to the Order of their Appearance.* At the Gilstrap Library at Newark is his interleafed copy of Ordoyno's *Flora* with interesting manuscript notes of about 1820. The four volumes of his herbarium 1821-24 at Bromley House, Nottingham, give valuable confirmation to records of some extinct or dubious plants. The *Botanical Calendars* themselves are written in the happily diffuse style of the time and show the author's aquaintance with both national and local botanical work. They contain interesting comments on Nottinghamshire botany and tantalising references to herbaria and interleafed floras belonging to Deering and his assistants, which were then still extant. One hundred species not mentioned in Deering and Ordoyno are recorded.

Jowett states his intention of writing a full scale flora. At his early death in 1832 the task passed to Dr. Godfrey Howitt, our great great uncle. He and Jowett were close friends and the most outstanding members of the Nottinghamshire botanical fraternity at this time. Godfrey Howitt was born at Heanor, Derbyshire, the seventh son of Thomas Howitt, a Quaker farmer. He graduated in medicine at Edinburgh and practised in Nottingham until he emigrated to Australia in 1839. On arriving at Melbourne, where he remained until his death in 1873, he set up a medical practice, became an original honorary physician to the Melbourne Hospital, an original member of the Council of Melbourne University, a member of the Acclimatization Society and a co-founder of the Royal Society of Victoria. He does not seem to have done much in the way of botany after going to Australia, there are no records or specimens of his in the National Herbarium; but he established a fine garden on his Collins Street property and grew a number of unusual subjects, including the commercial Date. In the Royal Botanic Gardens, South Yarra, is an historic date palm, raised by Godfrey Howitt in 1840 and donated by his son Dr. William Howitt in 1883: It is probably the oldest exotic tree in cultivation there. Howitt maintained an interest in entomology, bequeathing his insect collections to the University of Melbourne. His valuable library of scientific books, beautifully bound, has been kept intact; it also belongs to the University of Melbourne, but is on permanent loan to the National Museum. In 1856 Dr. Ferdinand Mueller, the colonial botanist, published a description of the genus *Howittia* (a handsome blue flowered Mallow), named in Godfrey Howitt's honour.

His nephew Alfred, son of William and Mary Howitt, continued in Australia the family interest in botany, his large plant collections are in the Melbourne Herbarium, and he wrote a paper on the *Eucalypti of Gippsland.* He was also an authority on entnology and geology and conducted the search party sent into the interior for the explorers Burke and Wallis.

Godfrey Howitt's *Flora of Nottinghamshire* is a slim volume of 142 pages hastily put together in the year before he left England. There is no introduction and only the barest notice of the distribution of each species, but the book does depict the plant life of the county before the sweeping changes caused by modern agriculture and industry. It includes a geological map. Jowett and Howitt were the first authors to appraise the botany of the county as a whole and to divide it on a geographical basis. The list of Nottinghamshire plants in the supplement to H. C. Watson's New Botanists Guide is drawn up from the advance sheets of Howitt's Flora, that in the N.B.G. itself from a marked catalogue accompanied by specimens submitted to Watson by Howitt through a T. H. Cooper, who added species drawn from Deering and earlier authors.

For the rest of the nineteenth century there was little botanical activity in the county and the few records we have stem chiefly from entries in the national botanical journals or in local guide books. The Revd. J. K. Miller is one of the few outstanding people. From 1819 to 1855 he was vicar of Walkeringham on the edge of the Carrs, a most interesting part of the county which had not been explored botanically. His "very accurate manuscript" was published by E. A. Woodruffe-Peacock as *Flora Walkeringhamiensis* in the *Naturalist* 1895.

E. J. Lowe of Highfields, Nottingham, was an authority on grasses and also on ferns and foliage plants, on which he published some handsome volumes. His *British Grasses* contains some Nottinghamshire records. He also wrote the Botany section for the report of the British Association Meeting for 1866. In 1880 Mrs. Ann Gilbert, a well-loved Nottingham lady, published *Botany for Beginners*, a collection of articles originally written for the *Forester*, the magazine of Nottingham High School. She has several new records, both of recent introductions, like *Claytonia perfoliata*, and of species not separated by the older botanists, and seems to have been a botanist of authority. John Bohler on the other hand, a Wingfield man who botanised chiefly on the Forest and in Nottingham Cemetery, appears to have been more likeable than accurate, though most of his records are sound.

In the eighties and nineties the Nottingham Naturalists Association, with R. A. Rolfe, Harry Fisher and the Rev. Hilderic Friend as its leading members, was stirring. There was talk of compiling a flora, but the scheme lapsed, possibly on Rolfe's appointment to Kew. Friend published various local lists. Harry Fisher, born in Nottingham in 1860, became a chemist and acquired a business in Stodman Street, Newark in 1886. In 1911 he became director and secretary of the Grantham Journal, and died at Grantham in 1935. He was botanist with the Jackson Harmsworth expedition to Franz Joseph Land in 1894, where he added arctic species and mosses to his considerable British herbarium. This collection, 10,000 species exclusive of mosses and arctic plants, he left to the Nottingham Natural History Museum at Wollaton Hall, where it still remains—in parcels. He compiled the botanical list for the 1893 meeting of the British Association, and added many new Nottinghamshire records, especially of *Rubus* and *Rosa*, and of aliens collected round Newark.

In 1886 John Wesley Carr was appointed Keeper of the Natural History Museum (then part of the Nottingham University College); in 1893 he was elected to the Chair in Natural Sciences. Carr was born in 1862 and awarded the M.A. degree by Cambridge University. Subsequently he became a Fellow of the Linnean Society and a Fellow of the Geological Society. He was an all round naturalist of wide scope, and published several geological studies and an invertebrate fauna of the county. In the *Victoria County History* he wrote not only all the botanical papers but those on Insects, Myriapoda, Spiders, Fishes, Reptiles, Batrachians and Mammals. His appointment marks the beginning of half a century of fruitful work for Nottinghamshire botany. The first major work was the preparation of the botanical section of the *Victoria County History* in 1906. This gives a sketch of previous botanists in the county and a statistical analysis of species. It also, most importantly, lays down the excellent system of geological divisions which he followed in his manuscript Flora, and which is substantially followed in the present work. Each species is listed under the appropriate division, and changes in the flora are noticed. At this period Carr was also publishing localised records in the *Trans. Nottingham Naturalists*. The Manuscript Flora itself was never published, owing to lack of support for the Invertebrate Fauna. This must always remain a great loss to the botany of the county. Though the University have most generously allowed us to incorporate Carr's material, its publication at the proper date would have been far more fruitful. The manuscript sheets themselves are written in a perfect sloping hand. They give the page reference for each work in which the plant has previously been noticed, its general habitat and distribution, and localities arranged according to divisions for the less common plants. In compiling the manuscript Carr used a card index now in the possession of Nottingham University, and a most ingenious forerunner of the recent 'grid cards'.

This was a printed list of parishes in the county, one for each species, the parishes arranged alphabetically within the divisions. Each parish where the plant had been found was marked. Several friends contributed to the flora, notably the Rev. John Roffey, the *Hieracium* expert who was curate at Long Eaton in 1885 and became curate at Worksop in 1887; and Mrs. Sandwith, wife of the vicar of Harworth, and mother of N. Y. Sandwith of Kew.

Dr. Butcher, who was born in Derbyshire and lived at Bramcote for many years, first encouraged the University to consider publishing Carr's MS., but he unfortunately left the county before this could be achieved. He did much botanical work in Nottinghamshire particularly on Batrachian Ranunculi and has always been a constant source of help and inspiration to us.

LIST OF RECORDERS

Column 1. Name of Recorder.

Column 2. Work from which record is taken or address of recorder.

Column 3. Date of work or records.

Adams, H.	B.S.B.I. Proceedings	1954
Bacon, H.	Herbarium in Nottingham City Library ..	1834
Becher, Rev. J.	Contributed to T. Ordoyno's Flora ..	1807
Bohler, J.	List in Allen's Nottingham and its Environs	1866
	List in White's Worksop and the Dukeries	1875
Bowen, H.	Records for B.S.B.I. Maps Scheme ..	1959
Bradley, B.	Naturalist I	1864
Bradley, Miss D.	Wild Flower Society Notts. Diary ..	1934 to 1937
Brown, J.	N.W. Naturalist XVII to XX	1942 to 1946
Brown, L.	Trowell, Notts.	1959
Bulley, Mrs.	late of Nottingham	*c.*1950
Butcher, R. W.	Burnham-on-Crouch, lately of Bramcote ..	1951 to 1962
Carr, J. W.	Trans. Nottingham Naturalists 51 to 56 ..	1903 to 1909
	Victoria County History of Nottinghamshire	1906
	Journal of Botany XLVII	1909
	Manuscript Flora	1909 to 1939
Carter, J.	A Visit to Sherwood Forest	1875
Chalk, H. H. O.	Glasgow (and Southwell, Notts.) ..	*c.*1958
Cole, Canon R. E. G.	Specimens in Herb. Lincoln Museum ..	1855 to 1899
	List for Woodruffe Peacock's Lincolnshire Check List	1855 to 1899
	Phytologist III	1859
Collinson, Mrs.	Contributed to Carrs MS.	*c.*1910
Cooper, T. H.	Records in Watson's New Botanists Guide	1835 to 1837
Creed, H.	Loudon's Magazine of Nat. Hist. V. ..	1832
Dallman, A. A.	N.W. Naturalist VII, IX, X	1932, 1934, 1935

Deering, Charles	Catalogus stirpium etc., or a Catalogue of Plants . . . about Nottingham	1748
	Historical Account of the Town of Nottingham	1751
Drabble, E. and H.	Journal of Botany	1909
	B.E.C. Report	1926
Druce, G. C.	Comital Flora of the British Isles	1932
Eddison, B.	Contributed to G. Howitt's Flora ..	1839
Evans, Rev. and Mrs. A. J.	Walesby, Notts.	*c.*1960
Fisher, H.	Handbook of the British Association Meeting at Nottingham (ed. J. W. Carr) ..	1893
	Trans. Nottingham Naturalists	1894
	Specimens in Herb. Grantham Museum	
Friend, Rev. H.	Trans. Nottingham Naturalists	1887
	List in Sisson's Beauties of the Sherwood Forest	1888
	Naturalist	1900
Gibbons, Miss E. J.	Holton-le-Moor, Lincs.	1959 to 1962
Gilbert, Mrs. A.	Botany for Beginners	1880
Goulding, R. W.	Botanical Exchange Club Report ..	1917
Hall, R. H.	Botanical Exchange Club Report—(Plant Records)	1946
Hopkinson, J. W.	Journal of Ecology XVI	1927
Horwood, A. R.	Botanical Exchange Club Report ..	1916
How, William	Phytologia Britannica	1650
Howitt, G.	Nottinghamshire Flora	1839
Hudson, William	Flora Anglica	1762
Hurt	Contributed to G. Howitt's Flora ..	1839
Jowett, T.	Records in his interleaved copy of Ordoyno in the Gilstrap Library, Newark ..	*c.*1820
	Herb. at Bromley House, Nottingham ..	1821 to 1824
	Botanical Calendars in the Nottingham Guardian, under name of Il Rosajo ..	1826
Jones, E. G. and W. A.	Mansfield	*c.*1957
Kaye, Sir Richard	MS List of plants. Memoir by R. Goulding in Journal Lincs. and Notts. Architectural Societies 1923	1774 to 1776
Leather, Miss V.	Wild Flower Society Notts. Diary ..	1934 to 1937
Lowe, E. J.	List in Allen's Nottinghamshire Handbook for the British Association	1866
	British Grasses	1871
Mason, Rev. W. W.	MS. Lincolnshire Check List	
Mather, J.	Kimberley	*c.*1948
McClintock, D.	B.S.B.I. Proceedings (Plant Records) ..	1953
Merrett, Christopher	Pinax	1650
Miller, Rev. J. K.	Naturalist 1895	1819 to 1855
Mitchell, J.	Bot. Gaz. I and see J. W. Carr's MS. Flora	1849
Moll, H.	A new Description of England and Wales ..	1724
Ordoyno, T.	Flora Nottinghamiensis	1807

Payne, R. M.	in litt	1952
Penrose, Rev. J.	Records in the Penroses of Fledborough Parsonage by A. B. Baldwin	1783 to 1829
Posnet, G.	Lincoln	1955
Potter, T. R.	'Rambles round Loughborough', in the Loughborough News	1868
Pulteney, Richard	MS. Leicester Museum	1749
	Philosophical Trans. XLIX	1757
	Contributed plants to Gough's Camdens Brit.	1789
	List in J. Nichol's Hist. of Leicestershire ..	1795
Ray, J.	Cat. Plantae Angl.	1640
	Phil. Letters, Dereham's Edn.	1718
	Synopsis. Dillenian Edn.	1724
Reynolds, Mrs. E.	see J. W. Carr's MS. Flora	
Roffey, Rev. J.	Contributed to J. W. Carr's MS. Flora ..	*c.*1900
Rolfe, R. A.	Contributed to J. W. Carr's MS. Flora ..	*c.*1900
Rose, K.	Watsonia	1950
Salt, J.	List of Plants . . . about Sheffield (E. Howarth 1889)	1796 to 1807
Sandwith, Mrs. and N.Y.	Contributed to J. W. Carr's MS. and in litt	*c.*1910 *et seq.*
Searle, H.	Journal of Botany XXIV	1886
Sidebotham, J.	Newman's British Ferns	1840
	Phytologist	1841, 1842
Staton, J.	late of Gedling	1918 *et seq.*
Stonehouse, Rev.	a correspondent of W. How and J. Ray ..	*c.*1650
Thornley, Rev. A.	Contributed to J. W. Carr's MS. Flora ..	*c.*1900
Turner, D. and Dillwyn, N. W.	Botanists Guide	1805
Tutin	A friend of C. Deering	*c.*1748
Watson, H. C.	New Botanists Guide	1835
	Topographical Botany	1873
Williams, F. N.	Journal of Botany	1909
Williams, R. G.	MS. List of Plants around Nottingham ..	1940 to 1946
Winn, J. R.	Contributed to J. W. Carr's MS. Flora ..	*c.*1910
Willisell, T.	A correspondent of C. Merrett	*c.*1650
Woodruffe, Peacock, E. A.	Lincolnshire Check List.	

Explanatory Notes

The order adopted is that of G. C. Druce's British Plant List 1928, except for stated critical genera.

Nomenclature. No particular list has been followed. The quotation of the authority for the scientific name should avoid confusion. The excessive splitting up of genera and families practised recently seems to obscure rather than elucidate plant relationships.

The records are arranged in chronological order within each division.

The recorder's name in italics follows each group of records attributed to him. The mark of certainty † indicates that we have also seen the plant in that locality.

RANUNCULACEAE

Clematis Vitalba L. *Traveller's Joy*

Native or Denizen. Hedges and rough ground. Not uncommon as a denizen especially in Divs. 1 and 3. In some places, as at Arnold and Burton Joyce (Div. 3) it has every appearance of being native. All Divs.

First Record: C. Deering, *Cat. Stirp.* 1738 "Here and there in Hedges, but rarely".

Thalictrum flavum L. *Meadow Rue*

Native. Damp meadows and woods. Frequent in the river valleys of Divs. 1, 2, and 3, rare in 4.

First Record: C. Deering, *Cat. Stirp.* 1738.

4 Broadholme.

Anemone Nemorosa L. *Wood Anemone*

Native. Woods and shady meadows. Common in 1 and 3, less so in 2 and 4, where it occurs chiefly on peaty or drift soils.

First Record: C. Deering, *Cat. Stirp.* 1738.

var. *purpurea* DC.

2 Harworth.
3 Saundby, Beckingham, North Wheatley.

Anemone Ranunculoides L.

Alien. Divs. 1 or 2.

Sowerby and Smith 3 Edn. 1887 quotes this plant as thoroughly naturalised in private grounds near Worksop. This record stems from M. Stovin *B. S. Lond.* 1843 but we have been unable to trace it.

Adonis annua L. *Pheasant's Eye*

Colonist. Very rare.

Only Record: *Bot. Chron.* 1863, Bingham (Div. 3).

Myosurus minimus L. *Mousetail*

Native. Gravelly meadows and arable fields. Very rare. Divs. 1, 3, 4.

First Record: C. Deering, *Cat. Stirp.* 1738.

1 Between Radford and Wollaton, *Deering*.
3 Thoroton, *Deering*; Upton, *Ordoyno*; Normanton-by-Southwell, *Becher*; Epperstone, *Carr* (1907); Meadow at Rolleston, *Leather*, still there 1950 *et seq*.
4 Coddington, *Ordoyno*.

Ranunculus repens L. *Creeping Buttercup*

Native. Damp grassland, waste ground, etc. A common weed. All Divs.

First Record: C. Deering, *Cat. Stirp.* 1738.

Ranunculus acris L. *Buttercup*

Native. Meadows, etc. Very common. All Divs.

First Record: C. Deering, *Cat. Stirp.* 1738.

Ranunculus auricomus L. *Goldilocks*

Native. Woods and hedges. Locally frequent. All Divs.

First Record: C. Deering, *Cat. Stirp.* 1738.

1 Frequent.
2 *Victoria County History.*
3 Common on both marls and gravels.
4 Willoughby; Widmerpool; Wysall.

Ranunculus bulbosus L. *Bulbous Buttercup*

Native. Meadows, etc. Very common. All Divs.

First Record: C. Deering, *Cat. Stirp.* 1738.

Ranunculus Lingua L. *Great Spearwort*

Native. Fen ditches and pools. Probably extinct. Divs. 2, 3.

First Record: C. Deering, *Cat. Stirp.* 1738. Jowett considered the plant to be *R. flammula* only.

2 Basford Scottum, *Deering*; Dykes at Misson; Misson Causeway; Idle Stop, Misson, *Miller*; Bulwell Bog, *Gilbert*; Marshes near Misson towards Bawtry in fair quantity, *Mrs. Sandwith* 1918.
3 Gamston Moor, (by Nottingham), *Deering*.

Ranunculus Flammula L. *Lesser Spearwort*

Native. Marshes and Bogs. Frequent in suitable habitats in all Divisions, but rarer in Div. 4.

First Record: C. Deering, *Cat. Stirp.* 1738.

Ranunculus arvensis L. *Corn Buttercup*

Native. Cornfields on strong clay. Locally frequent. All Divs.

First Record: C. Deering, *Cat. Stirp.* 1738.

1 Manor Cottage, Worksop, *Brown*; Huthwaite, *Carr MS.*
2 Most abundant in the sand district, *G. Howitt* (He was mixed); Misson, *Mrs. Sandwith*; Bramcote, *Carr MS.*
3 Fairly common.
4 Granby; Staunton; Kilvington; Harby.

Ranunculus sardous CR. *Hairy Buttercup*

Native. Fields and Meadows. Rare. No modern record. Divs. 3, 4.

First Record: C. Deering, *Cat. Stirp.* 1738. "These three (i.e. *R. repens*, *R. bulbosus* and *R. sardous*) flower everywhere in meadows and pastures." G. Howitt, *Fl. Notts.* 1839; "Moist gravelly places; frequent."

3 Moist Places between Granby and Bingham, *Cole.*
4 Barnstone, *Cole.*

Ranunculus sceleratus L. *Celery leaved Buttercup*

Native. Pool sides and marshy places. Common. All Divs.

First Record: C. Deering, *Cat. Stirp.* 1738.

Ranunculus parviflorus L. *Small Flowered Buttercup*

Native. Dry meadows. Very rare. Div. 3.

First Record: T. Jowett, *Bot. Cals.* 1826.

3 Clifton Lane (by Nottingham); Colwick Lodge, *Jowett*; Clifton Wood (by Nottingham), *G. Howitt*; Quarry beyond Lea Pool, *Williams*; Gotham Hill.

SECT. BATRACHIUM

The nomenclature of this section follows Dr. R. W. Butcher's *Illustrated British Flora.* We are always grateful to him for his help.

Ranunculus fluitans Lam. *Water Crowfoot*

Native. Deeper rivers and streams. Widespread, but less common than *R. calcareus.*

First Record: C. Deering, *Cat. Stirp.* 1738.

1 Lady Lee, Worksop.
2 Occurs in most of the tributaries of the R. Idle, but is decreasing owing to pollution from the pits.
3 The Trent at Nottingham, *Gilbert*; Newark weir†, *Fisher*; Clifton Grove; Dover Beck at Caythorpe; Common in the Idle.
4 Common in the Witham at Barnby.

Ranunculus circinatus Sibth. *Water Crowfoot*

Native. Deep still waters. Common in canals, gravel pits, etc. All Divs.

First Record: C. Deering, *Cat. Stirp.* 1738.

Ranunculus trichophyllus Chaix. *Water Crowfoot*

Native. Ditches and ponds. Frequent. All Divs.

First Record: J. W. Carr, *Tr. Nott. Nats.* 1904.

1 Nether Langwith, *Carr* 1904; Kirkby-in-Ashfield, *Carr* 1907; Cossall; Langold; Church Warsop.
2 Misson; Mattersey.
3 Common in the Trent Valley.
4 Balderton; Clipstone.

Ranunculus Drouetii F. Schultz. *Water Crowfoot*

Native. Ditches and ponds. Frequent. Divs. 1, 3, 4.

First Record: J. W. Carr, *Tr. Nott. Nats.* 1907.

1 Hills and Holes, Warsop, *Carr.*
3 Common in the Trent Valley.
4 Barnby.

Ranunculus heterophyllus Weber. *Water Crowfoot*

Native. Ditches and ponds. Very common. All Divs.

First Record: C. Deering, *Cat. Stirp.* 1738.

var. *submersus* Bab.

1 Lady Lee, Worksop.
3 Common.
4 Wysall.

var. *radians* Revel. Frequent in Div. 3.

Ranunculus peltatus Schrank. *Water Crowfoot*

Native. Ditches and ponds. Frequent. All Divs.

First Record: J. W. Carr, *Tr. Nott. Nats.* 1904, per H. Fisher.

1 Moor Green Reservoir.
2 Rufford Park, *Carr* 1907; Misson; Everton; Mattersey.
3 Common in the Trent Valley; Bunny Park; Bilsthorpe.
4 Brough.

var. *floribundus* Bab. 3 Old Trent Dyke, Newark†; Beeston, *Carr MS.*

forma *crenatus* Gluck. 4 Widmerpool.

Ranunculus calcareus Butcher. *Water Crowfoot*

Native. Shallower rivers and streams. Common. Divs. 1, 2, 3.

Ranunculus sphaerospermus Boiss. and Bl. *Water Crowfoot*

Native. Shallow rivers. Very rare. Div. 3.

Only Record: R. W. Butcher, In the River Greet, below Southwell Mill 1945.

Ranunculus Baudotii Godr. var *marinus* Arrh. and Fr.

Native. Lakes and canals. Rare. Divs. 2, 3.

First Record: R. W. Butcher 1951, Clumber Lake.

2 Clumber†; Welbeck, *Butcher*; Frequent in the Chesterfield Canal below Babworth.
3 Frequent in the Chesterfield Canal; Colwick gravel pit.

Ranunculus Lenormandi F. Schultz. *Water Crowfoot*

Native. Muddy ponds and streams. Very rare. Divs. 1, 2, 3.

First Record: J. W. Carr, *Tr. Nott. Nats.* 1905.

1 Hills and Holes, Warsop, *Carr* 1905.
2 Streams by Rufford Abbey, *Carr* 1907.
3 Beeston, *Mason*; Eaton, in a pond by a roadside.

Ranunculus hederaceus L. *Ivyleaved Crowfoot*

Native. Damp sandy places. Rare except in Div. 2. Divs. 1, 2, 3.

First Record: C. Deering, *Cat. Stirp.* 1738.

1 Startwood, Hucknall.
2 Frequent.
3 Edingley Moor, *Ordoyno*; Haughton; Besthorpe Fleet; Langford Fleet.

var *omiophyllus* 1 Startwood, Hucknall.

Ranunculus Ficaria L. *Lesser Celandine*

Native. Woods, hedges and meadows. Very common. All Divs.

First Record: C. Deering, *Cat. Stirp.* 1738.

Caltha palustris L. *Marsh Marigold*

Native. Bogs and marshy places. Common. All Divs.

First Record: C. Deering, *Cat. Stirp.* 1738.

Eranthis hyemalis (L.) Salisb. *Winter Aconite*

Alien. Woods and fields. A frequent garden escape and naturalised plant of ornamental woodland in all divisions. The following records are noteworthy.

4 "Thoroughly naturalized in an isolated wood at Langar"† *Carr*; "Some fields and copses in this neighbourhood are quite yellow with this plant". 'R.E.C.' of Elton, *Phytologist* 1859.

Aquilegia vulgaris L. *Columbine*

Native. Limestone Woodland. Very rare, only native in Div. 1. Divs. 1, 2, 3.

First Record: C. Deering, *Cat. Stirp.* 1738.

1 Aspley, *Deering*; Linby,† *Jowett*; Bulwell; Newstead; Pleasley, *G. Howitt*; Steetley Coppice, *Bohler* 1875; High Park Wood, Greasley, *Gilbert*; Skegby; Shireoaks; Teversall, *Carr* 1905; Scratta Wood, Shireoaks, *Roffey*; Nuthall, *Nott. Field Science Club* 1951.
2 Finningley; Budby, both escapes.
3 Naturalised in a hedge at North Leverton.

Helleborus viridis L. *Green Bears' Foot*

Native. Limestone Woodland. Very rare, only native in Div. 1, elsewhere a relic of cultivation. Divs. 1, 3.

First Record: G. Howitt, *Fl. Notts.* 1839, reported by B. Eddison.

1 Grives Wood, Kirkby, *G. Howitt*; Wallingwells, *Friend*, Still there in quantity.
3 Misterton, field on left going to the Soss, *Brown*. Naturalised at Kingshaugh, Darlton.

Helleborus foetidus L. *Stinking Bears' Foot*

Native or denizen. Ornamental grounds. Rare. Divs. 1, 4.

First Record: *T. Jowett, Bot. Cals.* 1826.

1 Kirby Woodhouse not far from the railroad, *Jowett*. This record is initialled "B.E." and might be an error for Eddison's record of *H. viridis*.
4 Old Vicarage garden at Elton.

Nigella damascena L. *Love-in-a-mist*

Alien. Casual. Occurs on rubbish tips and near gardens.

Delphinium Ajacis L. *Larkspur*

Alien. Has been found in various parts of the county near gardens and on rubbish tips, but is nowhere truly naturalised.

First Record: G. Howitt *Fl. Notts.* 1839. "Nottingham Park; Trentside near Wilford, perhaps not truly wild."

D. orientale J. Gay is also reported.

BERBERIDACEAE

Berberis vulgaris L. *Common Berberis*

Native or denizen. Hedges. Widely distributed, but uncommon and apparently decreasing. All Divs.

First Record: C. Deering, *Cat. Stirp.* 1738.

1 Strelley; Mansfield, *G. Howitt*; Carlton in Lindrick, *Friend*; About Sellars Wood, Bulwell, *Carr MS.*; Cossall; Hucknall.
2 Radford, *Deering*; Osberton, *Ordoyno*; Church Cemetery, Nottingham, *Bohler* 1866.
3 Clifton by Nottingham; Mapperley; Chilwell, *Deering*; Normanton; Holme Pierrepont; Fiskerton†, *Ordoyno*; Morton, *G. Howitt.*
4 Thorpe in the Glebe, *Carr MS.*; Owthorpe; Wysall.

Mahonia Aquifolium (Pursh.) Nutt. *Oregon Grape*

Alien. Denizen. Widely planted in woods for game cover and often persisting. All Divs.

NYMPHACEAE

Nuphar lutea (L.) Sm. *Yellow Water Lily*

Native. Pools, Canals and slow streams. Common, except in Div. 2.

First Record: C. Deering, *Cat. Stirp.* 1738.

2 Dyke at Park Drain Station, Misson, *Carr MS.*; Hesley; Wiseton Canal.

Nymphea alba L. *White Water Lily*

Native. River and Pools. Rare. All Divs.

First Record: C. Deering, *Cat. Stirp.* 1738.

1 River Erewash at Eastwood, *G. Howitt*; Pond near Old Moor Wood, Strelley, *Carr MS.*; Newstead; Shireoaks; Nuthall; Probably planted in these three localities.
2 Rainworth, Hesley and Wollaton Lakes. All probably planted.
3 Cheney Pool, Nottingham; Ditch between Lenton and Beeston, *Deering*; Langford Fleet; Ponds at Collingham†, *Ordoyno*; Beeston Canal at Lenton, *Jowett*; Pool on Fledborough Holme, *Penrose*; Mons Pool† and Black Pool, Besthorpe, *Fisher.*
4 Doctor's Pond, Coddington, possibly planted.

PAPAVERACEAE

Papaver somniferum L. *Opium Poppy*

Alien. Casual. Occurs on all rubbish tips and in waste places. All Divs.

First Record: G. Howitt, *Notts. Fl.* 1839 "Sandy fields and amongst rubbish".

Papaver Rhoeas L. *Field Poppy*

Native. Arable fields, roadsides and waste places. Still very common but decreasing. All Divs.

First Record: C. Deering, *Cat. Stirp.* 1738.

Papaver dubium L. *Longheaded Poppy*

Native. Arable fields, roadsides and waste places. Still very common but decreasing. All Divs.

First Record: T. Ordoyno, *Fl. Nott.* 1807.

Papaver Lecoqii Lamotte

Native. Arable fields. Distribution uncertain. Divs. 3, 4.

First Record: J. W. Carr, *Tr. Nott. Nats.* 1905, "*P. dubium* and *P. Lecoqii* occur in the County, but the former is the commoner."

3 Lowdham, *Carr* 1909; Bramcote, *Butcher*; Farndon.
4 Owthorpe; Kinoulton; Thorpe in the Glebe, *Carr MS.*

Papaver Argemone L. *Pale Poppy*

Native. Arable fields on light soils. Locally frequent. All Divs.

First Record: C. Deering, *Cat. Stirp.* 1738.

1 Bulwell†; Worksop, *Carr MS.*
2 Frequent.
3 Frequent on the gravels and Blown Sand.
4 Broadholme; Harby; West Leake; Wigsley, *Carr MS.*; Kilvington.

Meconopsis cambrica (L.) Vig. *Welsh Poppy*

Casual. Garden escape, nowhere naturalised.

Glaucium corniculatum (L.) Curtis *Red Horned Poppy*

Alien. Casual. Very rare. Div. 3.

Only Record: H. Fisher, *Rept. Brit. Ass.* 1893; Newark wharfs, plentifully.

Roemeria hybrida (L.) DC.

Alien. Casual. Very rare. Div. 3.

Only Record: H. Fisher, *Rept. Brit. Ass.* 1893; Newark Wharfs, rare.

Bocconia cordata Willd. *Mexican Plume Poppy*

Alien. A garden escape sometimes persisting in orchards and near houses.

Chelidonium majus L. *Greater Celandine*

Denizen. Roadsides and hedge banks near houses. Common. All Divs.

First Record: C. Deering, *Cat. Stirp.* 1738.

Eschscholtzia californica Cham.

Alien. Casual. Frequent as a garden escape and on rubbish dumps. All Divs.

FUMARIACEAE

Corydalis claviculata (L.) DC. *Climbing Fumitory*

Native. Damp woods on sand. Rare. Div. 2.

First Record: J. K. Miller, *Fl. Walk., Nat.* 1895.

2 Barrow Hills, near Bawtry, *Miller*; Hazel Gap, *Staton*; Norton; Oxton Bogs; Carburton; Lings Wood, Scaftworth; Mattersey Wood.

Corydalis bulbosa (L.) DC.

Alien. Divs. 1, 2.

First Record: G. Howitt, *Notts. Fl.* 1839.

1 In an old quarry at Mansfield, *G. Howitt*.
2 Near Annesley Church, *G. Howitt*; In the moat at Hodsock Priory; Shrubbery at Rainworth Lodge, *Carr MS*.

Corydalis lutea (L.) DC. *Yellow Fumitory*

Alien. Denizen. Frequently naturalised on walls. All Divs.

First Record: J. W. Carr, *Victoria County History* 1906.

Fumaria capreolata agg.

"By far the most common species in the neighbourhood of Nottingham." *Jowett*. "Frequent in the Sand District" (Div. 2), *G. Howitt*. There are no modern records of any of the species of this aggregate.

(**Fumaria muralis** Sonder is recorded with a query for Div. 1 in *V.C.H.* 1906)

Fumaria officinalis L. *Common Fumitory*

Native. Arable fields, gardens, waste places. Very common, especially on light soils. All Divs.

First Record: C. Deering, *Cat. Stirp.* 1738.

CRUCIFERAE

Cheriantus Cheiri L. *Wallflower*

Alien. Denizen. Old walls and rocks. Widespread but not common. Divs. 1, 2, 3.

First Record: C. Deering, *Cat. Stirp.* 1738.

1 Cresswell Crags; Worksop Priory.
2 Nottingham Castle†, *Deering*; Church Cemetery, Nottingham, *Bohler* 1866.
3 Garden Walls, Normanton (on-Soar), *Pulteney MS.*; Newark Castle† and Friary Walls†, *Ordoyno*; Aslockton.

Nasturtium officinale R.Br. *Watercress*

Native. Streams, ponds and marshes. Very common. All Divs.

First Record: C. Deering, *Cat. Stirp.* 1738.

Nasturtium microphyllum (Boenn.) Rchb. has not yet been recorded.

Rorippa sylvestris (L.) Besser. *Creeping Watercress*

Native. River sides. Locally common. Divs. 2, 3.

First Record: T. Ordoyno, *Fl. Nott.* 1807.

2 Farnsfield Carr; Oxton Stews, *Ordoyno*; Misson†; Lenton; Beeston, *Carr MS.*; Scaftworth.
3 Common on the Trent bank, in the tidal reach it is often dominant; Edingley Moor, *Ordoyno.*

Rorippa amphibia (L.) Besser. *Great Watercress*

Native. Beside rivers, ponds and streams. Common except in Div. 4. All Divs.

First Record: C. Deering, *Cat. Stirp.* 1738.

4 Owthorpe; Hickling.

Rorippa islandica (Oeder.) Borbas. *Marsh Watercress*

Native. River banks and marshes. Common except in Div. 4. All Divs.

First Record: C. Deering, *Cat. Stirp.* 1738.

4 Barnby-in-the-Willows.

Rorippa austriaca (Crantz) Besser.

Alien. Casual. Divs. 1, 2.

First Record: 1953, Eastwood.

1 Banks of the Erewash at Eastwood.
2 Drainsides, Misson.

Barbarea stricta Andrz. *Small Flowered Wintercress*

Denizen. Riversides, willow holts, damp waste land. Locally frequent and probably increasing. Divs. 2, 3.

First Record: J. Brown; *N.W.N.* 1944.

2 Misson; Mattersey; Drake Holes, *Brown*; Scaftworth; Everton; Scrooby. All these records are in the Idle Valley.
3 Frequent on the Trent side; Stanford-on-Soar.

Barbarea verna Asch.

Alien. Rare. Div. 3.

First Record: J. W. Carr MS. 1910.

3 Sneinton Dale, Nottingham, *Carr*; Roadside, Girton 1962.

Barbarea vulgaris R. Br.

Native. Riversides and damp places. Common in Divs. 2 and 3, less so in 1 and 4.

First Record: C. Deering, *Cat. Stirp.* 1738.

var. *arctuata* (Opiz) Fr. is occasionally recorded.

Barbarea intermedia Bor.

Alien. A casual of arable fields, particularly in grass leys. Widespread and occurring frequently in certain years. Divs. 1, 2, 3.

First Record: J. Brown, Misson 1950.

1 Nether Langwith.
2 Misson, *Brown*; Bestwood.
3 Bathley; Egmanton; Marnham; Clayworth; Holme Pierrepont; Clarborough.

Arabis hirsuta (L.) Scop. *Hairy Rock Cress*

Native. Limestone Rocks. Rare. Div. 1.

First Record: T. Ordoyno, *Fl. Nott.* 1807.

1 Newstead; Bulwell Lime Quarries, *Ordoyno*; Cinderhill; Nuthall; Between Shortwood and Hucknall, *Jowett*; Mansfield, *Bradley*; Pleasley Vale†, *G. Howitt*; Church Warsop†; Cresswell Crags†; Nether Langwith†, *Carr MS.*; Near Shireoaks, *Roffey*.

Turritis glabra L. *Tower Mustard*

Native. Sandy fields and roadsides. Very rare, or extinct. Div. 2.

First Record: C. Deering, *Cat. Stirp.* 1738.

2 Between Radford and Lenton, *Deering*; Blyth; Cuckney, *Ordoyno*; Bestwood Park; Wollaton, *Jowett*; Bulwell, *G. Howitt*; Barrow Hills, near Bawtry, *Carr* 1904; Near Gleadthorpe, Warsop, *Roffey*.

Cardamine pratensis L. *Cuckoo Flower*

Native. Damp meadows. Very common. All Divs.

First Record: C. Deering, *Cat. Stirp.* 1738.

Cardamine amara L. *Large Bittercress*

Native. Spongy ground near streams, woodland bogs, and willow holts. Frequent in Divs. 1 and 2, less so in 3 (where it is restricted to alluvial soils), absent from 4.

First Record: T. Ordoyno, *Fl. Nott.* 1807.

Cardamine impatiens L. *Narrow Bittercress*

Native. Stony places. Probably extinct. Div. 1.

Only Record: G. Howitt, *Notts. Fl.* 1839. "Banks of the Cromford Canal near Brinsley and Langley Mill."

Cardamine flexuosa With. *Wavy Bittercress*

Native. Marshes, drain sides, damp woods. Common except in Div. 4. All Divs.

First Record: Specimen in Herb. Jowett 1823 labelled '*C. hirsuta*'. A. Gilbert, *Botany for Beginners* 1888.

4 Langford; Rempstone.

Cardamine hirsuta L. *Hairy Bittercress*

Native. Sandy heaths, gardens, railway banks and tracks. Fairly common. All Divs.

First Record: T. Ordoyno, *Fl. Nott.* 1807.

1 Cossall; Wollaton, *Carr*; Hills and Holes, Warsop; Teversall railway.
2 Common both in natural habitats and on railways.
3 On all railways and as a garden weed.
4 Langford Moor; Kilvington railway.

Lunaria annua L. *Honesty*

Alien. Casual. A common plant of rubbish dumps and a garden escape.

Alyssum Alyssoides L. *Small Alison*

Alien. Colonist. Railway cuttings. Very rare. Divs. 2, 3.

First Record: J. W. Carr, *Victoria County History* 1906.

2 *Victoria County History*, in brackets.
3 Stanford-on-Soar; Bingham.

Alyssum incanum L.

Alien. Casual. Waste places. Div. 3.

Only Record: H. Fisher, *Rept. Brit. Ass.* 1893, Newark.

Alyssum maritimum Lam. *Sweet Alison*

Alien. Casual. A very common garden escape and rubbish dump plant, but not established. All Divs.

Eriophila verna (L.) Cheval *Whitlow Grass*

Native. Sandy and rocky places, railway tracks. Common. All Divs.

First Record: C. Deering, *Cat. Stirp.* 1738.

1 Hills and Holes, Warsop; Nuthall; Welbeck.
2 Common.
3 Common on the blown sand and river gravels, and on railways.
4 Langford Moor; Coddington; Wysall.

Cochlearia Armoracia L. *Horse Radish*

Alien, Denizen. Roadsides, waste places, river banks. Common. All Divs.

First Record: C. Deering, *Cat. Stirp.* 1738, 'grows only in Gardens.' T. Ordoyno, *Fl. Notts.* 1807; 'Sides of ditches, in gardens, Newark; Southwell.'

Cochlearia officinalis L. *Common Scurvy Grass*

Casual. Div. 2.

Only Record: C. Deering, *Cat. Stirp.* 1738. 'In several Places on Woollaton Walls but dare not say whether the Garden might not perhaps have furnished and the Wind sown the seed, it is commonly cultivated in Gardens . . . . .'.

Hesperis matronalis L. *Dames' Violet*

Alien. Denizen or casual. River banks, woods and dumps. Uncommon. Divs. 2, 3.

First Record: T. Jowett, *Bot. Cals.* 1826.

2 Annesley Forest.
3 Colwick Park; Clifton Hill, *Jowett;* Trent Bank, Beeston, *Williams*; Trent Bank, Farndon; Gamston Dump.

Sisymbrium Sophia L. *Flixweed*

Colonist. Arable land or waste places. Uncommon. Divs. 1, 2, 3.

First Record: C. Deering, *Cat. Stirp.* 1738. 'Not uncommon hereabout'.

1 Basford, *Deering.*
2 Between Nottingham and Radford, *Deering*; Bobber's Mill, *G. Howitt*; Harwell, *Mrs. Sandwith*; Parliament Oak, Warsop, *Williams*; Clipstone.
3 Southwell; Newark†, *Ordoyno*; Gringley Carr†, *Miller*; Gamston; Shelford Manor, *Carr MS.*; Arnold, *Williams.*

Sisymbrium altissimum L.

Alien. Rubbish Dumps, pit dumps, waste places and roadsides. Common. Increasing rapidly, and now nearly as frequent as the next species. Divs. 1, 2, 3.

First Record: H. Fisher, *Rept. Brit. Ass.* 1893.

Sisymbrium orientale L. *Eastern Rocket*

Alien. Similar situations to *S. altissimum.* Very common and probably still increasing. All Divs.

First Record: H. Fisher, *Rept. Brit. Ass.* 1893.

Sisymbrium officinale (L.) Scop. *Hedge Mustard*

Native. Roadsides and waste places. Very common. All Divs.

First Record: C. Deering, *Cat. Stirp.* 1738.

var. *leiocarpum* DC. occurs fairly frequently throughout the county.

Sisymbrium Thalianum (L.) Gay. *Thale Cress*

Native. Sandy heaths, walls, railway lines, gravel paths. Common in all Divs.

First Record: T. Ordoyno, *Fl. Nott.* 1807.

Sisymbrium Loeselii L.

Alien. This plant occurs in large quantities on Messrs. Boots' rubbish dump at Dunkirk, Nottingham. It is spreading into lanes and waste ground in Dunkirk Meadows, and onto Nottingham Corporation's tip close by. The firm tells us the seed was probably imported with liquorice root from Persia and the Near East. First found 1960. Div. 3.

Alliaria petiolata (Bieb.) Cavara and Grande. *Garlic Mustard*

Native. Hedge banks and under trees. Very common. All Divs.

First Record: C. Deering, *Cat. Stirp.* 1738.

Erysimum cherianthoides L. *Treacle Mustard*

Colonist. Arable fields on light soils. Locally common. All Divs.

First Record: J. K. Miller, *Fl. Walk.* 1819-55, *Nat.* 1895.

1 Broxtowe, *Gilbert*; Welbeck.
2 Forest Hill, Worksop, *Roffey*; Mattersey, *Brown*; Misson; Torworth; Rufford.
3 Common on river gravels, blown sand and on the Carrs.
4 Gotham Hills.

Conringia orientalis (L.) Dum.

Alien. Casual. Div. 3.

Only Record: H. Fisher, *Rept. Brit. Ass.* 1893, Newark.

Camelina sativa (L.) Crantz. *Gold of Pleasure*

Alien. Casual. Waste places. Rare. Divs. 2, 3.

First Record: R. E. G. Cole, sp. in Lincoln City Museum 1859.

2 Field between Styrrup and Serlby, *Brown*; Crossroads east of Styrrup, *Brown.*

3 Field on the footpath between Langar and Bingham, *Cole*; Newark Wharfs, *Fisher*; *Leather*; Nottingham Dump, frequently.

Camelina Alyssum (Mill). Thellung.

Alien. Casual. Divs. 1 or 2.

Only Record: A. Gilbert, *Bot. for Beginners* 'Cornfields at Kirkby', 1888.

Brassica campestris L. *'Trentside Rape'*

Denizen. River sides. This is the common cabbage on the banks of the Trent, Idle and Soar. Divs. 1, 3. Specimens have been identified by Mr. J. E. Lousley.

1 Roadside, Warsop.

Brassica nigra (L.) Koch. *Black Mustard*

Denizen or casual. Waste ground and roadsides. Frequent. All Divs.

First Record: C. Deering, *Cat. Stirp.* 1738, 'only met with in Gardens'. T. Ordoyno, *Fl. Nott.* 1809, 'Cornfields, ditch banks and roadsides; Newark'.

Brassica arvensis Kuntze. *Charlock, 'Ketlock'*

Native. Arable fields and waste places. Very common. All Divs.

First Record: C. Deering, *Cat. Stirp.* 1738.

Brassica alba (L.) Boiss. *White Mustard*

Alien. Casual. Roadsides and waste ground. A frequent relic of cultivation. All Divs.

First Record: C. Deering, *Cat. Stirp.* 1738, "only met with in Gardens". T. Ordoyno, *Fl. Nott.* 1807, "Cornfields, roadsides and in gardens; Newark; Southwell; Mansfield."

Brassica juncea Coss.

Alien. Casual. Div. 1.

Only Record: J. Brown 1950, 'Lady Lee, Worksop'.

Brassica gallica Willd.

Alien. Colonist or denizen. Div. 4.

Only Record: Barnstone Quarry 1950 *et seq.*

Diplotaxis tenuifolia (L.) DC.

Colonist or casual. Waste places. Rare. Divs. 1, 3, 4.

First Record: Barnstone 1950 *et. seq.*

1 Kimberley.
3 Thorney; Nottingham Dump.
4 Barnstone Quarry.

Diplotaxis muralis (L.) DC. *Stinkweed*

Alien. Casual or Colonist. Waste ground and railway lines. Widespread. All Divs.

First Record: H. Fisher, *Rep. Brit. Ass.* 1893.

1 Woodend, Worksop, *Brown*; Kimberley.
2 Kilton, Worksop, *Brown.*
3 Between Nottingham and Lenton, *Fisher*; Leenside, Nottingham, *Williams*; Welham, *Adams;* Newark; Nottingham Dump; Kilvington; Bingham; Granby.
4 Barnstone Quarry.

Capsella Bursa-pastoris (L.) Medic *Shepherd's Purse*

Native. Arable land, roadsides, waste places. Very common. All Divs.

First Record: C. Deering, *Cat. Stirp.* 1738.

Coronopus didymus (L.) Sm. *Lesser Swinecress*

Alien. Casual. Waste ground and corn fields. Rare. Divs. 1, 2, 3.

First Record: H. C. Watson, *Top. Bot.* specimen from Dr. B. Carrington, 1859.

1 Welbeck.
2 Radford, *Carrington*, specimen in Herb. Watson at Kew.
3 Lowdham; Newark; Nottingham Dump.

Coronopus squamatus (Forsk) Aschers. *Swinecress*

Native. Arable fields, gateways, farmyards, on heavy clays. Common in Div. 3 and 4, rare elsewhere. Divs. 2, 3, 4.

First Record: C. Deering, *Cat. Stirp.* 1738.

2 Wollaton, *Deering*; Misson.

Lepidium Draba (L.) *Hoary Pepperwort*

Alien. Denizen. Waste ground, roadsides, etc. Common and increasing, particularly in the industrial areas and the Trent Valley. Rare in 4, and on the clays of 3. All Divs.

First Record: Sp. in Lincoln City Museum from Herb. Canon R. E. G. Cole.

4 Roadside leaving Langar towards Cropwell, opposite Langar Church, *Cole*; Coddington.

(**Lepidium ruderale** L.

Recorded by R. G. Williams for waste ground at Wilford. Probably an error for *L. neglectum.*)

Lepidium campestre (L.) R.Br. *Pepperwort*

Native. Arable fields on light soils. Not common. All Divs.

First Record: R. Pulteney, MS. notebook in Leicester Museum, "Great Leke and in the little Leke Town 1746".

1 Broxtowe, *Gilbert.*
2 Ollerton, *Jowett*; Harworth, *Winn*; Common round Nottingham, *Williams* (not our experience); Misson; Gringley; Finningley.
3 West Leake Village, *Pulteney*; Besthorpe; Hawton; Rampton; Thorney; South Clifton; Clarborough; Misterton; West Drayton.
4 East Leake, *Pulteney*; West Leake.

Lepidium sativum L. *Garden Cress*

Alien. Casual. Occurs on rubbish dumps and near gardens and sewage works.

Lepidium Smithii Hook. *Smith's Cress*

Native. Div. 4.

Only Record: G. Howitt, *Notts. Fl.* 1839 "In chalky fields and on walls: rare. West Leake."

Lepidium neglectum Thellung.

Alien. Colonist. Rubbish dumps and waste ground. Often dominant over large areas. Divs. 1, 3.

First Record: Newark 1949 det. A. J. Wilmot.

1 Bulwell Dump.
2 Newark Dump; Nottingham Dump, and waste places in the City.

Thlaspi arvense L. *Field Pennycress*

Colonist. Arable fields. Common. All Divs. It appears to have increased in the last hundred years.

First Record: T. Ordoyno *Fl. Nott.* 1807, "Fields between Sutton-on-Trent and Marnham". G. Howitt, *Notts. Fl.* 1839 does not add any more records and considers it 'rare'.

Iberis umbellata L. *Candytuft*

Alien. Casual or colonist. Frequently found on rubbish dumps and is naturalised on a road embankment at Bunny, Div. 4.

Teesdalia nudicaulis (L.) R. Br. *Teesdalia*

Native. Sandy heaths. Locally common on the bunter, blown sand and gravel. Divs. 2, 3, 4.

First Record: Derham's Edition of J. Ray's *Philosophical Letters* 1718, "Frequent in the sandy grounds hereabout." (Wollaton) April 1670.

2 Frequent.
3 North Muskham, *Ordoyno*; Wigsley Wood; Girton; South Clifton.
4 Langford Moor, *Ordoyno*.

Euclydium syriacum (L.) R. Br.

Alien. Casual. Div. 3.

Only Record: H. Fisher, *Rept. Brit. Ass.* 1893, Newark.

Crambe orientalis L.

Alien. Casual. Div. 3.

Only Record: A. R. Horwood *Aliens from Notts., B. E. C. Rept.* 1915, Newark per Rev. A. Handel Smith.

Raphistrum rugosum (L.) All.

Alien. Casual. Dumps, wharfs, and waste places. Uncommon. Divs. 1, 2, 3.

First Record: H. Fisher, *Rept. Brit. Ass.* 1893.

1 Bulwell Dump.
2 Canal side, Worksop.
3 Newark, *Fisher*; Farndon kilns; Nottingham Dump; Wilford Dump.

Raphistrum hispanicum (L.) Crantz.

Alien. Casual. Div. 3.

Only Record: Nottingham Dump 1958.

Raphanus Raphanistrum L. *Wild Radish, "Lunch Bowl"*

Colonist. Arable land and waste places. Very common. All Divs.

First Record: T. Ordoyno, *Fl. Nott.* 1807.

var *raphanistrum* and var *flavus* are equally common, var *aureus* has not been recorded.

Raphanus sativus L. *Garden Radish*

Alien. Casual. Frequent on rubbish dumps and near gardens.

RESEDACEAE

Reseda lutea L. *Wild Mignonette*

Denizen. Waste places and roadsides. Uncommon. All Divs.

First Record: T. Ordoyno *Fl. Nott.* 1807, "Bulwell Lime Kilns".

1 Frequent.
2 Clipstone.
3 Railway bank near Aslockton, *Carr MS.*; Newark; Cropwell Bishop; Toton; Gringley; West Stockwith; Colwick; Walkeringham; Nottingham.
4 Willoughby-on-Wolds.

Reseda Luteola L. *Weld*

Native. Waste ground, riversides, arable land. Common. All Divs.

First Record: C. Deering. *Cat. Stirp.* 1738.

Reseda odorata L. *Garden Mignonette*

Alien. Casual. Common on rubbish dumps.

Reseda alba L.

Alien.

Only Record: H. C. Watson, *N.B.G.* 1835; Nottingham Castle, sp. C. Babington, "probably planted . . . not mentioned by Howitt". Div. 2.

CISTACEAE

Helianthemum Chamaecistus Mill. *Rock Rose*

Native. Meadows and rocks on calcareous soils. Rare and decreasing. Divs. 1, 2, 3.

First Record: C. Deering, *Cat. Stirp.* 1738.

1 Between Two Mile House and Nuthall, *Deering*; Aspley; Broxtowe; Bulwell, *Jowett*; Sutton; Mansfield, *Gilbert*; East Kirkby†; Church Warsop†; Shireoaks†; Linby; Teversall; Skegby; Sookholme Moor, *Carr MS.*; Annesley.
2 Nottingham Castle Rock, *Deering*.
3 Oxton Toll Bar, *Ordoyno*; Hayton Castle, *Miller*; Eaton†; Gamston, *Carr MS.*

VIOLACEAE

Viola Reichenbachiana Jord. *Wood Dog Violet*

Native. Woods and copses. Common. All Divs.

First Record: A. Gilbert, *Bot. for Beginners* 1888.

Viola Riviniana Reichb. *Common Dog Violet*

Native. Woods and hedgebanks. Very common. All Divs.

First Record: C. Deering, *Cat. Stirp.* 1738.

Viola canina L.—ssp. **canina** *Yellow Spurred Dog Violet*

var *ericetorum* Reichb.

Native. Heaths and sandy woods. Locally frequent. Divs. 2, 3, 4.

First Record: H. Fisher, *Brit. Ass. Rept.* 1893.

2 Frequent on the Forest and the Carrs.
3 Misterton Carr, *Miller* (this record might be ssp. *montana*); Haughton; Spalford.
4 Cotgrave; Langford Moor; Coddington; Barnby.

ssp. **montana** (L.) Fries.

Native. Peaty meadows. Rare. Div. 3.

3 Clifton by Nottingham; Gonalston, both det. Prof. D. H. Valentine.

Viola canina x Riviniana Reichb.

2 Lound.

Viola stagnina Kit. *Fen Violet*

Native. Peaty meadows. Very rare or extinct. Divs. 2, 3.

First Record: Specimen in Lincoln Museum from Revd. Owston 1840.

2 Between Misson and Misterton, *Owston*, *Miller* (as *V. lactea*). Between Misson and Newington† *Mrs. Sandwith.* The plant was flourishing in this station in 1952, but by 1956 the field had been ploughed and re-seeded. It may still survive on the headland.
3 Dyke near Oatland Farm, Gringley Carr 1909, *Carr MS.*

Viola odorata L. *Sweet Violet*

Native. Woods and hedgesides. Common. All Divs.

First Record: C. Deering, *Cat. Stirp.* 1738.

Viola x permixta Jord. (V. *odorata x hirta.*)

Occurs with the parents.

First Record: J. W. Carr, *Trans. Nott. Nats.*, Widmerpool and Clipstone. Div. 4.

Viola hirta L. *Hairy Violet*

Native. Banks and hedges on calcareous soils. Frequent except in Div. 2. All Divs.

First Record: T. Ordoyno, *Fl. Nott.* 1807.

2 Warsop, *Carr MS.*; Budby Forest.

Viola palustris L. *Marsh Violet*

Native. Bogs and boggy woods. Less frequent than formerly. All Divs.

First Record: T. Ordoyno, *Fl. Nott.* 1807.

1 Bulwell, *Jowett*; Greasley; Newstead.
2 Still frequent.
3 Girton; Spalford; New Park, Rufford.
4 Stapleford Moor, *Ordoyno.* (Probably in Lincolnshire.)

Viola tricolor L. *Heartsease*

Native. Arable fields. Common. All Divs.

First Record: C. Deering, *Cat. Stirp.* 1738.

Viola Lejeunei Jord.

Only Record: E. and H. Drabble *B. E. C. Rept.* 1926, Misson. Div. 2.

Viola arvensis Murr. *Field Pansy*

Native. Arable fields and waste ground, particularly on acid soil. Commoner than *V. tricolor.* All Divs.

Viola segetalis Jord.

First Record: J. W. Carr, *Trans. Nott. Nats.* 1908, per E. and H. Drabble. E. and H. Drabble, *B. E. C. Rept.* 1926.

1 Strelley; West Norbury, *Drabble.*
2 Misson, *Drabble.*

Viola Lloydii Jord. Var *insignis* Drabble.

First Record: J. W. Carr, *Trans. Nott. Nats.* 1908, per E. and H. Drabble. E. and H. Drabble, *B. E. C. Rept.* 1926.

1 Strelley.
2 Misson.

Viola obtusifolia Jord.

Only Record: J. W. Carr, *Trans. Nott. Nats.* 1908 per E. and H. Drabble, Misson, Div. 2.

Viola lepida Jord.

Native. Sandy fields and roadsides, sandy banks. Locally abundant in the North. Div. 2.

First Record: J. W. Carr, *Trans. Nott. Nats.* 1908, per E. Drabble. E. and H. Drabble, *B. E. C. Rept.* 1926.

2 Misson†; Everton†; *Drabble*; Finningley; Hesley; Scrooby; Scaftworth; Harworth.

Viola lutea Huds. *Mountain Pansy*

Native. Probably extinct. Div. 2.

Only Record: G. Howitt, *Notts. Fl.* 1839 "In upland pastures, rare; Bramcote."

POLYGALACEAE

Polygala serpyllifolium Hose. *Milkwort*

Native. Heaths and old pastures on acid soil. Decreasing. All Divs.

First Record: J. W. Carr, *Trans. Nott. Nats.* 1903.

1 East Kirkby, *Carr*; Cossall; Felley; Moor Green; Teversall.
2 Rather frequent.
3 Gamston by Retford, *Carr MS.*; Haughton; Eakring; Milton.
4 Langford Moor†, *Carr*; Brough.

Polygala vulgaris L. *Milkwort*

Native. Pastures and roadsides on basic soils. Commoner than *P. serpyllifolium* but not recorded for Div. 2. Divs. 1, 3, 4.

First Record: J. W. Carr, *Trans. Nott. Nats.* 1904, earlier records refer to the aggregate species.

Polygala oxyptera Reichb. *Milkwort*

Native. Old pastures. Rare. Divs. 1, 3.

First Record: J. W. Carr, *Trans. Nott. Nats.* 1905.

1 Between Moor Green Reservoir and High Park Wood, *Carr MS.*
3 Abundant in a field at South Wheatley, *Carr* 1905.

CARYOPHYLLACEAE

Dianthus deltoides L. *Maiden Pink*

Native. Around sandstone rocks. Extinct. Divs. 2, 3.

First Record: W. How, *Phytologia Britannica* 1650, per Mr. Stonehouse.

2 Nottingham Park, *Stonehouse*, *Deering*, *G. Howitt*; Nottingham Gallows, *Willisell*, *Deering*; Lenton Hollows, *Deering*; Nottingham Forest, *G. Howitt*.
3 Beeston Lane, *G. Howitt*.

Dianthus Armeria L. *Deptford Pink*

Denizen or casual. Frequent near gardens and on rubbish dumps.

Dianthus Caryophyllus L. *Clove Pink*

Alien. Denizen. Pastures and old walls. Div. 2.

Only Record: T. Jowett, *Bot. Cals.* 1826, 'Rufford, per Botham,' repeated by G. Howitt.

Saponaria officinalis L. *Soapwort*

Denizen. Hedgebanks. Usually near villages. Uncommon. All Divs.

First Record: C. Deering, *Cat. Stirp.* 1738.

1 Mansfield, *Deering*; Hucknall; Hempsall; Nuthall, *Deering's* MS. additions quoted by *Jowett*; Park Hall.
2 Between Mansfield and Sherwood Hall, *Ordoyno*; Between Mattersey and Everton, *Brown*; Blyth; Scrooby; Scaftworth; Harworth; Welbeck.
3 Cottam; Drake Holes; South Collingham; Misterton; West Stockwith; Bunny Park; Newark.
4 Harby.

Saponaria Vaccaria L.

Alien. Casual. Waste places. Rare. Div. 3.

First Record: H. Fisher, *Rept. Brit. Ass.* 1883.

3 Newark Wharfs, very abundant, *Fisher*; Garden weed at Farndon.

Silene Cucubalus Wibel *Bladder Campion*

Native. Grassy places and waste ground. Locally common. All Divs.

First Record: C. Deering, *Cat. Stirp.* 1738.

1 Common.
2 Nottingham Church Cemetery, *Bohler* 1866; Rainworth; Lindhurst; Scofton; Styrrup; Ranskill; Scrooby.
3 Clifton (by Nottingham), *Jowett*; Brinkley Railway Bridge, Southwell. Carr's MS. has some dozen records for this division.
4 Rather common.

Silene conica L. *Striated Catchfly*

Casual. Occurred as a weed in lawn seed at Farndon 1935.

Silene noctiflora L. *Nightflowering Catchfly*

Native. Arable fields on limestone and basic peat soils. Uncommon. All Divs.

First Record: G. Howitt, *Fl. Notts.*, 1839.

1 Between Mansfield and Sutton-in-Ashfield; Near Bilborough, *G. Howitt.*
2 Nottingham Castle Grounds, *Gilbert.*
3 Cotgrave; Holme Pierrepont; East Stoke.
4 West Leake; Gotham; Cotham; Balderton; Kinoulton.

Silene anglica L. *Small flowered Catchfly*

Native. Arable fields on sand. Very rare. Divs. 2, 4.

First Record: Specimen in Herb. Jowett 1821. No locality.

2 Near Mansfield; Farnsfield and Oxton Forests, *G. Howitt*; Finningley.
4 Cornfields, Langford Moor, *Fisher.*

Silene nutans L. *Nottingham Catchfly*

Native. Rocks and walls. Probably extinct. Div. 2.

First Record: J. Ray, *Cat. Plant. Angl.* 1670.

2 Nottingham Castle, *Ray per Mr. Willisel*; Sneinton Hermitage, *Deering*; Nottingham Park, *G. Howitt.*
Godfrey Howitt remarks on the spread of the plant after the Castle was burnt in the Reform Bill riots, but by 1880 Mrs. Gilbert describes it as rare. It was more or less exterminated by the restoration about 1890. In 1934 one plant was seen by Miss V. Leather flowering in a newly made rockery in the Castle grounds, but was destroyed before it could seed. It might reappear in similar circumstances, and should be watched for and given chance to re-establish itself.

Lychnis Flos cuculi L. *Ragged Robin*

Native. Damp meadows and marshes. Widespread but decreasing. Least common in Div. 4 when the clays produce few suitable habitats. All Divs.

First Record: C. Deering, *Cat. Stirp.* 1738.

Lychnis alba Mill. *White Campion*

Native. Arable fields, waste places and roadsides. Common. All Divs.

First Record: C. Deering, *Cat. Stirp.* 1738.

Lychnis x intermedia (*alba x dioica*)

Common with the parents.

Lychnis dioica L. *Red Campion*

Native. Woods and shady hedgerows. Common. All Divs.

First Record: C. Deering, *Cat. Stirp.* 1738.

Lychnis Githago (L.) Scop. *Corn Cockle*

Native. Arable fields. Formerly common, now extremely rare. All Divs.

First Record: C. Deering, *Cat. Stirp.* 1738, "Among the Corn, common."

3 Norwell 1952.

Cerastium quaternellum Fenzl. *Upright Mouse Ear Chickweed*

Native. Sandy heaths. Very rare, we have been unable to find this plant though many suitable habitats exist. Divs. 2, 3, 4.

First Record: T. Ordoyno, *Fl. Nott.* 1807.

2 Nottingham Park and Forest; Bulwell Forest, *Jowett*; 'Abundant in the neighbourhood of Nottingham,' *G. Howitt.*
3 Edingley Moor, *Ordoyno.*
4 Coddington Moor, *Ordoyno.*

Cerastium arvense L. *Field Mouse-ear Chickweed*

Native. Grassy places on sand. Locally common. All Divs.

First Record: J. Ray, *Phil. Letters* (Ed. 1718) "Frequent in the sandy grounds hereabout" (Wollaton).

1 Haggonfields, Worksop, *Roffey.*
2 Common.
3 Frequent on the river gravels and blown sand.
4 Thorney; Wigsley; Barnby; Coddington; Balderton.

Cerastium vulgatum L. *Common Mouse-ear Chickweed*

Native. Grassy places. Very common. All Divs.

First Record: C. Deering, *Cat. Stirp.* 1738.

Cerastium glomeratum Thuill. *Sticky Mouse-ear Chickweed*

Native. Meadows, heaths and arable fields. Common. All Divs.

First Record: C. Deering, *Cat. Stirp.* 1738.

Cerastium semidecandrum L.

Native. Heaths and sandy meadows, railway lines. Locally common. Divs. 2, 3, 4.

First Record: C. Deering, *Cat. Stirp.* 1738.

2 Common.
3 Frequent on the river gravels, blown sand and railways.
4 Wigsley; Barnby.

Cerastium tetrandrum Curt.

Rare or overlooked. Railway tracks. Div. 2.

Only Record: Railway between Chequer House Station and Worksop 1962, det. E. Milne Redhead.

Cerastium tormentosum L. *Snow-in-Summer*

Alien. A common and invasive garden plant, often naturalised around villages. All Divs.

Stellaria aquatica Scop. *Water Chickweed*

Native. River, drain and pond sides. Common, especially in the Trent Valley. All Divs.

First Record: C. Deering, *Cat. Stirp.* 1738.

Stellaria nemorum L. *Wood Stitchwort*

Native. Damp woodland. Very rare. Divs. 2, 3.

First Record: H. C. Watson, *N. B. G.* 1835, on the authority of T. H. Cooper, with no supporting specimen.

2 Budby, by the spring over the bridge, *B. Bradley*.
3 Clifton Grove, by Nottingham†, *Williams*.

Stellaria media (L.) Vill. *Chickweed*

Native. Arable land, woodland, waste places, etc. Very common All Divs.

First Record: C. Deering, *Cat. Stirp.* 1738.

Stellaria apetela Ucria. *Small Chickweed*

Native. Sandy places. Perhaps frequent in Div. 2.

First Record: J. Brown, *N. W. Nat.* 1944.

2 Pusto Hill, Everton; Carlton-in-Lindrick, *Brown*; Welbeck.

Stellaria neglecta Weihe. *Greater Chickweed*

Native. Shady places. Uncommon. All Divs.

First Record: T. Jowett, *Bot. Cals.* 1826, records a decandrous variety of *S. media* in Clifton Grove. H. Fisher, *Trans. Nott. Nats.* 1894.

1 Papplewick; Linby, *Fisher*; Kirkby, *Carr* (1909).
2 Hodsock.
3 Clifton Grove, by Nottingham†, *Jowett*; Grassthorpe.
4 Staunton.

Stellaria Holostea L. *Greater Stitchwort*

Native. Hedgesides and woods. Common. All Divs.

First Record: C. Deering, *Cat. Stirp.* 1738.

Stellaria palustris Retz. *Marsh Stitchwort*

Native. Marshy meadows on light soils. Decreasing. Divs. 2, 3, 4.

First Record: T. Jowett, *Bot. Cals.* 1826.

2 Bulwell, *Jowett*; Scrooby†, *Miller*; Misson; Scaftworth; Everton; Lound.
3 Nottingham; Clifton by Nottingham†; Wilford, *Jowett*; Gringley Carr, *Miller*; Nr. Gamston, *Roffey*; Laxton, *Thornley*; Newark; Saundby; *Carr MS.*; Farndon; Spalford; Averham; Ragnall; Misterton; Cottam.
4 Between Coddington and Barnby, *Fisher*.

Stellaria graminea L. *Lesser Stitchwort*

Native. Grassy places. Common. All Divs.

First Record: C. Deering, *Cat. Stirp.* 1738.

Stellaria Alsine Grimm. *Bog Stitchwort*

Native. Stream, pond and drain sides. Common. All Divs.

First Record: C. Deering, *Cat. Stirp.* 1738.

Arenaria trinerva L. *Three-nerved Sandwort*

Native. Woods and shady hedgerows. Common. All Divs.

First Record: T. Ordoyno, *Fl. Nott.* 1807.

Arenaria serpyllifolia L. *Thyme leaved Sandwort*

Native. Walls and dry places. Common. All Divs.

First Record: C. Deering, *Cat. Stirp.* 1738.

Arenaria leptoclados (Rchb.) Guss.

Native.

Only Record: J. W. Carr, *Trans. Nott. Nats.* 1907, "Owthorpe, Div 4."

Arenaria verna L. *Vernal Sandwort*

H. C. Watson, *N. B. G.* 1835, on the authority of T. H. Cooper. No locality or supporting specimen.

Sagina nodosa (L.) Fenzl. *Knotted Pearlwort*

Native. Drainsides and damp places. Now confined to the Carrs and the Magnesian Limestone. Rare. Divs. 1, 2, 3.

First Record: T. Ordoyno, *Fl. Nott.* 1807.

1 Mansfield; Pleasley; Sutton-in-Ashfield, *G.Howitt*; Haggonfields, Worksop, *Friend*; Sookholme Moor, *Carr*; Hills and Holes, Warsop.
2 Farnsfield Carr; Oxton Bottoms, *Ordoyno*; Misson†; Finningley†, *Carr.*
3 Edingley Moor, *Ordoyno*; Stockwith to Haxey Road, *Miller.*

Sagina ciliata Fr. *Ciliate Pearlwort*

Native. Sandy places, pathways, walls. Common. All Divs.

First Record: H. C. Watson, *Top. Bot.* 1883.

Sagina apetala L. *Small Pearlwort*

Native. Similar situations to the last species. Common, but less so than the last species. All Divs.

First Record: C. Deering, *Cat. Stirp.* 1738.

Sagina procumbens L. *Procumbent Pearlwort*

Native. Walls, damp grassland and paths. Very common. All Divs.

First Record: T. Ordoyno, *Fl. Nott.* 1807.

Spergula arvensis L. *Corn Spurrey*, "*Dother*"

Native. Arable fields on light soils. Very common in all suitable soils. All Divs.

First Record: C. Deering, *Cat. Stirp.* 1738.

Spergula pentandra L.

Only Record: T. Ordoyno, *Fl. Nott.* 1807, "Farnsfield" (2 or 3).

Spergularia rubra (L.) J. O. C. Presl. *Sand Spurrey*

Native. Dry sandy fields and paths. Locally common. All Divs.

First Record: T. Ordoyno, *Fl. Nott.* 1807.

1 Shireoaks.
2 Common.
3 Gravel walks at Southwell, *Ordoyno*; Wigsley; Bilsthorpe; Hawton; Winkburn (adventive).
4 Coddington Moor, *Ordoyno*; South Scarle; Brough; Langford Moor; Barnby; Normanton-on-Soar.

PORTULACACEAE

Claytonia Alsinoides Sims.

Alien. Found near old gardens in Sherwood, Nottingham (Div. 2) by Mr. A. Dobb's pupils, of the Arnot Vale School, 1956.

Claytonia perfoliata Wild.

Alien. Colonist. Sandy fields, old walls. Uncommon. Divs. 2, 3, 4.

First Record: A. Gilbert, *Botany for Beginners*, 1880 "Garden in Villa Road, Nottingham, an officious weed among strawberry beds."

2 Ollerton†, *Friend*; Ranby, *Dallman*; Farnsfield, *Leather*; Boughton†, *Carr* 1904; Bramcote, *Bowen*; Thoresby forestry nursery.

3 Nottingham, *Gilbert*; Kneesall Wood (presumably imported from Thoresby).

4 Garden Wall at Staunton Hall.

Montia fontana L. *Blinks*

Native. Damp hollows. Local. Commonest in gravelly hollows in the Trent Valley. Divs. 2, 3, 4.

First Record: C. Deering, *Cat. Stirp*. 1738.

2 Oxton Bottoms, *Ordoyno*; Mansfield Forest; Bulwell Forest; Nottingham Park, *Jowett*.

3 Edingley Moor, *Ordoyno*; North Collingham; Besthorpe; Rolleston; Kelham; Manzer Gorse, Eakring.

4 Coddington Moor, *Ordoyno*; Langford Moor, *Peacock*. Specimens submitted to S. M. Walters have been determined as ssp. *chondrosperma* (Fenzl) W. which is probably our common species.

HYPERICACEAE

Hypericum Androsaemum L. *Tutsan*

Extinct or error. Divs. 1 or 2, 3.

1 or 2 Kirkby-in-Ashfield, *Kaye*. Nottingham Castle, *Babington* sp., in Watson's N.B.G. 1835.

3 Colwick Wood, *Gough's Camden's Britannia* 1789.

Hypericum calycinum L. *Rose of Sharon*

Alien. Commonly naturalised in shrubberies.

Hypericum montanum L. *Mountain St. John's Wort*

Native. Bushy places on limestone. Very rare. Divs. 1, 3.

First Record: T. Jowett, *Bot. Cals.* 1826.

1 Between Bulwell and Nuthall; Wood about a mile from Bulwell, *Jowett*; Wood near Skegby, *Carr* 1927.
3 Mapperley Hills, *G. Howitt.*

Hypericum hirsutum L. *Hairy St. John's Wort*

Native. Woods and hedges. Common on strong land in Divs. 1, 3, 4, rare in 2.

First Record: C. Deering, *Cat. Stirp.* 1738.

2 Beeston; Bramcote; Rufford, *Carr MS.*; Misson.

Hypericum pulchrum L. *Slender St. John's Wort*

Native. Woods and shady places. Widespread but not common. All Divs.

First Record: C. Deering, *Cat. Stirp.* 1738.

1 Linby; Langwith; Bulwell.
2 Larkdale, Nottingham, *Deering*; Blidworth; Boughton; Budby; Thoresby.
3 Colwick, *Deering*; Westhorpe Dumble, Southwell, *Ordoyno*; Wigsley Wood, Winkburn; Caunton; Rufford.
4 Barnby; Between Balderton and Coddington, *Ordoyno*; Langford; Clipstone; Brough; Stanton-on-Wolds; Wigsley; Thorney.

Hypericum tetrapterum Fr. *Square stalked St. John's Wort*

Native. Beside streams and ditches. Common. All Divs.

First Record: C. Deering, *Cat. Stirp.* 1738.

Hypericum dubium Leers. *Imperforate St. John's Wort*

Native. Banks and sandy woods. Very rare. Divs. 2, 3.

First Record: G. Howitt, *Fl. Notts.* 1839, quoting Miss C. Churchill.

2 By Harlow Wood Hospital, *Gibbons.*
3 "On the roadside from Edwalton to Nottingham, near West Bridgford," *Churchill.*

Hypericum perforatum L. *Common St. John's Wort*

Native. Woods, heaths and banks. Widespread and frequent, preferring lighter soils. All Divs.

First Record: C. Deering, *Cat. Stirp.* 1738.

Hypericum humifusum L. *Trailing St. John's Wort*

Native. Heaths and sandy fields. Locally frequent. All Divs.

First Record: C. Deering, *Cat. Stirp.* 1738.

1 Langwith; Bramcote.
2 Frequent.
3 Edingley Moor; Radley, near Thurgarton, *Ordoyno*; Halloughton Wood; West Drayton, *Carr MS.*; Wigsley; Spalford; Epperstone Wood; Caunton.
4 Coddington and Langford† Moors, *Ordoyno*; Gotham Hills, *Williams*; West Leake; Brough; Wigsley; Barnby; Clipstone Wolds.

MALVACEAE

Althea rosea L. *Hollyhock*

Alien. Casual. Roadsides and dumps. Frequent, particularly on the Fosse road between Newark and Saxondale, but does not appear to establish itself.

Malva moschata L. *Musk Mallow*

Native. Grassy banks and open woodland. Widespread but not common. All Divs.

First Record: C. Deering, *Cat. Stirp.* 1738.

1 Haggonfields, *Friend*; Pleasley Vale; Church Warsop; Huthwaite; Kimberley; Skegby.
2 Frequent.
3 Formerly widely distributed. Modern Records; Cropwell Bishop; Epperstone; Kelham.
4 Gotham Hills; Upper Broughton.

Malva sylvestris L. *Common Mallow*

Native. Roadsides and waste places. Very common. All Divs.

First Record: C. Deering, *Cat. Stirp.* 1738.

Malva neglecta Wallr. *Dwarf Mallow*

Native. Waste places, roadsides and particularly around farmyards. Sporadic. All Divs.

First Record: C. Deering, *Cat. Stirp.* 1738.

1 Mansfield, *Ordoyno*; Nether Langwith; Holbeck; Styrrup, *Carr MS.*; Kirkby.
2 Scaftworth; Everton; Finningley; Misson; Hodsock. It appears to avoid the Forest villages.
3 Frequent.
4 Harby; Keyworth; Granby; Langar; Flawborough, *Carr MS.*; Staunton; Bunny.

Malva pusilla With.

Alien. Casual. Div. 3.

Only Record: A. R. Horwood, *B.E.C. Rept.* 1915, "Kingston-on-Soar."

TILIACEAE

Tilia platyphyllos Scop. *Large leaved Lime*

Denizen. Div. 1.

Only Record: Found in Scratta Wood, Shireoaks by J. Brown. Most of the wood is now cut down, but in 1962 there were still several trees in the remaining portion, and in shelter belts left by the farmer.

Tilia x vulgaris Hayne *T. platyphyllos x cordata* *Common Lime*

Alien. Denizen. Very commonly planted in all parts of the county. It regenerates freely.

Tilia cordata Mill *Small leaved Lime*

Certainly native in Divs. 1 and 3. Woods and hedges. Locally frequent. All Divs.

First Record: Sp. Herb. Salt, Sheffield *c.*1800. G. Howitt, *Fl. Notts.* 1839.

1 Nether Langwith: Scratta Wood, Shireoaks†, *Carr MS.*; Hucknall; Bilborough; Pleasley Vale.
2 Nottingham Park, *Salt*; Scrooby Churchyard; Clumber Park; Babworth; Welbeck; Osberton, (all planted).
3 Frequent.
4 Harby, possibly planted.

LINACEAE

Radiola Linoides Roth. *All-seed*

Native. Damp hollows on heaths. Probably extinct. Divs. 2 and 4.

First Record: T. Ordoyno, *Fl. Nott.* 1807.

2 About Farnsfield and Ollerton, *G. Howitt.*
4 "In the lane leading to Stapleford Moors from the Sleaford Turnpike," *Ordoyno.*

Linum catharticum L. *Purging Flax*

Native. Dry banks and meadows, particularly on basic soils. Common except in Div. 2. All Divs.

First Record: C. Deering, *Cat. Stirp.* 1738.

2 Nottingham Church Cemetery, *Bohler* 1866; Misson; Harworth; Clumber Park.

Linum usitatissimum L. *Common Flax*

Alien. Casual. Occurs frequently on roadsides and dumps and as a relic of cultivation; sometimes persisting for several years. All Divs.

First Record: G. Howitt, *Nott. Fl.* 1839 "In cultivated fields; rather rare."

GERANIACEAE

Geranium sanguineum L. *Bloody Cranesbill*

Native. Limestone Rocks. Probably extinct. Div. 1.

Only Record: G. Howitt, *Notts. Fl.* 1839, Cresswell Crags, per B. Eddison.

Geranium pratense L. *Meadow Cranesbill*

Native. Damp meadows, roadsides and willow holts. Common in Divs. 1 and 3, less so in 2 and 4.

First Record: C. Deering, *Cat. Stirp.* 1738.

Geranium phaeum L. *Dusky Cranesbill*

Alien. Denizen. Very rare. Divs. 1, 3.

First Record: G. Crabbe in Turner and Dillwyn's *Botanist's Guide* 1805.

1 Between Nottingham and Alfreton, *Crabbe.*
3 Plentifully in Fledborough Churchyard.

Geranium pyrenaicum Burm. fils. *Mountain Cranesbill*

Denizen. Roadsides, etc. Local. All Divs.

First Record: H. C. Watson, *N.B.G.* 1837, per Cooper, probably erroneous. J. W. Carr, MS.; Roadside Winthorpe.

1 Pleasley Vale, *Brown.*
2 Hodsock.
3 Frequent.
4 Cropwell Bishop; Sutton Bonington. Old Church yard, Colston Bassett.

Geranium columbinum L. *Long Stalked Cranesbill*

Native. Dry pastures, particularly on basic soils. Very rare. All Divs.

First Record: C. Deering, *Cat. Stirp.* 1738.

1 Mansfield, *Ordoyno*; Mansfield Woodhouse, *G. Howitt*; Annesley; Kirkby, *Gilbert*; Church Warsop†, *Carr* (1904).
2 Larkdale, Nottingham, *Deering*; Lane between Rayton and Worksop, *Roffey*; Lane east of Harworth; Barrow Hills, Everton, *Mrs. Sandwith.*
3 Southwell; Newark, *Ordoyno*; Sneinton Wood, *G. Howitt.*
4 Wigsley in one field, plentiful.

Geranium dissectum L. *Cut-leaved Cranesbill*

Native. Roadsides, borders of fields, waste places. Common except in Div. 2, where it is practically confined to the Carrs. All Divs.

First Record: C. Deering, *Cat. Stirp.* 1738.

Geranium molle L. *Dove's Foot Cranesbill*

Native. Waysides and grassland, arable land. Very common. All Divs.

First Record: C. Deering, *Cat. Stirp.* 1738.

Geranium pusillum Burm. fils. *Small Flowered Cranesbill*

Native. Arable land and roadsides, on sand. Frequent in Div. 2 and on the sand in Divs. 3 and 4.

First Record: C. Deering, *Cat. Stirp.* 1738.

Geranium lucidum L. *Shining Cranesbill*

? Native. Walls and rocks. Very rare. Divs. 1, 2, 3.

First Record: C. Deering, *Cat. Stirp.* 1738.

1 Kirkby Hardwick, *Carr* 1907.
2 Larkdale, Nottingham, *Deering*; Shaws Lane, Nottingham, *Jowett.*
3 Thrumpton Ferry, *Carr MS.*; Winthorpe, *Leather*; Tuxford.

Geranium Robertianum L. *Herb Robert*

Native. Woods, hedges, waste ground. Very common. All Divs.

First Record: C. Deering, *Cat. Stirp.* 1738.

Geranium nodosum L.

Alien. Div. 3. H. Friend, *Trans. Nott. Nats.* 1887, records finding a fruiting plant he supposed to be this species at Eakring, opposite the windmill.

Erodium maritimum Sm.

Sandy banks. Probably extinct. Div. 2.

First Record: T. Jowett, *Bot. Cals.* 1826.

2 By the Rock Houses, Mansfield, *Jowett*; Near Sherwood Hall, *G. Howitt*, per *Hurt*. G. Howitt's specimens are in the Watson Herb. at Kew.

Erodium moschatum L'Herit. *Musk Stork's Bill*

Native or casual. Sandy fields, waste ground. Very rare. Divs. 2, 3.

First Record: C. Deering, *Cat. Stirp.* 1738. "Here and there on Banks".

2 Nottingham Lammas Fields, *G. Howitt.*
3 Kingston-on-Soar, *Horwood.*

Erodium cicutarium L. *Common Stork's Bill*

Native. Sandy fields, roadsides, etc. Locally common. All Divs.

First Record: C. Deering, *Cat. Stirp.* 1738.

1 Nether Langwith; Worksop, *Carr MS.*; East Kirkby.
2 Common.
3 Common on the blown sand; Frequent in the Trent Valley.
4 Common on the sand; Rempstone.

ssp *dunense* Andrews. 2 Pusto Hill, Everton, det. E. F. Warburg.

Tropaeolum majus L. *Nasturtium*

Alien. Casual. Common on rubbish dumps and as a garden escape.

Oxalis Acetosella L. *Wood Sorrel*

Native. Damp woods. Common in Divs. 1 and 3, and in the damper woods of Div. 2. Absent from Div. 4.

First Record: C. Deering, *Cat. Stirp.* 1738.

Oxalis corniculata L. *Yellow Oxalis*

var *microphylla* Hook. fils.

Alien. A common and invasive garden weed throughout the county. A purple leaved variety also occurs.

var *atropurpurea* Van Houtte ex Planch.

Alien. A common and invasive garden weed throughout the county.

Oxalis europea Jord. *Upright Oxalis*

Alien. Garden weed. Rare. Div. 3.

3 In several gardens at Farndon. Known since 1900.

Oxalis articulata Sav.

Alien. Occurs in gardens throughout the county but cannot be considered naturalised.

Oxalis corymbosa DC.

Alien. Garden weed. ?Frequent. Divs. 1, 2, 3.

1 Mansfield.
2 Wollaton Hall.
3 Several gardens at Farndon, known since 1900. Nottingham dump.

Oxalis incarnata L.

Alien. Garden weed, but less invasive than the foregoing species. Previously thought to be tender. Rare. Divs. 2, 3.

2 Rufford; Cuckney.
3 Farndon, sporadically since 1930, and in the lane; Lowdham; Bingham; West Stockwith.

The exact distribution of the last four species is imperfectly known as it is sometimes difficult to botanise in people's gardens.

Impatiens capensis Meer. *Orange Balsam*

Alien. Denizen. Willow holts. Rare. Divs. 1, 3.

First Record: R. H. Hall, *B. E. C. Rept.* 1946.

1 Linby†, *Hall*; Newstead.
3 Farndon; Averham; South Muskham; Shelford.

Impatiens parviflora DC. *Small flowered Balsam*

Alien. Denizen. Riversides, waste ground. Uncommon. Divs. 1, 3.

First Record: F. G. Williams MS. 1940.

1 Watnall, roadside.
3 Clifton Grove (by Nottingham)†, *Williams*; Newark, waste ground; Nottingham; Winthorpe, roadside; Farndon Holt.

Impatiens glandulifera Royal. *Himalayan Balsam*

Alien. Denizen. Riversides. Locally common. Divs. 1, 2, 3.

First Record: J. Staton, Radcliffe-on-Trent Viaduct, *c.*1918.

1 Canal side, Shireoaks; On the banks of the Erewash, throughout its length, *Butcher*.
2 Common by the Rivers Meden and Idle; Hodsock; Bobber's Mill, Nottingham.
3 Common on the Trent bank from the Derbyshire border to the beginning of the tidal reach at Cromwell; Tuxford.

ILICACEAE

Ilex Aquifolium L. *Holly*

Native in Div. 1, planted or bird sown elsewhere. Hedges, woods and rough pastures (in 1). Common. All Divs.

First Record: C. Deering, *Cat. Stirp.* 1738.

CELASTRACEAE

Euonymus europaeus L. *Spindle Tree*

Native. Hedges and woods on basic soils. Common in Divs. 1 and 3, less so in Div. 2, very rare in 4.

First Record: C. Deering, *Cat. Stirp.* 1738.

4 Elton, *Carr MS.*

RHAMNACEAE

Rhamnus catharticus L. *Buckthorn*

Native. Hedges and woods. Generally common, but less so in Divs. 2, 4.

First Record: C. Deering, *Cat. Stirp.* 1738.

Rhamnus Frangula L. *Alder Buckthorn*

Native. Hedges, woods and drainsides, on moist sand or peat. Uncommon. All Divs.

First Record: T. Jowett, *Bot. Cals.* 1826.

1 Bulwell†, *Jowett*; Shireoaks†; Newstead; Teversall, *Carr MS.*; Sookholme; Hucknall; Nether Langwith; Warsop.
2 Mattersey†, *Brown*; Newstead; Hesley; Everton; Bothamsall.
3 South Clifton, *Carr MS.*; Wigsley; Winkburn; Spalford.
4 Brough; Thorney; South Scarle.

VITACEAE

Various species of *Parthenocissus* (Virginia Creeper) are commonly cultivated and frequently found on waste ground in and around towns.

HIPPOCASTANACEAE

Aesculus Hippocastanum L. *Horse Chestnut*

Alien. Denizen. Commonly planted and reproducing freely from seed. All Divs.

ACERACEAE

Acer Pseudo-platanus L. *Sycamore*

Alien. Denizen. Woods, hedges and waste ground. Very common. Since myxamatosis seedlings are smothering the ground flora in many places.

First Record: C. Deering, *Cat. Stirp.* 1738, "very common about Gentlemen's Seats and Churchyards . . . I have observed some of them in Nottingham Coppice, and upon Clifton Hill."

Acer campestre L. *Maple*

Native. Hedges, wood verges. Very common. All Divs.

First Record: C. Deering, *Cat. Stirp*. 1738.

Acer Platanoides L. *Norway Maple*

Alien. Denizen. Often planted round villages and occasionally in woods. It reproduces freely from seed.

LEGUMINOSAE

Lupinus polyphyllus L. *Lupin*

Alien. Casual or denizen. Dumps, waste places and old army camps. Frequent. All Divs.

Laburnum Anagroides Medic.

Alien. Commonly planted and often occurring in hedges far from habitation.

Genista anglica L. *Needle Furze*

Native. Boggy places. Rare and decreasing. All Divs.

First Record: C. Deering, *Cat. Stirp*. 1738.

1 Sookholme, *Jones*.
2 Bulwell; Papplewick, *Jowett*; Sutton near Retford; near Osberton, *Mrs. Sandwith*; South edge of Harlow Wood; Mansfield, *Carr MS.*; Lyndhurst Heath, *Hopkins*; Clipstone; Rufford Park and Forest; Newstead Forest.
3 Bridgeford Gorse, *Deering*; Edingley Moor, *Ordoyno*; Bramcote Moor, *Jowett*.
4 Langford Moor, *Ordoyno*.

Genista tinctoria L. *Dyer's Greenweed*

Native. Banks and hillsides, particularly on calcareous soils. Locally frequent. All Divs.

First Record: C. Deering, *Cat. Stirp*. 1738.

1 Frequent.
2 Hesley.
3 Rather frequent.
4 Widmerpool†; Cropwell Bishop; Cotgrave; Bunny; Keyworth; Stanton-on-Wolds; Leake Hills†; Wysall, *Carr MS*.

Spartium junceum L.

Alien. Div. 2.

Thoresby Pit Dump, *Evans*. Planted by the County Council on Scaftworth-by-pass.

Ulex europaeus L. *Gorse*

Native. Heaths, hedges and woods on light soils. Common, especially in Div. 2. All Divs.

First Record: C. Deering, *Cat. Stirp.* 1738.

Ulex Gallii Planch. *Dwarf Furze*

Native. Heaths. Local. Divs. 1, 2, (4).

First Record: C. Deering, *Cat. Stirp.* 1738, "*Genista Spinosa minor*," probably refers to this species, which is commoner than *U. minor.* J. W. Carr, *Trans. Notts. Nats.* 1894, records the segregate.

1 Wollaton Old Pits, *Deering*; Huthwaite.
2 Mansfield Forest, near Fountain Dale, *G. Howitt*; Birklands, *Bohler* 1875; Bulwell†, *Carr* 1894; Blidworth, *Williams*; Rufford Forest; Mansfield: Stapleford; Budby Forest; Walesby; Boughton; Thoresby; Clumber; Osberton.
(4 Ordoyno's locality is in Lincolnshire.)

Ulex minor Roth.

Native. Heaths, growing with *U. gallii*, but not in such quantity. Rare. Divs. 2, 3.

First Record: J. W. Carr, *Trans. Nott. Nats.* 1907.

2 Perlethorpe, *Carr;* Lyndhurst Heath, *Hopkinson*; Budby Forest†, *Brown*; Boughton Breck; Walesby; Mansfield Forest; Many places on the Osberton estate.
3 On heathy gravel at Gamston.

Sarothamnus scoparius (L.) Wimmer *Broom*

Native. Heaths, woods and rough land on light soils. Common. All Divs.

First Record: C. Deering, *Cat. Stirp.* 1738.

Ononis repens L. *Restharrow*

Native. Rough grassland. Not common. All Divs.

First Record: C. Deering, *Cat. Stirp.* 1738.

1 Kirkby; Lady Lee, Worksop; Church Warsop; Langwith.
2 Chapel Bar, Nottingham, *Deering*; Blidworth, *Ordoyno*; Everton; Scaftworth; Babworth; Misson; Bulwell.
3 Clifton Hall, (by Nottingham), *Deering*.
4 Langar Lane Covert.

Ononis spinosa L. *Prickly Restharrow*

Native. Rough grassland on basic soils. Frequent. Divs. 2, 3, 4.

First Record: C. Deering, *Cat. Stirp.* 1738.

2 Radford Hollows, *Deering*; Carburton.
3 Common on the clays and river gravels.
4 Common on the clay.

Trigonella caerulea (L.) Druce.

Casual. Alien. Div. 3.

Only Record: A. R. Horwood, *B. E. C. Rept.* 1915: "Kingston-on-Soar."

Trigonella ornithopoides (L.) DC.

?Native. Probably extinct. Div. 2.

Only Record: J. Bohler in Allen's "*Nottingham and its Environs*" 1866, "Nottingham Church Cemetery."

Medicago falcata L. *Sickle Medick*

Casual or Denizen. Waste places and roadsides. Rare. Divs. 2, 3.

First Record: J. Bohler in Allen's *Nottingham and its Environs* 1866.

2 Nottingham Church Cemetery, *Bohler*; Scaftworth, *Brown*; Roadside at Everton, apparently established with grass seed.
3 Newark Wharfs†, *Fisher*.

Medicago x varia Martyn (*falcata x sativa*)

Casual. Rare. Div. 3.

First Record: Newark Wharfs 1953.

3 Newark Wharfs; Toton sidings; Nottingham Dump 1961.

Medicago sativa L. *Lucerne*

Alien. Denizen or casual. Waste places roadsides, railway banks, etc. Common. All Divs.

First Record: T. Ordoyno, *Fl. Nott.* 1807. "Meadows, pastures and ditch banks, cultivated at Newark, Mansfield; Hoveringham."

Medicago hispida Gaertn. *Toothed Medick*

Native. Sandy places. Very rare. Div. 2.

First Record: Mrs. Sandwith 1918.

2 In two fields on Barrow Hills, Everton, *Mrs. Sandwith*; Waste land near Blyth with *M. arabica*, *J. Brown*, det. A. J. Wilmot.

Medicago arabica (L.) All. *Spotted Medick*

Native. Sandy and gravelly banks, particularly the Trent terraces and old flood banks. Local. Divs. 2, 3, 4.

First Record: C. Deering, *Cat. Stirp.* 1738, no locality.

2 Bobber's Mill, Nottingham; Nottingham Castle, *Gilbert*; Gateford, Worksop, *Carr MS.*; Blyth, *Brown.*
3 Between Newark and Kelham; outside the Churchyard at Averham†, *Ordoyno*; Carlton; Colwick; Burton Joyce, *Jowett*; Walkeringham, *Miller*; Muskham, *Fisher*; Fiskerton; Bingham, *Carr MS.*; Farndon; Rolleston; Girton; Newark; Rampton; Besthorpe; Ratcliffe-on-Soar; Thrumpton.
4 Beacon Hill, Newark, *Fisher*; By foot path from Rempstone to Stanford, *Carr MS.*

Medicago lupulina L. *Black Medick*

Native. Dry banks, roadsides, waste places. Very common. All Divs.

First Record: C. Deering, *Cat. Stirp.* 1738.

Melilotus altissima Thuill. *Melilot*

Native or Denizen. Waste places, roadsides, etc. Very common. All Divs.

First Record: C. Deering, *Cat. Stirp.* 1738.

Melilotus alba Desr. *White Melilot*

Alien. Casual or Denizen. Waste places, arable land. Uncommon. All Divs.

First Record: H. Fisher, *Brit. Ass. Rept.* 1893.
1 Sookholme; Blanchard's Bakery, Watnall; Old railway track, Greasley.
2 Farnsfield; Finningley; Misson; Mansfield.
3 Newark†, *Fisher*; Cotgrave, *Carr MS.*; Nottingham; Toton Sidings; Spalford.
4 *Victoria County History.*

Melilotus officinalis (L.) Lam. *Field Melilot*

Alien. Casual or denizen. In similar situations to *M. altissima* but less common. Widespread. All Divs.

First Record: H. Fisher, *Rept. Brit. Ass.* 1893 'Newark.'

Melilotus indica (L.) All.

Alien. Casual. Dumps and waste ground. Rare. Divs. 2, 3.

First Record: H. Fisher, *Brit. Ass. Rept.* 1893.

2 Edwinstowe Dump.
3 Newark, *Fisher*; Nottingham Dump; Wilford Dump.

Trefolium medium Huds. *Zig zag Clover*

Native. Old grassland, especially on basic soils. Rather common, less so in Div. 2. All Divs.

First Record: C. Deering, *Cat. Stirp.* 1738.

Trefolium pratense L. *Red Clover*

Native. Meadows, roadsides and grassy places. Very common. All Divs.

First Record: C. Deering, *Cat. Stirp.* 1738.

Trefolium ochroleucon Huds. *Sulphur Clover*

Native. Meadows. Probably extinct. Div. 3.

Only Record: G. Howitt, *Notts. Fl.* 1839, "Field by Wilford Osier Holt."

Trefolium incarnatum L. *Crimson Clover*

Alien. Rare. Div. 3.

First Record: J. W. Carr, *Victoria County History* 1906.

3 Southwell, *Leather.*

Trefolium arvense L. *Hare's Foot Clover*

Native. Disturbed ground on light soils. Locally common. All Divs.

First Record: C. Deering, *Cat. Stirp.* 1738.

1 Welbeck, *Kaye*; Mansfield.
2 Common.
3 Newark†; Hawton; Balderton, *Ordoyno*; Frequent on the blown sand; Gringley by-pass.
4 Thorney; Wigsley.

Trefolium striatum L. *Knotted Clover*

Native. Meadows and banks on sandy soils. Locally common. All Divs.

First Record: C. Deering, *Cat. Stirp.* 1738.

1 Warsop.
2 Frequent.
3 Frequent on the river gravels and blown sand; Bunny Park.
4 North Collingham, *Carr MS.*; Balderton.

Trefolium subterraneum L. *Subterranean Clover*

Native. Gravelly meadows and banks. Local, with *T. striatum*, but less common. Divs. 2, 3.

First Record: C. Deering, *Cat. Stirp.* 1738.

2 Nottingham Park, *Deering*; Sherwood Forest, *Ordoyno*; Bulwell Forest, *Gilbert*; Near Sloswicks, *Roffey*.
3 Quonce Hill Close, Newark†; Langford, *Ordoyno*; Walkeringham, *Miller*; Kelham; Muskham, *Fisher*; Colwick; Fiskerton, *Carr MS.*; Farndon; Rolleston; Besthorpe; South Collingham; Girton; Rampton.

Trefolium fragiferum L. *Strawberry Headed Clover*

Native. Hollows on the river gravels where water stands in winter, paths, banks. Local. All Divs.

First Record: Specimen in Herb. Jowett 1821. No locality.

1 Mansfield; Sutton-in-Ashfield; Kirkby Hardwick, *G. Howitt*; Between Annesley and Selston; Carlton-in-Lindrick; Styrrup, *Carr MS.*; Shireoaks.
2 Everton.
3 Frequent in the Trent Valley.
4 Widespread in J. W. Carr's time; Barnby, Witham Meadows; Hickling.

Trefolium hybridum L. *Alsike*

Alien. Denizen. Naturalised on roadsides, field borders and waste places throughout the county. All Divs.

First Record: *Victoria County History*. 1906.

var *elegans* Savi, occurs in several places, especially disturbed ground round gravel pits.

First Record: E. Cole, *Phyt. M. S.* 1859.

1 East Kirkby.
2 Everton; Finningley.
3 Nottingham Dump.
4 Barnstone, *Cole.*

Trefolium repens L. *White or Dutch Clover*

Native. Meadows, roadsides, etc. Very common. All Divs.

First Record: C. Deering, *Cat. Stirp*. 1738.

Trefolium campestre Schreb. *Hop Trefoil*

Native. Banks, dry meadows, roadsides, etc. Common. All Divs.

First Record: C. Deering, *Cat. Stirp*. 1738.

Trefolium dubium Sibth. *Lesser Trefoil*

Native. In all grassy places. Common. All Divs.

First Record: C. Deering, *Cat. Stirp*. 1738.

Trefolium micranthum Viv. *Slender Trefoil*

Native. Lawns and open grass communities. Rare or overlooked. Divs. 2, 3.

First Record: T. Jowett, *Bot. Cals*. 1826.

2 Mansfield, *Gilbert* (or 1); White Water Bridge, Perlethorpe.
3 Kelham, *Leather*; Southwell; Farndon; Clarborough.

Trefolium lappaceum L.

Alien. Casual. Div. 3.

Only Record: A. R. Horwood, *B.E.C. Rept.* 1915, "Kingston-on-Soar."

Trefolium resupinatum L. *Reflexed Clover*

Alien. Casual. Div. 3.

Only Record: H. Fisher, *Brit. Ass. Rept.* 1893, Newark.

Anthyllis Vulneraria L. *Kidney Vetch*

Native. Banks and well drained grassland, disturbed ground. Local. All Divs.

First Record: C. Deering, *Cat. Stirp.* 1738.

1 Frequent in natural habitats and on waste land.
2 Frequent on railway banks, stoneheaps, etc.
3 Fields at Mapperley, *Deering*; Ruddington Hills, *Pulteney* 1756; Newark; Averham; Oxton; Southwell, *Ordoyno*; Gringley Hill, *Miller*; Averham, *Fisher*; Newark; Holme; Tuxford railway, *Carr MS.*; Hawton; North Muskham railway bank; Balderton railway bank.
4 Canal bank, Cropwell Bishop; Colston Bassett, *Carr MS.*; Upper Broughton railway bank.

Lotus uliginosus Schkuhr. *Greater Birds Foot Trefoil*

Native. Damp meadows, marshes, drain sides. Common. All Divs.

First Record: C. Deering, *Cat. Stirp.* 1738.

Lotus corniculatus L. *Birds Foot Trefoil*

Native. Dry grassy places on both sand and clay. Common. All Divs.

First Record: C. Deering, *Cat. Stirp.* 1738.

Lotus tenuis Waldst. and Kit. *Slender Birds Foot Trefoil*

Native. Grassy places on basic soils. Uncommon. All Divs.

First Record: J. Salt, *List of Plants* . . . 1796 to 1807.

1 Worksop and banks of the canal, *Salt*; Lady Lee Quarry, Worksop,† *Brown*; Sankey's clay pits, Bulwell.
2 Near Harworth brickyard, *Mrs. Sandwith.*
3 East Leake, *Carr MS.*; Hare Hills, Kersall.
4 Between Gotham and West Leake, *G. Howitt*; Kinoulton, *Carr* 1904; East Leake Hills; Crow Wood Hill; West Leake; Widmerpool, *Carr MS.*; Clipstone Wolds; Bunny; Cotgrave Forest.

Galega officinalis L. *Goat's Rue*

Alien. Naturalised on roadsides and in woods. Rare. Divs. 1, 3.

First Record: Trowell roadside 1953.

1 Trowell; A fair quantity in woodland at Carlton-in-Lindrick.
3 Nottingham Dump.

Robinia Pseudo-Acacia L.

Alien. Frequently planted in woods in the Dukeries. Div. 2.

First Record: Rufford 1958.

Colutea arborescens L. *Bladder Senna*

Alien. Nottingham Dump. 1960 *et seq.* Div. 3.

Astragalus glycyphyllos L. *Milk Vetch*

Native. Roadsides on both sand and clay, probably preferring a basic soil. Sporadically throughout the county. Divs. 1, 2, 3.

First Record: C. Deering, *Cat. Stirp.* 1738.

1 Between Wollaton and Bilborough, *Jowett*; Nether Langwith.
2 Between Cow Lane and Nottingham Gallows; Larkdale, *Deering*; Nottingham Park, *Jowett*; Misson.
3 Colwick Wood, *Deering*; Between Newark and Hawton; Thorpe Lane Toll Bar; Stoke Hill, *Ordoyno*; Clifton (by Nottingham), *Jowett*; Beeston Lane, *G. Howitt*; Hayton; Clayworth, *Miller*; Bingham Road, *Gilbert*; Ruddington to Plumtree†, *Fisher* (Grantham); Colwick Park, *Staton*; North Clifton, a lot; Eaton; Wilford.

Astragalus odoratus Lam.

Alien. Around malt kilns. Rare. Div. 3.

Only Record: Well established on railway sidings near Quibell's works, Newark 1952 and still persisting.

Glycyrrhiza ? **glabra** L. is mentioned by Deering as being cultivated about Worksop, but has not established itself.

See also Gibson's *Camden* 1695.

Coronilla varia L. *Crown Vetch*

Alien. Casual. Rare. Div. 3.

Only Record: Waste ground by Tolney Lane, Newark 1951.

Ornithopus perpusillus L. *Common Bird's Foot*

Native. Sandy fields and grass land. Common on the Bunter and Eastern river gravels. Divs. 2, 3, 4.

First Record: C. Deering, *Cat. Stirp.* 1738.

2 Common.
3 Newark, *Ordoyno*; Besthorpe; Girton; Spalford; South Clifton; North Muskham; Balderton.
4 Wigsley; Langford Moor; Thorney.

Hippocrepis comosa L. *Horseshoe Vetch*

Native. Grassy places on basic soil. Extinct. Div. 2.

Only Record: C. Deering, *Cat. Stirp*. 1738, "In Nottingham Park, but not very common."

The plant could not be found by Ordoyno or Jowett but there seems no reason to doubt the record, as other calicole species, *Silene nutans*, *Helianthemum vulgare* etc., grew in the Park and on the Castle Rock.

Onobrychis viciifolia Scop. *Saintfoin*

Denizen or casual. Grassy places and railway banks. Rare. Divs. 1, 4.

First Record: J. Salt, *List of Plants* . . . 1796 to 1807.

1 Lady Lee, Worksop, *Salt*; Kirkby Hardwick, *G. Howitt*, *Carr MS.*; Bulwell Lime Quarries, *Jowett*, *Carr MS.*
4 Beacon Hill, Newark, *Ordoyno*; Railway bank, Balderton.

Vicia sylvatica L. *Wood Vetch*

Native. Clay woodland. Local. Div. (2), 3.

First Record: T. Ordoyno, *Fl. Nott*. 1807.

(2 Oxton Forest, in great profusion, *Sidebotham*. An unlikely locality, the record might refer to the part of Oxton in Div. 3 or even Epperstone.)
3 Epperstone Park†, Flintham Wood; Manzer Gorse, Eakring, *Ordoyno*; Wellow Park†; Mapperley Hills, *Jowett*; Gringley Wood, *Miller*; Roselle Wood, Oxton; Bevercotes Park†; Grove†, *Carr MS*.

Vicia Cracca L. *Tufted Vetch*

Native. Roadsides and rough ground. Common. All Divs.

First Record: T. Ordoyno, *Fl. Nott*. 1807.

Vicia bithynica L. *Bithynian Vetch*

Native. Among scrub. Very rare. Div. 3.

Only Record: Hare Hills, Kersall 1952.

Vicia sepium L. *Bush Vetch*

Native. Roadsides and meadows. Very common. All Divs.

First Record: C. Deering, *Cat. Stirp*. 1738.

Vicia sativa L. *Common Vetch*

Denizen. Roadsides, waste places and as a relic of cultivation. Very common. All Divs.

First Record: C. Deering, *Cat. Stirp.* 1738.

Vicia angustifolia L. *Narrow Leaved Vetch*

Native. Roadsides, heaths and meadows on light soils. Common in Div. 2, confined to sands and gravels elsewhere.

First Record: T. Jowett, *Bot. Cals.* 1826. No locality.

Vicia Lathyroides L. *Spring Vetch*

Native. Dry fields and roadsides on the bunter and blown sand. Uncommon. Divs. 2, 3.

First Records: J. Ray, *Phil. Letters*, Dereham's Ed. 1718, mentions, "a sort of small vetch I have not before observed," growing with *Teesdalia* in Nottingham Park. T. Jowett, *Bot. Cals.* 1826.

2 Nottingham Park, in association with *Teesdalia*, *?Ray*, *Jowett*; Bowling Alley Fields, Nottingham, *Jowett*; Bulwell Forest, *Gilbert*; Carlton-in-Lindrick†, *Brown*; Finningley; Everton; Manton; Ollerton; Boughton; Walesby; Osberton estate.
3 North Collingham; Besthorpe; South Clifton; Girton.

Vicia hirsuta L. *Tare*

Native. Arable fields, waste ground, roadsides, etc. Very common. All Divs.

First Record: C. Deering, *Cat. Stirp.* 1738.

Vicia tetrasperma (L.) Schreb. *Smooth Tare*

Native. Roadsides, waste ground and grassy places. Common. All Divs.

First Record: T. Ordoyno, *Fl. Nott.* 1807.

Lathyrus latifolius L. *Everlasting Pea*

Alien. Denizen. Near gardens and frequently on railway banks. Rather frequent. All Divs.

First Record: Railway bank at Plumtree, 1948, R. W. Butcher.

1 Lady Lee Quarry, Worksop; Nuthall.
2 By gardens at Rainworth.
3 Plumtree, *Butcher*; North Clifton; East Leake; Bingham; Clarborough.
4 Upper Broughton.

Lathyrus sylvestris L. *Wood Everlasting Pea*

Native. Rough woods and bushy places. Very rare. Div. 3.

First Record: Turner and Dillwyn, *Bot. Guide* 1805.

3 Colwick Park pales, *Turner and Dillwyn* per *Mr. Brunton*; Debdon Hill Toll Bar (i.e. Debdale Hill near Averham), *Ordoyno*; Between Clifton and Barton; Mapperley Hills, *Jowett*; Newark.

Lathyrus palustris L. *Marsh Pea*

Native. Among rough grass, hedges and drain sides on fen peat. Very rare and decreasing. Div. 2.

2 Fenny field between Misson and Newington†, *Mrs. Sandwith* 1909. The plant grows in several places in Misson parish both towards Newington and Idle Stop, but is in danger of extermination by increased drainage.

Lathyrus pratensis L. *Meadow Pea*

Native. Meadows, roadsides and all grassy places. Very common. All Divs.

First Record: C. Deering, *Cat. Stirp.* 1738.

Lathyrus hirsutus L.

Alien. Casual. Div. 3.

Only Record: Nottingham Dump 1961.

Lathyrus Nissolia L. *Grass Vetchling*

Native. Rough grassland. Very rare. Divs. 3, 4.

First Record: T. Ordoyno, *Fl. Nott.* 1807, on the sides of cornfields on Beacon Hill, Newark.

3 Hockerton 1830, sp. in *Herb. Reader* of Leicester, see *Carr MS.*
4 It is quite abundant in Messrs. Cafferata's old brick pits on Beacon Hill, but these are now being used as the town dump and will doubtless soon be built on.

Lathyrus Aphaca L.

Casual. Rare.

Only Records: J. W. Carr MS.; Welbeck (Div. 1); Newark Malt Kilns (Div. 3).

Lathyrus montanus (L.) Bernh. *Tuberous Pea*

Native. Wood verges, rough grassland and railway banks. Locally common. All Divs.

First Record: C. Deering, *Cat. Stirp.* 1738.

1 Common, especially on the coal measures.
2 Nottingham Coppice, *Deering*; Babworth, *Carr MS.*; Bulwell; Hesley.
3 A widespread woodland plant, but never growing abundantly.
4 West Leake; Wigsley Wood, *Carr MS.*

ROSACEAE

Prunus Padus L. *Bird Cherry*

Native in Divs. 1 and 2. Planted elsewhere. Damp woodland. Uncommon. Divs. 1, 2, 3.

First Record: T. Ordoyno, *Fl. Nott.* 1807.

1 Linby (?planted); In several small woods at Skegby; Woods near Park Hall, Mansfield Woodhouse.
2 Nottingham Church Cemetery, *Bohler* 1866; Clumber Park, *Bohler* 1875, both records would appear doubtfully native; Oxton Bogs, *Carr MS.*; Woods near Carburton, *Jones*; By the River Poulter at Elkesley, in quantity; Babworth.
3 Norwood Park, *Ordoyno*; Colwick Wood, *Jowett*, *Gilbert* (possibly native); Treswell (planted).

Prunus avium L. *Wild Cherry*

Native. Woods and hedges, particularly on light soils. Common. All Divs.

First Record: J. W. Carr, *Victoria County History* 1906. The older botanists did not distinguish this species and the next, but Ordoyno's record probably and perhaps Deering's also, refers to this species.

Prunus Cerasus L. *Sour Cherry*

Denizen. Woods and hedges. Rare or overlooked. Recorded in the *Victoria County History*, for Div. 1 with a query. C. Deering, *Cat. Stirp.* 1738 "I have observed some in Nottingham Park . . . but doubt the Birds have sown them," may refer to this species.

Prunus domestica L. and **Prunus cerasifera** Ehrh. are found frequently in hedges near villages and on the sites of old cottages and are sometimes planted for game cover and food for pheasants (as at Blue Barn, Welbeck).

Prunus institia L. *Bullace*

Denizen. Hedges. Uncommon or overlooked. Divs. 2, 3, 4.

First Record: C. Deering, *Cat. Stirp.* 1738.

2 Bulwell, *Jowett*,(O); Clumber Park, *Bohler* 1875.
3 Colwick Lane, *Deering*; Normanton by Southwell, *Ordoyno*; Egmanton.
4 Wigsley; Widmerpool.

Prunus spinosa L. *Blackthorn*

Native. Hedges, woods and rough ground. Very common. All Divs.

First Record: C. Deering, *Cat. Stirp.* 1738.

Prunus Lauro-Cerasus L. *Common Laurel*

Alien. Commonly planted in woods.

Prunus lusitanica (L.) Coste. *Portuguese Laurel*

Alien. Frequently planted in parks, especially in the Dukeries, and occasionally in woods.

Spiraea salicifolia L. *Willow Spiraea*

Alien. Naturalised near a garden in Kirkby Dumble. Div. 1.

Spiraea Ulmaria L. *Meadow Sweet*

Native. Damp meadows, watersides and marshes. Common. All Divs.

First Record: C. Deering, *Cat. Stirp.* 1738.

Spiraea Filipendula L. *Dropwort*

Native. Calcareous grassland. Local. Decreasing. All Divs.

First Record: C. Deering, *Cat. Stirp.* 1738.

1 Frequent.
2 On the roadside from Sandhills to Radford Church, *Deering*.
3 Still fairly frequent on calcareous gravels and marls.
4 Fosse Road, Cotgrave; Widmerpool; Hickling, *Carr MS.*; Clipstone; Stanton; Gotham; Upper Broughton.

Rubus Very little work has been done in Notts. on this genus. Our own records of critical species have been determined by Mr. E. S. Edees, whom we would like especially to thank. H. Fisher's specimens were submitted to W. O. Focke, J. G. Baker or W. Moyle Rodgers. All his records quoted here are from the *Report of the British Association Meeting in Nottingham*, 1893. The order followed is that of J. E. Dandy's *British Plant List* 1958.

(**Rubus saxatilis** L.

Error. Recorded in Watson's *N.B.G.* on the authority of Cooper's catalogue. No specimens.)

Rubus Idaeus L. *Raspberry*

Native. Damp woods and hedgesides. Very common. All Divs.

First Record: C. Deering, *Cat. Stirp.* 1738 "between Brockstow and Nuttal."

R. caesus L. *Dewberry*

Native. Damp woods and willow holts. Very common. All Divs.

First Record: C. Deering, *Cat. Stirp.* 1738, "Between Clifton Hall and Barton," etc.

R. caesus x ulmifolius: Averham, Div. 3 det. Watson.

Rubus suberectus sensu lato.

Native. Divs. 2 and 4.

First Record: G. Howitt, *Notts. Fl.* 1839.

2 Near Farnsfield, *G. Howitt*; Swinnow Wood, Harworth; Scaftworth.
4 *Victoria County History.*

Rubus scissus W.C.R. Wats.

Native. Div. 1.

Only Record: Cuckney Hay, Langwith, 1960.

Rubus conjungens (Bab.) Watson

Native. Divs. 2, 3, 4.

First Record: H. Fisher 1893.

2 Mansfield.
3 Newark, *Fisher.*
4 Thorney.

Rubus sublustris Lees.

Native. Div. 3.

First Record: T. Ordoyno, *Fl. Nott.* 1807. (R. *corylifolius* of Smith's *Flora Brittanica*) "Not unfrequent." G. Howitt (E.B. 827) "Very common." A. Gilbert: "North Notts."

2 Canal Side, Retford.
3 Spalford.

Rubus scabrosus P. J. Muell.

Native.

First Record: H. Fisher (*R. dumetorum* W. and N., incl. *tenuiarmatus* Lees.) "Generally distributed."

Rubus gratus Focke.

Native. Div. 3.

Only Record: H. Fisher, "Newark to Farndon."

Rubus nemoralis P. J. Muell.

Native. Div. 2.

First Record: Idle Stop, Misson 1959.

2 Idle Stop: Sadler's Breck, Carburton: Budby North Forest.

Rubus Lindleianus Lees.

Native. Divs. 2, 3.

First Record: H. Fisher, 1893.

2 Oxton Forest, *Fisher*; Everton; Harworth.
3 Edingley Moor, *Fisher*.

Rubus Maassii Focke ex Bertram and R. Muenterii Marss.

Native. Div. 2, etc.

First Record: H. Fisher as *R.? dumosus* Lefr. incl. *R. Maarssii* Focke and *R. Muenterii Marss*. "Rather common especially about the Forest."

Rubus Schlechtendalii Weihe ex Link.

Native. Div. 3.

Only Record: H. Fisher (as *R. macrophyllus* W. and N., b. *Schlechtendalii* W.) "Sconce Hills, Newark".

Rubus pyramidalis Kalt.

Native. Div. 3.

First Record: Farndon, 1959.

Rubus incurvatus Bab.

Native. Divs. 1, 2.

First Record: J. W. Carr, *Tr. Nott. Nats.* 1905, det. Moyle Rodgers.

1 Felley Mill; Selston, *Carr*.
2 South Forest, Mansfield Woodhouse, *Carr*.

Rubus villicaulis Koel. ex W. and N.

Native. Div. 3.

Only Record: H. Fisher, Fiskerton.

Rubus polyanthemus Lindeb.

Native. Divs. 2, 3, 4.

First Record: H. Fisher (as *R.? dumosus* Lefr. var. *pulcherrimus* Neum.).

2 Osberton Ash Holt.
3 or 4 Barnby Lane, near Newark, *Fisher*.

Rubus rhombifolius Weihe ex Boenn.

Native. Div. 3.

Only Record: J. W. Carr, *Tr. Nott. Nats.* 1905 (as *R. argenteus* W. and N.) Clifton. det. W. Moyle Rodgers.

Rubus cardiophyllus Muell and Lefeu.

Native. Div. 2.

First Record: A. Gilbert, *Botany for Beginners* (as *R. rhamnifolius*).

2 Oxton Bogs, *Gilbert*; Rainworth; Oxton, *Fisher* (as *R. rhamnifolius* angl. "Non W. and N.").

Rubus ulmifolius Schott.

Native. Frequent. All Divs. (*V.C.H.*)

First Record: G. Howitt (E.B. 715), "Frequent." H. Fisher "generally distributed."

3 Averham (det. Watson); Farndon.

Rubus choocladus W.C.R. Wats.

Recorded in the *Victoria County History* (as *pubescens* Weihe.) No division is mentioned.

Rubus procerus P. J. Muell.

Alien. Div. 3.

Only Record: Naturalised on the canal bank at West Bridgford 1959.

Rubus falcatus Kalt.

Native. Div. 3.

First Record: H. Fisher (as *R. thrysoides* Wimm.) "From Sconce Hills to Farndon and Hawton."

Rubus vestitus W. and N.

Native. Divs. 1, 2, ?3.

First Record: G. Howitt, *Notts. Fl.* 1839 (as *leucostachys* E.B. 2631 ?) "Near Nottingham frequent."

1 Crags Quarry, Holbeck.
2 Clipstone Forest; Sandpit, Carlton-in-Lindrick.

Rubus criniger (E. F. Linton.) Rodgers.

Native. Div. 2.

Only Record: Ollerton Corner 1960.

Rubus radula Weihe ex Boenn.

Native. Div. 3.

Only Record: H. Fisher, Flintham Wood.

Rubus discerptus P. J. Muell.

Native. Div. 3.

First Record: H. Fisher, (as *R. echinatus* (W. and N.) Lindl.).

2 Osberton, old airfield.
3 Spring Wood, Averham; Edingley Hill; Southwell, *Fisher*.

Rubus apiculatus W. and N.

Native. Div. 3.

Only Record: H. Fisher (as *R. anglosaxonicus* Gelert.), Spring Wood, Averham.

Rubus Koehleri W. and N.

Native. ?2, 3.

First Record: 1835, H. C. Watson *N.B.G.* from Cooper's catalogue per G. Howitt. G. Howitt *Notts. Fl.* 1839.

3 Nr. Nottingham, *G. Howitt*; Mapperley Plains, *Sidebotham*; Oxton (or 2); Hawton Road, Newark, *Fisher*.

Geum urbanum L. *Avens*

Native. Woods, hedges, etc. Common. All Divs.

First Record: C. Deering, *Cat. Stirp.* 1738.

Geum rivale L. *Water Avens*

Native. By streams and in damp woods. Local. Divs. 1, 2, 3.

First Record: C. Deering, *Cat. Stirp.* 1738.

1 Very frequent, both in woods and in the open.
2 Newstead.
3 Near Radley, *Ordoyno*; Bevercotes Park, *Carr MS.*; Kelham, *Leather*; Kneesall Wood; Roe Wood, Winkburn; Wellow Park; Gamston Wood; Treswell; Mather Wood, Caunton.

Geum x intermedium Ehrh. (*rivale x urbanum*)

Damp woodland, with the parents. Rare. Divs. 1, 3.

First Record: G. Howitt, *Notts. Fl.* 1839.

1 Pleasley Wood and a wood between Linby and Newstead, *G. Howitt*; Aspley Wood; Linby, *Carr MS.*
3 Bevercotes Park; Treswell Wood, *Carr MS.*; Mather Wood, Caunton; Gamston Wood; Wellow Park.

Fragraria moschata Duchesne. *Hautbois*

Alien. Div. 1.

Only Record: T. Jowett, *Bot. Cals.* 1826, Woods near Pleasley.

Fragraria vesca L. *Wild Strawberry*

Native. Woods, hedges. Common, less so in Div. 2. All Divs.

First Record: C. Deering, *Cat. Stirp.* 1738.

Fragraria x ananassa Duchesne (*chiloensis x virginiana*). *Garden Strawberry*

Alien. Denizen. Frequently naturalised on railway banks and in waste places.

Potentilla Anserina L. *Silverweed*

Native. Roadsides, waste ground, fields, etc. Very common. All Divs.

First Record: C. Deering, *Cat. Stirp.* 1738.

Potentilla argentea L. *Hoary Cinquefoil*

Native. Heaths and sandy tracksides. Local, chiefly on the bunter and river gravels. Divs. 2, 3, 4.

First Record: C. Deering, *Cat. Stirp.* 1738.

2 Fairly frequent.
3 Sneinton, *Deering*; Quonce Hill Close, Newark†, *Ordoyno*; Chilwell, *Jowett*; Girton; North Clifton; Gringley.
4 Upon Cotgrave and Stanton Wolds, *Pulteney* 1736.

Potentilla reptans L. *Cinquefoil*

Native. Roadsides, grassland, waste ground. Very common. All Divs.

First Record: C. Deering, *Cat. Stirp.* 1738.

Potentilla anglica Laich. *Trailing Tormentil*

Heaths, meadows and woodland rides on light soils. Local. All Divs.

First Record: T. Ordoyno, *Fl. Nott.* 1807.

1 Wollaton, *Jowett*; Langold, *Mrs. Sandwith*; Sookholme; Moor Green; Kirkby.
2 Lenton; Farnsfield; Mansfield Forest, *G. Howitt*; Misson, *Mrs. Sandwith*; Blidworth, *Williams*; Finningley†, *Brown*; Carburton; Thoresby; Rufford; Osberton.
3 Manzer Gorse, Eakring, *Ordoyno*; Nottingham, *G. Howitt*; Muskham Wood†, *Fisher*; Syerston; Ordsall, *Carr MS.*
4 Turf Moor, Brough.

Potentilla erecta (L.) Rausch. *Tormentil*

Native. Heaths, woods and rough meadows on light soils. Common. All Divs.

First Record: C. Deering, *Cat. Stirp.* 1738.

Potentilla erecta x reptans occurs frequently with the parents.

Potentilla sterilis (L.) Garke. *Barren Strawberry*

Native. Woods and Meadows. Common. All Divs.

First Record: T. Ordoyno, *Fl. Nott.* 1807.

Potentilla intermedia L.

Alien. Div. 2.

Only Record: J. Brown in litt. 1951, Pusto Hill, Everton, det. R. W. Butcher.

Potentilla recta L.

Alien. Rare. Div. 2.

Only Record: A few plants in 'seeds' at Osberton Grange. The next week we discovered many well established plants on the edge of Osberton old airfield. They were nowhere near the huts and lupins and appeared to have been quite accidentally introduced, possibly also with grass seed. 1961.

Potentilla palustris (L.) Scop. *Marsh Cinquefoil*

Native. Acid Bogs. Uncommon and decreasing. Divs. 2, 3.

First Record: C. Deering, *Cat. Stirp.* 1738.

2 Modern Records; Rainworth; Ranby; Misson; Scaftworth; Bestwood Duckponds; Vicar Water, Clipstone; Osberton.
3 Moor Lane, Calverton, *Carr MS.*; Girton.

Alchemilla vulgaris agg. *Lady's Mantle*

First Record: C. Deering, *Cat. Stirp.* 1738.

Alchemilla vestita (Buser) Raunk. *Lady's Mantle*

Native. Woodland rides and damp meadows. The common species in Notts. All Divs.

First Record: R. W. Butcher in Carr's MS. Our thanks to Dr. S. M. Walters for determining our specimens.

1 Very common.
2 Newstead; Ollerton; Papplewick.
3 Frequent in woods.
4 Owthorpe.

Alchemilla conjuncta Bab.

Denizen. Div. 1.

Only Record: Naturalised on rocks near houses in Pleasley Vale, 1952.

Aphanes arvensis L. *Parsley Piert*

Native. Arable fields and open communities on light soils. Common, except in Div. 2. All Divs.

First Record: C. Deering, *Cat. Stirp.* 1738.

Aphanes microcarpa (Bois. and Reut.) Rothm. *Parsley Piert*

Native. Heaths, open grassland and arable fields on acid soils. Uncommon except in Div. 2. Divs. 2, 4.

First Record: Langford Moor 1951, det. S. M. Walters.

2 Common.
4 Langford Moor; Turf Moor, Brough.

Agrimonia Eupatoria L. *Common Agrimony*

Native. Roadsides and rough grassland. Common. All Divs.

First Record: C. Deering, *Cat. Stirp.* 1738.

Agrimonia odorata (Gouan) Mill. *Fragrant Agrimony*

Native. Grassland on light soils. Uncommon. Divs. 2, 3, 4.

First Record: J. W. Carr, *Trans. Nott. Nats.* 1903.

2 Clumber Park; Thoresby Park; Hazel Gap.
3 Farnsfield, *Carr.*
4 Thorney.

(*Aremonia Agrimoniodes* (L.) Neck. is recorded in the *Comital Flora* 1932 for V. C. 56. (Notts.))

Poterium polygamum Walst. and Kit.

Alien. Rare. Divs. 2, 3.

First Record: A. R. Horwood, *B.E.C. Rept.* 1915.

2 Misson, *Mrs. Sandwith, Butcher*; Pusto Hill, Everton, *Brown.*
3 Kingston-on-Soar, *Horwood.*

Poterium Sanguisorba L. *Salad Burnet*

Native. Banks and meadows, chiefly on basic soils. Common except in Div. 2, where it is most frequent on the Carrs. Formerly sown in grass seeds. All Divs.

First Record: C. Deering, *Cat. Stirp.* 1738.

2 Misson; Scaftworth; Newstead; East Kirkby.

Sanguisorba officinalis L. *Great Burnet*

Native. Meadows and grassy places on rich alluvial soils. Frequent throughout the county. All Divs.

First Record: C. Deering, *Cat. Stirp.* 1738.

Rosa The classification of this genus follows A. H. Wolley-Dod 1924. Our thanks are due to Dr. R. Melville of Kew who has checked our records. More work is required on this section.

Rosa arvensis Huds. *Field Rose*

Native. Hedges, woods and scrub. Common. All Divs.

First Record: T. Ordoyno, *Fl. Nott.* 1807. "Southwell; Newark."

Rosa spinosissima L. *Burnet Rose*

Appeared to grow plentifully for the ancient Botanists. Some records may be misidentifications of *R. arvensis*, but some reputable people record both. It is recorded for Leicestershire (*Horwood and Gainsborough* 1933.) with specimens still extant.

First Records: C. Deering, *Cat. Stirp.* 1738, "very plentifully about the Sand Hills." G. Howitt, *Notts. Fl.* 1837 "In stony places. In many places on both the Magnesian and Lias Limestones, and also in the Sand District."

1 *G. Howitt*, No locality.
2 Nottingham sandhills, *Deering* and *Jowett*; Nottingham Park; Larkdale; Bulwell, *Jowett*; Bulwell Forest, *Gilbert.*
3 Newark; Southwell, *Ordoyno*; Stanford-on-Soar, *Potter*; Between Newton and North Clifton, *Cole.*
4 Leake; Bunny, *Pulteney*; Near E. and W. Leake, *Nicholls*; G. *Howitt*, no locality.

Rosa x Sabini Woods (*spinosissima x villosa*).

Only Record: J. W. Carr *J. B.* 1909; Bunny Hill, Div. 4. as *R. involuta* Sm. var *Sabini* Woods.

Rosa rugosa Thumb.

Alien. Denizen. Woods. Thoroughly naturalised in the Dukeries. Div. 2.

First Record: Gleadthorpe Breck 1959.

2 Gleadthorpe Breck; Hatfield Plantation; Rufford.

Rosa canina L.

Native. Woods, hedges and scrub. Common. All Divs.

First Record: C. Deering, *Cat. Stirp.* 1738. "Common in hedges."

var *lutetiana* Baker.

First Record: H. Fisher, *Brit. Ass. Rept.* 1893. "Common." *Victoria County History*. 1906. Divs. 1, 3.

var *oxyphylla* (Rip.) W. Dod.

Only Records: Red Bridge, Osberton; Thievesdale, Osberton 1961, Div. 2.

var *sphaerica* Dumort.

First Record: H. Fisher, *Brit. Ass. Rept.* 1893, Kelham. Div. 3.

var *dumalis* Dum.

First Record: T. Jowett, *Bot. Cals.* 1826, "common." H. Fisher 1893, "common." *Victoria County History*, Divs. 1, 3.

2 Blyth.
3 Roe Wood, Winkburn.
4 Leake Hills.

var *medioxima* (Desegl.) Rouy.

Only Records: Carlton-in-Lindrick, Div. 1; Serlby Div. 2. 1962.

var *eriostyla* (Rip.) W. Dod.

Only Record: Langwith, Div. 1, 1960.

var *viridicata* (Pug.) Rouy.

Only Record: Birklands, Div. 2. 1960.

var *fraxinoides* (H. Br.) W. Dod.

First Record: Div. 3, Little Gringley 1953.

3 Little Gringley; Roe Wood, Winkburn.

var *recognita* Rouy.

Only Records: Ruins Plantation, Wallingwells, Div. 1; Red Bridge, Osberton, Div. 2.

var *sylvularum* (Rip.) Rouy.

Only Record: Turners Green, Shireoaks, 1962, Div. 1.

var *andevagensis* Desp.

First Record: H. Fisher, *Brit. Ass. Rept.* 1893 "Newark District."

var *Blondaeana* Rouy.

First Record: H. Fisher, *Brit. Ass. Rept.* 1893 "Farndon; Newark; Muskham Wood."

All Div. 3 (as var. *marginata* Wallr,) "a form which differs from the type by its reflexed sepals."

var *spuria* (Pug.) W. Dod.

Only Record: Osberton, Div. 2, 1961.

Rosa dumetorum Thuill.

Native. "Thickets and hedges, common," *G. Howitt*.

First Record: T. Jowett, *Bot. Cals.* 1826 "common."

var *urbica* Lem.

First Record: H. Fisher *Brit. Ass. Rept.* 1893, "Newark to Flintham." Div. 3.

var *semiglabra* (Rip.) W. Dod.

First Record: Cottam, Div. 3, Aug. 1951.

var *calophylla* Rouy.

First Record: Birklands 1960.

2 Birklands.
3 Trent Lane, Nottingham.

var. *sphaerocarpa* (Pug.) W. Dod.

First Record: Kirkby Bogs, Div. 1, 1959.

var. *mercica* W. Dod is recorded in *Victoria County History*, for Div. 1 or 2 (as *R. arvatica* Baker).

Rosa Afzeliana Fries. (*glauca* Vill.).

Native. Woods and scrub. Div. 3, 4.

First Record: H. Fisher, *Brit. Ass. Rept.* 1893.

3 Newark; Mons Pool, Collingham, *Fisher*.
4 Potter Hill, Collingham, *Fisher*.

var *Reuteri* (God.) W. Dod.

Balderton Div. 4, Aug. 1952.

Rosa corifolia Fries.

Native. Div. 3.

Only Record: H. Fisher, *Brit. Ass. Rept.* 1893; "Rare." Near Hazleford; Kirklington Mill.

Rosa tormentella Lem.

var *Borreri* W. Dod. *Victoria County History*. No division (as *R. obtusifolia* Desv. var. *Borreri* (Woods)).

var *obtusifolia* W. Dod. *Victoria County History*. Div. 3 (as R. *obtusifolia* Desv. var. *tormentella* (Lem.)).

Rosa mollis Sm.

Native. "In hedges." Uncommon. Div. 1.

First Record: T. Jowett, *Bot. Cals.* 1826.

1 Bramcote Moor, *Jowett*; Aspley; Near Wollaton, *G. Howitt*.

Rosa omissa Desegl. var *Sherardii* W. Dod.

Only Record: T. Jowett, *Bot. Cals.* 1826. (as *R. subglobosa* Sm.) "?Bulwell." Div. 1 or 2.

Rosa tormentosa Sm. agg.

Native. Hedges and woods. Frequent in 3 and probably in 1, Divs. 1, 3, 4.

First Record: T. Ordoyno, *Fl. Notts.* 1807 as *R. villosa* of Smith's *Flora Brit.* "Before you reach Kirklington turnpike . . . from Normanton."

var *tormentosa*

Frequent, *G. Howitt.*

1 Warsop Wood; Wallingwells Wood, Carlton-in-Lindrick, plentifully and in the lane by Lingy Wood; Scratta Wood, Shireoaks.
3 Roe Wood, Winkburn.

var *eglandulosa* W. Dod.

First Record: Roe Wood, Winkburn, Div. 3 1960.

var *pseudo cuspidata* Rouy.

First Record: Eakring, Div. 3 1956.

var *scabriuscula* Sm.

First Record: T. Jowett; *Bot. Cals.* 1826 "common." G. Howitt "more frequent than *tormentosa.*"

Rosa rubiginosa L. *Sweet Briar*

Native. Hedges etc. Rare or overlooked. Divs. 1, 2, 3.

First Record: C. Deering, *Cat. Stirp.* 1738.

1 Beauvale; Bulwell, *Jowett*; Steetley, *Bohler.*
2 Edwinstowe, *Bohler.*
3 Colwick Hills, *Deering*, *Gilbert*; Clifton, *Jowett*; Between Walkeringham and Beckingham, *Miller.*

Rosa micrantha Sm.

Native. Bushy places. Very rare. Divs. 1, 2.

First Record: T. Jowett, *Bot. Cals.* 1826.

1 In an old stone quarry near Bulwell Wood Hall, *Jowett.*
2 Meadows between Chequer Bridge and Bilby, Osberton, a form between f. *Briggsii* and f. *trichostyla*, det. R. Melville 1961.

Rosa agrestis Savi.

Native. Very rare.

Only Record: H. Fisher, *Brit. Ass. Rept.* 1883 (as *R. sepium* Thuill) "An undescribed form of this a long way from the type, between Upton and Spring Wood; Edingley Moor (Div. 3)."

Pyrus Malus L. *Crab Apple*

Native. Hedges and edges of woods. Common. All Divs.

First Record: C. Deering, *Cat. Stirp.* 1738.

Pyrus communis L. *Pear*

Alien. Hedges, etc. On the sites of old gardens. Rare. Divs. 2, 3, 4.

First Record: T. Ordoyno, *Fl. Nott.* 1807 "Woods and Hedges."

2 Scaftworth; Ranby.
3 East Stoke†, *Leather*; Eaton; East Bridgeford.
4 South Scarle.

Sorbus aucuparia L. *Rowan*

Native. Woodland on light soils. Locally common. All Divs.

First Record: C. Deering, *Cat. Stirp.* 1738.

1 Common on the coal measures.
2 Common.
3 Common on the blown sand.
4 Thorney; Wigsley; Langford.

Sorbus intermedia Ehrh. *Whitebeam*

Alien. Denizen. Waste Places. Rare. Div. 3.

Only Record: Mapperley Brick pits, plenty of young trees, 1958.

Sorbus Aria (L.) Crantz. *Whitebeam*

Native in Div. 1, planted elsewhere, woods, rough ground and hedges. Rare. All Divs.

First Record: J. Bohler, White's *Worksop and the Dukeries* 1875.

1 Tranker Wood, Shireoaks; Styrrup; Langold; Oldcotes (planted).
2 Clumber Park; Rufford, *Bohler*; Cockglade, Edwinstowe.
3 Winthorpe; Ossington; Weston.
4 Wigsley.

Sorbus torminalis (L.) Crantz. *Wild Service Tree*

Native. Woods and hedges, especially on clay. Locally frequent. Divs. 1, 3, 4.

First Record: C. Deering, *Cat. Stirp.* 1738, "Not uncommon in hedges."

1 Shireoaks; Hucknall; Creswell Crags; Warsop.
3 Colwick Park, *Jowett*; Mapperley Hills, *G. Howitt*; Walkeringham, *Miller*; Egmanton Wood; Winkburn; Kirton; Eakring; Caunton; Thurgarton; Epperstone.
4 Hedge at Cotham.

Crataegus monogyna Jacq. *Hawthorn*

Native. Woods, scrubland and hedges. Very common. All Divs.

First Record: C. Deering, *Cat. Stirp.* 1738.

Crataegus x media Bechst. *monogyna x oxyacanthoides*

Occurs frequently with the parents.

Crataegus oxyacanthoides Thuill. *Midland Hawthorn*

Native. Woods, scrubland and hedges. Frequent throughout the county and common in the Trent Valley. All Divs.

First Record: H. Fisher, *Rept. Brit. Ass.* 1883.

(**Cotoneaster microphyllus** Wallich. is recorded for V.C. 56 (Notts.) in the *Comital Flora* 1932.)

SAXIFRAGACEAE

Saxifraga granulata L. *Meadow Saxifrage*

Native. Banks in meadows. Local, chiefly in the Trent Valley. Divs. 2, 3, 4.

First Record: C. Deering, *Cat. Stirp.* 1738. "In all meadows and Pastures."

2 Church Cemetery, Nottingham, *Bohler* 1866, *Williams*; Common, gravelly soils in the Sherwood Forest, *Bohler* 1875; Harworth, *Mrs. Sandwith*; Woodthorpe; Arnold; Lenton; Bulwell; Bramcote, *Carr MS.*; Rufford, *Jones*; Welbeck Park.
3 Southwell; Quonce Close, Newark; Averham; Edingley; Kirklington, *Ordoyno*; Eakring, *Friend*; Dorket Head; Arnold; Clifton Grove, *Williams*; Trent Hills at Elston and Flintham; Kelham; Hawton; Rempstone; Newark. Prof. Carr has a dozen more records for this decreasing species.
4 Harby, *Carr MS.*

Saxifraga tridactylites L. *Rue Leaved Saxifrage*

Native. Old walls and quarries. Uncommon. All Divs.

First Record: C. Deering, *Cat. Stirp.* 1738.

1 Mansfield, *Deering*; Nuthall; Felley Mill, *Jowett*; Langwith; Haggonfields, *Roffey*; Sookholme; Cresswell Crags, *Carr MS.*; Church Warsop.
2 Lenton; Nottingham, *Deering*; Newstead; Papplewick; Welbeck.
3 Southwell; Newark, *Ordoyno*; Walkeringham, *Miller*; Sneinton, *Gilbert*; Epperstone; Woodborough; East Bridgford; Gunthorpe, *Carr MS.*; Winkburn, *Leather*.
4 Wysall Churchyard, *Butcher*.

Chrysosplenium alternifolium L. *Alternate Golden Saxifrage*

Native. Very wet 'alder carr' type woods by streams in Div. 2. Local. Divs. 2, 3.

First Record: T. Ordoyno, *Fl. Nott.* 1807.

2 Carbanks Field (Farnsfield); Fountaindale; Bogs near Farnsfield, *G. Howitt*; Budby Carr; Rainworth; Clumber Park; Thoresby Ash Holt; Osberton, in quantity.
3 Epperstone Park, *Ordoyno*; Thurgarton Gorse, *Leather*.

Chrysosplenium oppositifolium L. *Golden Saxifrage*

Native. Wet woods and Dumbles. Locally frequent in Divs. 1, 2 and 3.

First Record: C. Deering, *Cat. Stirp.* 1738.

Parnassia palustris L. *Grass of Parnassus*

Native. Bogs, often on calcareous formations. Very rare and decreasing. Divs. 1, 2, 3.

First Record: C. Deering, *Cat. Stirp.* 1738.

1 Papplewick, *Deering*; Kirkby-in-Ashfield, *Kaye*; Many places in the course of the Leen; Pleasley, *Jowett*; Cresswell Crags, *Bohler*; Shireoaks; Haggonfields, *Friend*; Church Warsop; Sookholme Bath.
2 Basford Scottum, *Deering*; Ollerton, *Jowett*.
3 Southwell; Halam; Kirklington; Bleasby, *Ordoyno*; Morton; Clifton by Nottingham, *Jowett*; Edingley Moor, *Fisher*.

Philadelphus coronarius L. *Mock Orange*

Alien. Sometimes planted in woods.

First Record: R. G. Williams MS. 1940, "Abundantly naturalised in Gedling Moor."

Ribes Uva-crispa L. *Gooseberry*

Native. Damp woods and hedges. Common. All Divs.
First Record: T. Ordoyno, *Fl. Nott.* 1807.

Ribes nigrum L. *Blackcurrant*

Native. Wet woods. Common, especially in willow holts in the Trent Valley. All Divs.

First Record: C. Deering, *Cat. Stirp.* 1738.

Ribes sylvestre (Lam.) Mert. and Koch. *Red Currant*

?Native. Wet woods. Common, especially in willow holts in the Trent Valley. All Divs.

First Record: C. Deering, *Cat. Stirp.* 1738, "I cannot say I have yet observed them wild." T. Ordoyno, *Fl. Nott.* 1807, "In a hedge near Papplewick Bridge . . . also at Basford".

Ribes alpinum L. *Mountain Currant*

Native. Marshy woods. Very rare. Div. 1.

First Record: G. Howitt, *Fl. Notts.* 1839.

1 Felley Mill, *G. Howitt*; Shireoaks, one bush by the stream, *Roffey*; Pleasley Vale, by the Mill; Skegby, apparently wild, *Carr MS.*; Dovedale Wood, Teversall, a lot; Wallingwells Wood, Carlton-in-Lindrick.

CRASSULACEAE

Tillaea muscosa L. *Mossy Tillaea*

Native. Gravel Rides. Very rare. Div. 4.

Only Record: Mrs. Foggitt, *B.E.C. Rept.* 1926 'Stapleford Wood, Notts.' It grows both at Stapleford, Lincs, and on rides on the adjacent Langford Moor, Notts.

Sedum Telephinum L. *Orpine*

Native. Hedges and woods. Very rare. Divs. 1, 2, 3.

First Record: G. Howitt, *Notts. Fl.* 1839.

1 Gateford Lane, Worksop, *G. Howitt.*
2 Carlton Road, Worksop, *G. Howitt*; Barrow Hills, Everton, *Miller*; Elkesley, *Carr MS.*
3 Gamston Wood, very little.

var *purpurascens* (Koch.) F. Arechoug.

Only Record: J. K. Miller, *Fl. Walk.* 1819-55, *Nat.* 1845 "Harwell Hills." Sp. in Herb. Lincoln Museum.

Sedum reflexum L. *Reflexed Stonecrop*

Alien. Denizen. Walls and waste ground. Fairly common. All Divs.

First Record: C. Deering, *Cat. Stirp.* 1738 "In Nottingham Park and on many thatched Houses in this Town."

var *albescens* Haw.

G. Howitt, *Notts. Fl.* 1839 includes this on the authority of C. Deering's *S. minus haematoides* Syn. 269. "is very common in the hollow Ways about this Town." Howitt had not seen it himself.

Sedum acre L. *Wall Pepper*

Native. Walls, rocks, heaths, railways. Common. All Divs.

First Record: C. Deering, *Cat. Stirp.* 1738.

Sedum album L. *White Stonecrop*

Alien. Denizen. Walls and rocks. Rare. Divs. 2, 3.

First Record: G. Howitt, *Notts. Fl.* 1839.

2 Rocks at the entrance to Nottingham Park, *G. Howitt.*
3 Lock wall, Kingston-on-Soar.

Sedum dasyphyllum L. *Thick Leaved Stonecrop*

Alien. Walls. Div. 1.

Only Record: T. Ordoyno, *Fl. Nott.* 1807. "Walls near Kirkby Church."

Sedum anglicum Huds.

Denizen. Walls. Rare or extinct. Divs. 1, 2.

First Record: T. Jowett, *Bot. Cals.* 1826.

1 Walls at Mansfield Bottoms, *G. Howitt* per *Mr. Deakin.*
2 Fountain Dale, *Jowett*; Nottingham Castle Rock, *Sidebotham.*

Sempervivum tectorum L. *Houseleek*

Alien. Denizen. Roofs and old walls. Commonly planted and frequently spreading spontaneously, as at Farndon.

First Record: C. Deering, *Cat. Stirp.* 1738, "Very common on thatched Houses and Barns in most Villages about Nottingham."

DROSERACEAE

(**Drosera intermedia** Drev. and Heyne. *Long Leaved Sundew*

G. Howitt, *Notts. Fl.* 1839, records this species for Stapleford Moor, the record is probably in Lincolnshire.)

Drosera rotundifolia L. *Sundew*

Native. Peat bogs. Probably extinct. Divs. 2, 3, 4.

First Record: C. Deering, *Cat. Stirp.* 1738.

2 Oxton; Caudwell Brook, Mansfield, *Deering*; Papplewick and Bulwell Forest, *Jowett*; "Frequent," *G. Howitt*; Occurred at Oxton Bogs till about 1900, *Carr MS.*
3 Edingley Moor, *Ordoyno*; Epperstone, *Jowett.*
4 Coddington and Langford Moors, *Ordoyno.*

HALORAGACEAE

Hippuris vulgaris L. *Mare's Tail*

Native. Ponds and drains, mostly in base rich waters. Common in Div. 1 and on the Carrs, rare elsewhere.

First Record: G. Pulteney, *Phil. Trans.* 1756.

1 Common.
2 Gringley Carr†, *Miller*; Misson; Everton Carr; Annesley; Hucknall; Thoresby Lake; Welbeck Lake; Langwith.
3 West Leake, *Camden*; Trent above Wilford, *G. Howitt*; Gringley Carr; Misterton Carr; Walkeringham; Trentside, West Stockwith; Subsidence pool on Nottingham Meadows.

Myriophyllum spicatum L. *Water Milfoil*

Native. Ponds, drains, canals and gravel pits. Common. All Divs.

First Record: T. Ordoyno, *Fl. Nott.* 1807 (aggregate). J. W. Carr, *Victoria County History* 1906 (segregate).

Myriophyllum alterniflorum DC. *Water Milfoil*

Only Record: H. Fisher, quoted by J. W. Carr, *Trans. Nott. Nats.* 1904, 'Newark'—An unlikely locality.

Myriophyllum verticillatum L. *Whorled Water Milfoil*

Ponds and drains in base rich waters. Rare. Divs. 1, 2, 3.

First Record: C. Deering, *Cat. Stirp.* 1738.

1 Shireoaks Lake.
2 *Victoria County History.*
3 "In the Trent below Colwick, on the opposite side of the River," *Deering*; Pool in Nottingham Meadows, *G. Howitt*; Pool in Attenborough Meadows; Drain on Misterton Carr.

Callitriche aquatica agg. *Water Starwort*

First Record: C. Deering, *Cat. Stirp.* 1738.

Callitriche stagnalis Scop. *Water Starwort*

Native. Ponds, drains etc. Common. All Divs.

First Record: J. W. Carr and H. Fisher, *Trans. Nott. Nats.* 1904.

Callitriche obtusangula Hegelm. *Water Starwort*

Native. Streams and ditches. Rare. Div. 3.

Only Records: J. W. Carr, *Tr. Nott. Nat.* 1904, Fairham Brook . . . at Wilford; Bingham.

(**Callitriche vernalis** Koch. is recorded in the *Victoria County History*, probably on the authority of G. Howitt's record. This record would appear to refer to the aggregate.)

Callitriche hamulata Kutz. *Water Starwort*

Native. Ponds. Rare. Div. 2.

Only Record: Pond in Martin Wood, Hesley, det. J. P. Savidge 1959. H. Fisher's plant was *C. truncata.*

(**Callitriche autumnalis** L. is recorded with a query in the *Victoria County History*, probably on the authority of T. Ordoyno. This record would appear to refer to the aggregate.)

Callitriche truncata Guss. *Water Starwort*

Slow streams, canals and large drains. Local. Chiefly in the North. Divs. 2, 3.

First Record: H. Fisher, see J. W. Carr, *Tr. Nott. Nats.* 1904. Fisher identified this plant as a *C. hamulata* Kutz. and it appears under this name in the *Rept. Brit. Ass.* 1893. On submission to A. Bennett it was determined as *C. truncata.*

2 Rainworth Water, *Fisher*; Clumber, *Mrs. Sandwith*; R. Poulter at Cuckney, *Butcher*; In the Chesterfield Canal at Retford, Wiseton, Osberton and Gringley; In the Ryton at Scrooby; Scaftworth; Wollaton.

3 Chesterfield Canal at Clarborough†, Hayton† and Misterton†, *Carr* 1905; Mother Drain, Sturton; Hecdyke, West Stockwith; R. Greet, Rolleston.

LYTHRACEAE

Peplis Portula L. *Water Purslane*

Native. Damp places where water has stood. Local. Chiefly on sand. Divs. 2, 3, 4.

First Record: C. Deering, *Cat. Stirp.* 1738.

2 Farnsfield Carr, *Ordoyno*; Finningley.

3 Edingley Moor, *Ordoyno*; Clifton Grove, *Williams*; Winkburn; Spalford; Haughton Decoy.

4 Coddington and Langford† Moors, *Ordoyno.*

Lythrum Salicaria L. *Purple Loosestrife*

Water sides and marshes, willow holts. Common. All Divs.

First Record: C. Deering, *Cat. Stirp.* 1738.

Lythrum Hyssopifolia L. *Grass Poly*

Native. Extinct. Div. 3.

Only Record: C. Deering, *Cat. Stirp.* 1738, "grows in Places where sometimes Water Stagnates, a little below Wilford Boat."

ONAGRACEAE

Epilobium angustifolium L. *Rosebay*

Denizen. Derelict and open woodland, heaths, waste ground. Very common. All Divs.

First Record: A. Gilbert, *Botany for Beginners* 1880, "Canal side near Wollaton."

Epilobium hirsutum L. *Great Willow Herb*

Native. Riversides, marshes, willow holts. Very common. All Divs.

First Record: C. Deering, *Cat. Stirp.* 1738.

Epilobium parviflorum Schreb. *Hoary Willow Herb*

Native. Riversides and marshes. Common. All Divs.

First Record: T. Ordoyno, *Fl. Nott.* 1807.

Epilobium adnatum Gris. *Square stemmed Willow Herb*

Native. Damp places. In more open habitats than the next and often on waste ground. Local. All Divs.

First Record: C. Deering, *Cat. Stirp.* 1738, the aggregate species H. Fisher, *Tr. Nott. Nats.* 1894, segregate.

1 Bulwell.
2 Between Rainworth and Inkersall; Rufford Forest, *Fisher*; Ranskill; Ordsall; Annesley; Thoresby Pit Dump.
3 Fiskerton, *Williams*; Southwell; Arnold Dump.
4 West Leake.

Epilobium obscurum Schreb. *Square stemmed Willow Herb*

Native. Damp shady places. Rather frequent. All Divs.

First Record: J. W. Carr, *Tr. Nott. Nats.* 1904.

Epilobium roseum Schreb. *Pale Willow Herb*

Native. Waste ground in towns, where it partly replaces *E. montanum* as a garden weed. Local. Divs. 1, 2, 3.

First Record: G. Howitt, *Notts. Fl.* 1839.

1 Teversall; Skegby, *Carr MS.*; Pleasley Vale, *Carr MS.* and *Butcher*.
2 Blyth; Mansfield Woodhouse, *Carr MS.*; Worksop; Mansfield; Arnot Hill, Arnold.
3 Frequent in the vicinity of Nottingham and in many places in the Trent Vale, *G. Howitt*; Clifton Grove; Thurgarton, *Carr MS.*

Epilobium montanum L. *Broad leaved Willow Herb*

Native. Damp places and gardens. Common. All Divs.

First Record: C. Deering, *Cat. Stirp.* 1738.

(**Epilobium alpinum** L. is recorded in Turner and Dillwyn's *Botanists Guide* and various other works on the authority of C. Deering's *Lysimachia siliquosa glabra minor*.)

Epilobium palustre L. *Marsh Willow Herb*

Native. Bogs and marshes, chiefly on light land.

First Record: C. Deering, *Cat. Stirp.* 1738.

1 Kirkby Bogs.
2 Very frequent.
3 Frequent, especially in the river valleys.
4 Coddington; Langford Moor.

Oenothera biennis L. *Evening Primrose*

Alien. Denizen. Rubbish dumps, railway sidings and waste ground generally. Common. All Divs.

First Record: Waste ground, Newark, 1949.

Oenothera erythrosepala Borbas. *Evening Primrose*

Alien. Denizen. Waste ground, dumps and near gardens. Uncommon, but probably increasing. Divs. 2, 3.

First Record: Smith's Wood yard, Newark, 1958.

Circaea lutetiana L. *Enchanter's Nightshade*

Native. Damp woods. Common, least so in Div. 2. All Divs.

First Record: C. Deering, *Cat. Stirp.* 1738.

CURCURBITACEAE

Cucumis sativus L. Cucumber and **Curcurbita Pepo** L. Vegetable marrow, both occur very frequently on dumps.

Bryonia dioica Jacq. *White Bryony*

Native. Hedges. Very common. All Divs.

First Record: C. Deering, *Cat. Stirp.* 1738.

UMBELLIFERAE

Hydrocotyle vulgaris L. *Marsh Pennywort*

Native. Peaty bogs and drainsides. Still fairly common, but decreasing. All Divs, least common in 4.

First Record: C. Deering, *Cat. Stirp.* 1738.

4 Harby; Thorney, *Carr MS.*; Langford and Turf Moors on the river gravels; Rempstone old Churchyard on sandy boulder clay.

Sanicula europaea L. *Wood Sanicle*

Native. Damp woods on all formations. Common, least so in Div. 2. All Divs.

First Record: C. Deering, *Cat. Stirp.* 1738.

Conium maculatum L. *Hemlock*

Native. Dry, disturbed ground, near roads, streams, waste places. Common. All Divs.

First Record: C. Deering, *Cat. Stirp.* 1738.

Smyrnium Olusatrum L. *Alexanders*

Alien. Denizen. Rare. Near old buildings. Divs. 2, 3.

First Record: J. Ray, *Phil. Letts.* (*Dereham's Ed.*) 1718, per Mr. Sherard.

2 Nottingham Castle Rock, *Ray.* It is still there in great quantity.
3 About Bingham, *Crabbe.*

Bupleurum rotundifolium L. *Hare's Ear*

Probably native in Div. 1. Cornfields and waste ground. Rare. Divs. 1, 3, 4.

First Record: G. Howitt, *Notts. Fl.* 1839.

1 Cornfields near Cresswell Crags, *G. Howitt* per *Mr. B. Eddison.*
3 Newark Wharfs, *Fisher*; Garden in Victoria Street, Newark, formerly used as a fowl run.
4 Roadside at Cotham, possibly native.

Apium Dulce Mill., the garden celery, occurs on rubbish tips.

Apium graveolens L. *Wild Celery*

Native. Ditches and marshes. Apparently extinct. Divs. 2, 3, 4.

First Record: C. Deering, *Cat. Stirp.* 1738.

2 Lenton, *Deering*; Basford, *G. Howitt.*
3 Kirklington Toll Bar; Halam Cross; Thurgarton, *Ordoyno*; Lowdham, *Jowett*; Banks of the Leen, *G. Howitt*; North Leverton, *Carr MS.*
4 Costock Town, *Deering.*

Apium nodiflorum (L.) Lag. *Fool's Watercress*

Native. Ditches, pools and stream sides. Very common. All Divs.

First Record: C. Deering, *Cat. Stirp.* 1738.

Apium inundatum (L.) Rchb. *Lesser Apium*

Native. Pools and drains, chiefly in the Trent Valley and the Carrs. Very local. Divs. 2, 3, 4.

First Record: T. Ordoyno, *Fl. Nott.* 1807.

2 Bulwell, *Jowett* (or 1); Misson.
3 Gravel Pits near Kirklington Mill, *Ordoyno*; Nottingham Meadows, *G. Howitt*; Gringley Carr, *Miller*; Leenside, *Gilbert*; Rolleston; Collingham; South Muskham.
4 Thorney; Harby; Wigsley.

Cicuta virosa L. *Cowbane*

Native. River and pond sides. Extinct. Div. 2.

First Record: R. Pulteney, *Phil. Trans.* 1756.

2 Pool in Nottingham Park, *Pulteney*; Ditches at the foot of Nottingham Castle Rock (beside the Leen), *Becher.* Both these stations were extinct by G. Howitt's time.

Ammi majus L.

Alien. Casual. Div. 3.

Only Record: A. R. Horwood, *B.E.C. Rept.* 1915, "Kingston-on-Soar."

Carum Carvi L. *Caraway*

Alien. Casual. Meadows and gardens. Rare. Divs. 1, 2, 3.

First Record: T. Ordoyno, *Fl. Nott.* 1807.

1 Between Hucknall under Huthwaite and Whitborough, *G. Howitt.*

2 Nottingham Forest Toll Bar, *G. Howitt.*
3 Newark Meadows, *Ordoyno*; Nottingham Meadows, *G. Howitt*; Between Walkerith and Stockwith, *Miller*; Clayworth; North Wheatley, *Carr MS.*; Garden weed at Farndon; Newark Dump; Nottingham Dump.

Carum Petroselinum (L.) B. and H. *Parsley*

Alien. Denizen or casual. Walls and rocks. Rare. Divs. 1, 2.

First Record: T. Jowett, *Bot. Cals.* 1866.

1 Wall at Cinder Hill, *Gilbert.*
2 Rocks in Nottingham Park, *Jowett*; Nottingham Church Cemetery, *Bohler* 1866; Roadside, Everton.

Carum segetum B. and H. *Corn Caraway*

Native. Arable fields on basic soils. Rare. Div. 3, 4.

First Record: H. C. Watson *Top. Bot.* 1883, from Mrs. Russell's Catalogue.

3 Kilvington.
4 Stanford-on-Soar, *Carr* 1904; Barnby in the Willows; Kilvington.

Sison Amomum L. *Hedge Sison*

Native. Hedge sides and among bushes on heavy clay. Locally frequent. Divs. 3, 4.

First Record: T. Ordoyno, *Fl. Nott.* 1807.

3 Frequent.
4 Near East Leake and Bunny, *G. Howitt*; Hickling; Kinoulton; Widmerpool.

Falcaria vulgaris Bernh. *Long Leaf*

Alien. Denizen. Naturalised on the Lias.

The plant is thoroughly established in a grass field at Kilvington (Div. 4) and on the adjoining railway banks (1951).

Sium latifolium L. *Great Water Parsnip*

Native. Sides of drains and fen pools. Rare and decreasing. Divs. 2, 3.

First Record: J. Salt, *List of Plants* . . . 1796 to 1807.

2 Everton Common, *Salt*; Misson†, *Carr*; Beckingham, *Roffey*; Everton Carr.
3 Old Trent Dyke, Averham; By the Greet at Southwell, *Ordoyno*; Misterton†, *Carr MS.* where there is still a little by the Gate Inn.

Sium erectum Huds. *Lesser Water Parsnip*

Native. Sides of streams, ponds and particularly canals. Common. All Divs.

First Record: Notts. taken specimen in Salt's Herbarium at Sheffield, 1803.

Aegopodium Podagraria L. *Gout Weed*

Roadsides and gardens and frequently in woods. Very common. All Divs.

First Record: C. Deering, *Cat. Stirp.* 1738, "I only observed it going from Nottingham Castle towards the Leen . . . and also a little lower down . . . pretty plentifully".

Pimpinella major (L.) Huds. *Great Burnet Saxifrage*

Native. Meadows, roadsides and rough ground on calcareous soils. Locally frequent. All Divs.

First Record: C. Deering, *Cat. Stirp.* 1738.

1 Frequent.
2 Hodsock.
3 Frequent on the clay.
4 Thorney; Stanton; Harby.

Pimpinella Saxifraga L. *Burnet Saxifrage*

Native. Meadows, roadsides and grassland. Common in Divs. 1, 3, 4, less so in 2.

First Record: C. Deering, *Cat. Stirp.* 1738.

2 Nottingham Lings, *Deering*; Lyndhurst; Wiseton; Everton; Farnsfield.

Conopodium majus (Gouan) Loret and Barr. *Earthnut*

Native. Meadows, roadsides and grassland, woods. Common. All Divs.

First Record: C. Deering, *Cat. Stirp.* 1738.

Myrrhis odorata (L.) Scop. *Sweet Cicely*

?Denizen. Meadows. Rare. Divs. (2), 3.

First Record: G. Howitt, *Notts. Fl.* 1839.

3 "In pastures; rare. Nr. Bramcote," *G. Howitt* (or 2); Naturalised in the grounds of Orston Hall.

Chaerophyllum temulum L. *Rough Chervil*

Native. Roadsides, woods and bushy places. Common. All Divs.

First Record: C. Deering, *Cat. Stirp.* 1738.

Scandix Pecten-veneris L. *Venus' Comb*

Native. Cornfields, especially on clay. Locally common. All Divs.

First Record: C. Deering, *Cat. Stirp.* 1738.

1 Kirkby-in-Ashfield; Teversall, *Carr MS.*; Shireoaks; Huthwaite; Mansfield Woodhouse.
2 Everton.
3 and 4 Frequent.

Anthriscus sylvestris (L.) Bernh. *Hedge Parsley*

Native. Hedges, roadsides, woods and meadows. Very common. All Divs.

First Record: C. Deering, *Cat. Stirp.* 1738.

Anthriscus neglecta Boiss. and Reut. *Bur Chervil*

Native. Sandy ground, especially on the bunter and blown sand. Local. Divs. 2, 3.

First Record: C. Deering, *Cat. Stirp.* 1738.

2 About Nottingham, *Deering*, *G. Howitt*; Everton†, *J. Brown*; Carlton-in-Lindrick; Manton; Ollerton; Osberton Estate.
3 Newark; Kelham to Muskham, *Fisher*; Under Colwick Wood; Wilford Hill; Orston; Langford; Girton; North Collingham†; Besthorpe†, *Carr MS.*; Saundby Dump.

Anthriscus Cerefolium (L.) Hoffm. *Garden Chervil*

Alien. A rare casual. Divs. 1, 3.

First Record: Herb. Jowett, 1821.

1 On a wall at Nuthall, *G. Howitt.*
3 Trentside below Clifton Hall, *Jowett.*

Foeniculum vulgare Mill. *Fennel*

Denizen or casual. Dumps, waste ground and roadsides. Frequent. Often established on sandy gravel. Divs. 1, 2, 3.

First Record: C. Deering, *Cat. Stirp.* 1738, "In plenty about the Rock of Nottingham Castle." It is still there.

Oenanthe aquatica (L.) Poir. *Fine leafed Water Dropwort*

Native. Around deep muddy ponds and ditches. Rare, except in the Trent Valley. All Divs.

First Record: T. Ordoyno, *Fl. Nott.* 1807.

1 Banks of R. Erewash below Eastwood, *G. Howitt.*
2 Misson†; Finningley†, *Carr MS*; Sutton Moor.
3 Frequent in the Trent Valley; Canal at Cropwell Bishop.
4 Broadholme†, *Carr.*

(**Oenanthe crocata** L. recorded for Nottingham Meadows by A. Gilbert is probably an error for the preceding species.)

Oenanthe silaifolia Bieb.

Native. Moist meadows. Very rare. Not all Notts. records are reliable, the specimen sent to Watson by Cooper was *Oe. Lachenalii.* Div. 3.

First Record: T. Ordoyno *Fl. Nott.* 1738, he does not record *O. Lachenalii.*

3 Halam Bottoms; About the Cotton Mill at Southwell, *Ordoyno*; Spalford Meadows, det. J. E. Lousley, sp. Herb. *R. C. L. Howitt.*

Oenanthe Lachenalii C.C. Gemel. *Parsley Water Dropwort*

Native. Damp meadows on basic soils. Local. All Divs.

First Record: T. Jowett, *Bot. Cals.* 1826.

1 Bulwell, *Jowett*; Sookholme Moor†; Hills and Holes, Warsop†, *Carr MS.*
2 Farnsfield Carr, *G. Howitt*; Burns Green, Warsop, *Carr MS.*
3 Morton, *Jowett*; Clifton Cow Pasture, *G. Howitt*; Misterton, *Miller*; Sutton-by-Granby; Treswell, *Carr MS.*
4 Cotgrave; Gotham; Wysall, *Carr MS.*; West Leake; Hickling; Kinoulton.

Oenanthe fistulosa L. *Water Dropwort*

Native. Pondsides and damp meadows. Common in the Trent Valley, less so elsewhere. All Divs.

First Record: C. Deering, *Cat. Stirp.* 1738.

1 Sutton-in-Ashfield; Worksop, *Carr MS.*; Shireoaks.
2 Frequent on the Carrs.
3 Common in the valleys of the Trent and its tributaries.
4 Several places on the Grantham Canal; Thorney; Harby; Wigsley.

Aethusa Cynapium L. *Fool's Parsley*

Native. A weed of cultivated ground. Common. All Divs.

First Record: T. Ordoyno, *Fl. Notts.* 1809.

Silaum Silaus (L.) Schinz and Thell. *Pepper Saxifrage*

Native. Meadows and grassy places. Frequent except in Div. 2. All Divs.

First Record: C. Deering, *Cat. Stirp.* 1738.

1 Greasley; Kirkby; Sookholme; Church Warsop; Annesley.
2 On the Line Bank at Misson; Clipstone.
3 and 4. Frequent.

Selinum Carvifolia L.

Native. Boggy meadows. Very rare or extinct. Div. 1.

Only Record: J. W. Carr *Tr. Nott. Nats.* 1907 and *J. Bot.* 1909, "Newbound Mill, Teversall." The plant was growing in a boggy meadow beside the R. Meden. When we visited the place in 1952 the field had been drained a few years previously. It was still extremely wet, but the farmer, who remembered the plant, said it had disappeared after drainage.

Angelica sylvestris L. *Wild Angelica*

Native. Damp meadows and woods. Common. All Divs.

First Record: C. Deering, *Cat. Stirp.* 1738.

Angelica Archangelica L. *Angelica*

Alien. Denizen. Riversides and damp woods. Uncommon. Divs. 1, 3.

First Record: T. Jowett, *Bot. Cals.* 1826.

1 King's Mill Reservoir.

3 "Wellow Park (Wood), undoubtedly indigenous," *Jowett*; Trentside, North Leverton; Canal Banks in Nottingham; Trentside, Burton Joyce; Trentside, Farndon.

Peucedanum palustre (L.) Moench. *Milk Parsley*

Native. Extinct or error. Div. 1.

Only Records: T. Jowett, *Bot. Cals.* 1826 and G. Howitt, *Fl. Nott.* 1839, "By the side of a small stream between Mansfield Woodhouse and Park Hall, *Hurt* and *Ramsbottam*"; Aspley, *G. Howitt.*

J. W. Carr, supported by Arthur Bennett, considered this plant was *Selinum Carvifolia*, which had not been recorded for Britain in 1826. The localities are in the same area as his station for *Selinum.* The Mansfield Woodhouse one is very close, and also on the R. Meden.

(**Peucedanum officinale** L.

C. Deering records this "In Colwick Wood and near bank sides, not uncommon." From these situations Deering probably intended *Sison Amomum*, which he does not record.)

Pastinaca sativa L. *Wild Parsnip*

Native. Roadsides, banks and waste ground. Common in all Divisions except 2.

First Record: C. Deering, *Cat. Stirp.* 1738.

2 Papplewick; Rufford; Budby; Mansfield; Ollerton. Always a ruderal.

Heracleum Spondylium L. *Cow Parsnip, Hogweed*

Native. Roadsides, meadows and all grassy places. Very common. All Divs.

First Record: C. Deering, *Cat. Stirp.* 1738.

ssp. *angustifolium* Huds. is frequent.

Coriandrum Tordyloides

Alien. A rare casual.

Only Record: H. Fisher, *Rept. Brit. Ass.* 1893, Newark. Div. 3.

Daucus Carota L. *Wild Carrot*

Native. Dry banks, roadsides and pastures. Common in Divs. 1, 3, 4, rare in 2 where it only occurs in artificial habitats.

First Record: C. Deering, *Cat. Stirp.* 1738.

Torilis japonica (Houtt) DC. *Upright Hedge Parsley*

Native. Roadsides, banks and dry places. Common All Divs.

First Record: T. Ordoyno, *Fl. Nott.* 1807.

Torilis arvensis (Huds.) Link. *Spreading Hedge Parsley*

Casual. Arable fields. Rare. Divs. 3, 4.

First Record: Herb. Jowett 1821.

3 Gamston Moor; Clifton about the Broadsick Closes, *Jowett*; Cornfield, Kingston-on-Soar, *Thornley*; Fiskerton, in Lucerne with *Centaurea Solstitialis.*

4 Between Gotham and West Leake, *G. Howitt.*

Torilis nodosa (L.) Gaertn. *Knotted Hedge Parsley*

Native. Dry clay banks. Uncommon. Divs. 3, 4.

First Record: T. Jowett, *Bot. Cals.* 1826.

3 Widely distributed, but not common.

4 By the canal bridge at Owthorpe, *Carr MS.*; Kilvington; Balderton.

Caucalis Lappula (Weber.) Grande. *Small Bur Parsley*

Alien. A rare casual. Div. 3.

Only record: H. Fisher *Rept. Brit. Ass.* 1893. Newark.

Caucalis latifolia L. *Great Bur Parsley*

Alien. A rare casual. Div. 3.

Only Record: H. Fisher, *Rept. Brit. Ass.* 1893, Newark.

ARALIACEAE

Hedera Helix L. *Ivy*

Native. Walls, rocks, hedges and woodland. Very common. All Divs.

First Record: C. Deering, *Cat. Stirp.* 1738.

var *ovata* is naturalised in woods at Pleasley Vale and Mansfield Woodhouse. Div. 1.

CORNACEAE

Cornus sanguinea L. *Dogwood*

Native. Hedges and scrub, avoiding acid soils. Common except in Div. 2. All Divs.

2 Hodsock.

Cornus alba L. and **C. stolonifera** Michx. are frequently planted for game cover and become naturalised, as at Teversall and Harworth.

CAPRIFOLIACEAE

Adoxa Moschatellina L. *Town Hall Clock*

Native. Damp woods. Common in Divs. 1, 3, less so in Div. 2 and absent from Div. 4.

First Record: C. Deering, *Cat. Stirp.* 1738.

Sambucus nigra L. *Common Elder*

Native. Hedges, scrub and woodland. Very common. All Divs.

First Record: C. Deering, *Cat. Stirp.* 1738.

var *lacinata* L.

2 "Hedge of Mr. Collier's Vinyard on the Castle Rock" (Nottingham), *Deering*; Bulwell.

var *viridis* Ait.

3 Graves Lane, Farnsfield, per *Mr. Tutin*, *Deering*.

Sambucus Ebulus L. *Danewort*

Native or Denizen. Roadsides and by ruins. Now very rare. All Divs.

First Record: C. Deering, *Cat. Stirp.* 1738.

1 Beauvale Priory, Greasley†, *Carr MS.*
2 Blidworth, *G. Howitt*; About Ollerton, *Jowett.*
3 Gamston (by Nottingham); Bunny, *Deering*; Normanton (on-Soar) churchyard, *Pulteney MS.*; Bleasby, *Jowett*; Beeston Canal beyond Lenton, *G. Howitt*; Walkeringham, *Miller.*
4 Great Leake Churchyard, *Pulteney MS.*

Viburnum Opulus L. *Guelder Rose*

Native. Damp woods and hedges. Common except in Div. 4 where it is chiefly found on the sands.

First Record: T. Ordoyno *Fl. Nott.* 1807.

Viburnum Lanata L. *Wayfaring Tree*

Native or planted. Hedges and woods. Very rare. Divs. 1, 2, 3.

First Record: T. Jowett, *Bot. Cals.* 1826.

1 Fishponds Lodge, between Cuckney and Warsop, *Jones.*
2 Clumber Park, *Bohler* 1875.
3 Colwick Wood, *Jowett*, *Gilbert*; Cocking Hill, Boughton, *Jones.*

Symphoricarpos rivularis Suksdorf. *Snowberry*

Alien. Denizen. Commonly planted as game cover in woods, and near villages and now naturalised. All Divs.

First Record: J. W. Carr, *Manuscript Flora c.*1930.

Lonicera Caprifolium L. *Perfoliate Honeysuckle*

Only Record: A. Gilbert, *Botany for Beginners*, "Escape from cultivation."

Lonicera Peri-Clymenum L. *Honeysuckle*

Native. Woods and hedges. Common, especially on light soils. Rare in Div. 4 except on the sand and drift. All Divs.

First Record: C. Deering, *Cat. Stirp.* 1738.

RUBIACEAE

Galium Mollugo L. *Hedge Bedstraw*

Native. Hedges and rough meadows on basic soil. Locally frequent. All Divs.

First Record: C. Deering. *Cat. Stirp.* 1738.

1 Very frequent.
2 Widely scattered.
3 Frequent, particularly on the clay.
4 Gotham Hill; Newark; Collingham; Sutton Bonington.

Galium erectum Huds. *Erect Hedge Bedstraw*

Native or Denizen. Rare. Divs. 2, 4.

First Record: H. C. Watson, *Top. Bot.* 1883 per Mrs. Russell *MS.*

2 Bulwell railway bank, well established.
4 Casual in grass seed at Balderton, *Fisher.*

Galium saxatile L. *Heath Bedstraw*

Native. Heaths and sandy fields. Common on the light soils in all divisions, especially on the bunter and the sands east of the Trent.

First Record: C. Deering, *Cat. Stirp.* 1738.

Galium pumilum Murray *Slender Heath Bedstraw*

A rare casual. Div. 4.

Only Record: H. Fisher, *Rept. Brit. Ass.* 1893, "In grass seed at Balderton with *G. erectum.*"

(R. G. Williams record, as 'frequent' probably refers to *G. saxatile.*)

Galium uliginosum L. *Fen Bedstraw*

Native. Bogs, especially in less acid situations. Decreasing. All Divs.

First Record: T. Ordoyno, *Fl. Nott.* 1807. T. Jowett and G. Howitt "Frequent."

1 and 2 Frequent.
3 Modern Records: Maplebeck; Thorney.
4 Coddington Moor, *Ordoyno*; Rempstone Old Churchyard.

Galium palustre L. *Marsh Bedstraw*

Native. Marshes and watersides. Common. All Divs.

First Record: C. Deering, *Cat. Stirp.* 1738.

var *Witheringii* Sm.

3 Edingley Mill, *Jowett*; "Several places in the neighbourhood of Farnsfield" (or 2) *G. Howitt*, per *Miss A. Lindley.*

Galium verum L. *Lady's Bedstraw*

Native. Meadows and grassland. Common. All Divs.

First Record: C. Deering, *Cat. Stirp.* 1738.

Galium tricorne Stokes. *Rough Corn Bedstraw*

Native or colonist. Cornfields and waste places. Extinct or rare. Divs. 1, 3, 4.

First Record: C. Deering, *Cat. Stirp.* 1738.

1 Wollaton Old Pits, *Deering.*
3 Cornfields at Kingston-on-Soar and East Leake, *Carr MS.*
4 Between Barnstone, Harby and Langar, *Cole*; Cornfields at Crow Wood Hill, West Leake; Owthorpe; Kinoulton; Cotham, *Carr MS.*

Galium Aparine L. *Goosegrass*

Native. Hedges, woods and waste places. Very common. All Divs.

First Record: C. Deering, *Cat. Stirp.* 1738.

Galium Cruciata (L.) Scop. *Crosswort*

Native. Roadsides and grassy places. Common. All Divs.

First Record: C. Deering, *Cat. Stirp.* 1738.

Galium saccharatum All.

Alien. A rare casual. Div. 3 or 4.

Only Record: G. Howitt, *Notts. Fl.* 1839 "In a cornfield between Gotham and West Leake."

Asperula odorata L. *Sweet Woodruff*

Native. Damp woodland on clay soil. Frequent in Divs. 1 and 3, rare in 2 and absent from 4.

First Record: C. Deering, *Cat. Stirp.* 1738.

2 Sutton-in-Ashfield; Carlton-in-Lindrick, *Carr MS.*

Asperula arvensis L.

Alien. Rare casual.

Only Record: H. Fisher, List of aliens in *Rept. Brit. Ass.* 1893.

Sherardia arvensis L. *Field Madder*

Native. Arable fields. Frequent. All Divs.

First Record: T. Ordoyno, *Fl. Nott.* 1807.

VALERIANACEAE

Valeriana officinalis L. *Valerian*

Native. Damp woods, hedgebottoms and streamsides. Common. All Divs.

First Record: C. Deering, *Cat. Stirp.* 1738.

Valeriana dioica L. *Marsh Valerian*

Native. Boggy and peaty meadows. Decreasing. All Divs.

1 and 2 Still frequent, particularly near limestone streams in Div. 1.
3 Southwell Parks, *Ordoyno*; Calverton†; Boughton; Gringley; Misterton†; Eakring; *Carr MS.*, Gamston Wood; Clifton by Nottingham.
4 Harby†; Broadholme, *Carr MS.*; Rempstone.

Centranthus ruber (L.) DC. *Red Valerian*

Alien. Denizen. Widespread. Naturalised on walls, dry banks, clay pits etc., near houses.

First Record: Road cutting at Mansfield 1952.

Valerianella locusta (L.) Betcke. *Lamb's Lettuce*

Native. Railway banks, hedge sides, and arable fields. Frequent. All Divs.

First Record: C. Deering, *Cat. Stirp.* 1738.

Valerianella eriocarpa Desv. *Cornsalad*

A rare casual.

Only Record: H. Fisher, List of aliens in *Rept. Brit. Ass.* 1893.

Valerianella dentata (L.) Poll. *Narrow fruited Corn Salad*

Native. Arable fields on basic soils. Uncommon. All Divs.

First Record: T. Jowett's interleaved Ordoyno 1822.

1 Basford; Cinder Hill; Bulwell, *Jowett*; Mansfield, *G. Howitt*; Nether Langwith, *Carr MS.*; Shireoaks.

2 Radford, *Gilbert*; Barrow Hills, Everton; Finningley, *Carr MS.*; Misson, *Mrs. Sandwith, Butcher.*

3 Ollerton, *Jowett*; Fiskerton; Treswell; Misterton, *Carr MS.*

4 West Leake; Owthorpe†; Balderton, *Carr MS.*; Bunny; Cotgrave; Harby.

DIPSACACEAE

Dipsacus sylvestris Huds. *Wild Teasel*

Native. Banks, woodland rides, waste places. Common, especially in Div. 4. All Divs.

First Record: C. Deering, *Cat. Stirp.* 1738.

Dipsacus pilosus L. *Small Teasel*

Native. Edges of woods. Rare. Divs. 1, 3.

First Record: C. Deering, *Cat. Stirp.* 1738.

1 Pleasley Forge, *Deering*; Pleasley Vale; Beauvale Abbey, *G. Howitt.*

3 Flintham Wood; Epperstone Wood, *Ordoyno*, *Carr*; Thurgarton, *Ordoyno*; Kneeton Wood, *Fisher*; Trent Hills, Elston; near Kirton Church, *Carr MS.*; Hedges near Thistly Coppice, Gonalston.

Scabiosa Columbaria L. *Small Scabious*

Native. Calcareous grassland. Fairly frequent, but decreasing. All Divs.

First Record: C. Deering, *Cat. Stirp.* 1738.

Modern Records:
1 Kirkby Grives; Cresswell Crags; Church Warsop; Annesley.
2 Barrow Hills, Everton, *Gibbons.*
3 Farndon; Lowdham; Spalford; Gamston.
4 Cotham; Coddington.

Scabiosa Succisa L. *Devil's Bit Scabious*

Native. Meadows and woodland rides. Common, particularly on the coal measures, but rather rare in Div. 4, where it is chiefly on the drift soils. All Divs.

First Record: C. Deering, *Cat. Stirp.* 1738.

Scabiosa arvensis L. *Field Scabious*

Native. Roadsides and edges of arable fields. Common, especially in Div. 2. All Divs.

First Record: C. Deering, *Cat. Stirp.* 1738.

Scabiosa lutea L. *Yellow Scabious*

Alien. Occasionally on rubbish tips. Established in Cossall Marsh (Div. 1).

COMPOSITAE

Eupatorium cannabinum L. *Hemp Agrimony*

Native. Streamsides and damp places. Common in the West and the Trent Valley, rare in Div. 4. All Divs.

First Record: C. Deering, *Cat. Stirp.* 1738.

4 Thorney, *Carr MS.*

Solidago Virgaurea L. *Golden Rod*

Native. Banks and woods on sand. Very rare. Divs. 2, (3) 4.

First Record: C. Deering. *Cat. Stirp.* 1738.

2 Radford Lings, *Deering*; Kirkby-in-Ashfield, *Kaye*; Carbanks Woods near Mansfield, *Hurt*; By Alexandrina Plantation, Wollaton, *Carr MS.*, still there in great quantity, 1962.
3 Colwick, *Mason.* An unlikely place.
4 Bank between Coddington and Barnby, *Ordoyno*; Near Barnby, *Fisher.*

Solidago canadensis L. *Garden Golden Rod*

Alien. A common plant on rubbish dumps and near camps and houses. Often persisting. All Divs.

First Record: Farndon gravel pits 1950.

Bellis perennis L. *Daisy*

Native. Grassland. All Divs. Very common, less so on the acid sands of Div. 2.

First Record: C. Deering, *Cat. Stirp.* 1738.

Callistephus chinensis (L.) Nees. *Garden Aster*

Alien. Frequent on dumps. Near camps.

Aster novi-belgii L. *Michaelmas Daisy*

Alien. Common on rubbish dumps, round camps, and naturalised on roadsides. All Divs.

Aster novae-angliae L. *Michaelmas Daisy*

Alien. On rubbish dumps—Less common than the last.

Aster Tripolium L. *Sea Aster*

Native. Tidal mud banks of the Trent, etc. Rare. Divs. 2, 3.

First Record: J. W. Carr *Tr. Nott. Nats.* 1904.

2 In quantity in the Warping Drain at Misson, *Carr.*
3 Trent Bank, West Stockwith: Trent Bank, Saundby.

Erigeron acris L. *Blue Fleabane*

Native. Dry banks on limestone and gravel. Common in Div. 1. In Div. 2, 3 and 4 chiefly on railway banks and disturbed ground. Increasing.

First Record: *Gough's Camdens Britannia* 1789: "Near Mansfield."

Erigeron canadensis L. *Canadian Fleabane*

Alien. Colonist. Waste ground on light soils and in towns. Still rather uncertain in its occurrence. Divs. 1, 2, 3.

First Record: J. Brown, *N.W. Nat.* 1946.

1 Bulwell.
2 Budby; Hazel Gap, *Brown*; Nottingham Castle and Cemetery, *Butcher*; Worksop; Everton; Retford; Babworth.
3 Sporadically on disturbed ground in the Trent Valley.

Filago germanica L. *Cudweed*

Native. Barren sandy ground. Locally common. All Divs.

First Record: C. Deering, *Cat. Stirp.* 1738.

1 Nether Langwith; Styrrup, *Carr MS.*; Warsop; Cresswell Crags.
2 Common.
3 Common on the river gravels and blown sand.
4 Thrumpton; Upper Broughton, *Carr MS.*; Common on the gravels east of the Trent.

Filago minima L. *Slender Cudweed*

Native. Barren sandy ground. Less common than the last. Divs. 2, 3, 4.

First Record: C. Deering, *Cat. Stirp.* 1738.

2 Common.
3 Newark, *Carr MS.*; Between Nottingham and Carlton; Frequent on the blown sand.
4 Langford Moor†; Wigsley†, *Carr MS.*; Thorney.

Antennaria dioica (L.) R. Br. *Cat's Foot*

Native. Heaths. Very rare or extinct. Div. 2.

First Record: W. How, *Phytologia Brit.*, per Mr. Stonehouse.

2 Bescot (i.e. Bestwood) Park, *Stonehouse*; Mansfield Forest, *G. Howitt*; Annesley, *Gilbert*.

Gnaphalium uliginosum L. *Marsh Cudweed*

Native. Damp places and where water has stood. Common. All Divs.

First Record: C. Deering, *Cat. Stirp.* 1738.

Gnaphalium sylvaticum L. *Wood Cudweed*

Native. Heaths and sandy woods. Local. Divs. 2, 3, 4.

First Record: C. Deering, *Cat. Stirp.* 1738.

2 Common.
3 West Drayton, *Carr MS.*; North Collingham; Wigsley; Misterton.
4 Near Leake, *Ordoyno*; Frequent on the gravels; Clipstone Wolds.

Inula Helenium L. *Elecampane*

Alien. Roadsides etc. Probably extinct. Div. 3.

First Record: C. Deering, *Cat. Stirp.* 1738, "In gardens only."

3 Oak Lane, Walkeringham; Trentside near Walkerith Ferry, *Miller*.

Inula Conyza DC. *Ploughman's Spikenard*

Native. Banks, quarries and disturbed ground. Increasing. Divs. 1, 2, 3.

First Record: Sir Richard Kaye 1774, *Trans. Lincs. and Notts. Archit. Socy.* 1923.

1 Frequent.
2 Mansfield, *G. Howitt*; Osberton, *Ordoyno*; Welbeck; Clipstone; Babworth.
3 Clarborough Tunnel; Stanford-on-Soar; Beacon Hill, Newark.

Pulicaria dysenterica (L.) Bernh. *Fleabane*

Native. Damp meadows and roadsides. Common. All Divs.

First Record: C. Deering, *Cat. Stirp.* 1738.

Buphthalmum speciosum (Schreb.) Dr.

Alien. Naturalised in a derelict garden at Cockglade. Div. 2.

Helianthus annuus L. *Sunflower*

Alien. Common on rubbish dumps and occasionally on the Trent Bank. All Divs.

Helianthus tuberosus L. (Jerusalem Artichoke), **H. decapetalus** L. (Perennial Sunflower) and **H. rigidus** (Cass.) Desf. are all frequent on rubbish dumps.

Guiotzia abyssinica Cass.

Alien. Casual. Occasionally on rubbish dumps. Divs. 1, 3.

1 Bulwell 1958; Sookholme 1960.
3 Nottingham 1958 et seq.; Wilford 1958; Farndon, Fosse Road side 1961.

Bidens cernua L. *Nodding Bur Marigold*

Native. Ponds, anciently on peat, now chiefly around towns in foul water. Locally frequent. Divs. 1, 2, 3.

First Record: C. Deering, *Cat. Stirp.* 1738.

1 Langold; Carlton-in-Lindrick, *Mrs. Sandwith*; Cossall.
2 Nottingham Park, *Deering*; Farnsfield Carr, *Ordoyno*; Annesley, *Gilbert*; Nottingham Canal side†, *Carr MS.*; Mansfield, plentifully at Clarborough; Lound; Ollerton; Eaton.
3 Collingham Fleet; Edingley Moor, *Ordoyno*; Nottingham Meadows and Stoke Bardolph Sewage Farm in quantity; and as a casual on the Trent and Soar banks.

Bidens tripartita L. *Common Bur Marigold*

Native. River and canal sides. Common except in Div. 4. All Divs.

First Record; Sir Richard Kaye 1774, *Trans. Lincs. and Notts. Archit. Socy.* 1923.

4 Canal Banks at Kinoulton; Owthorpe; Hickling.

Bidens frondosa L.

Alien. Div. 3.

Only Record: Several plants in Farndon Willow Holt 1961. Seed has either come down the river or from our garden.

Galinsoga parviflora Cav. *Gallant Soldier*

Alien. Naturalised in waste places, especially in and about Nottingham. Divs. 1, 2, 3.

First Record: Goulding, *B.E.C. Rept.* 1917.

1 Welbeck, *Goulding*, Still in the gardens; Bulwell.
2 Nottingham.
3 Stoke Bardolph Sewage Farm†, *Williams*; Nottingham; Wilford; Farndon, garden and lane, inadvertently introduced.

Galinsoga ciliata (Raf.) Blake.

Alien. Naturalised in several places. Divs. 2, 3.

First Record: D. McClintock, *B.S.B.I.Proc.* 1952.

2 Garden weed, Walesby†, *Evans.*
3 West Bridgford, McClintock; Nottingham Dump.

Achillea Millefolium L. *Yarrow*

Native. Grassland. Very common. All Divs.

First Record: C. Deering, *Cat. Stirp.* 1738.

Achillea Ptarmica L. *Sneezewort*

Native. Marshy places and streamsides. Frequent. All Divs.

First Record: C. Deering, *Cat. Stirp.* 1738.

Anthemis tinctoria L. *Yellow Chamomile*

A rare alien. Div. 3.

Only Record: H. Fisher, *Rept. Brit. Ass.* 1893, "Newark."

Anthemis nobilis L. *Chamomile*

Native. Sandy fields. Rare. Divs. 1, 2.

First Record: T. Jowett, *Bot. Cals.* 1826.

1 In a field of mangolds at Bilborough, *Carr MS.*
2 Bestwood Park, *Jowett*; Several places near Nottingham, *G. Howitt.*

Anthemis arvensis L. *Corn Chamomile*

Native. Sandy fields. Local. All Divs.

First Record: G. Howitt, *Notts. Fl.* 1839.

1 Sookholme, *Carr MS.*
2 Widely distributed.
3 Kirklington; Newark, *Carr MS.*; Wigsley; Spalford; Thorney.
4 Wigsley; Harby; Cotgrave; Kinoulton.

Anthemis Cotula L. *Stinking Mayweed*

Native. Arable fields and roadsides. Decreasing, less common than the last. All Divs.

First Record: T. Ordoyno, *Fl. Nott.* 1807.

1 Mansfield, *Ordoyno*; Warsop Windmill.
2 Welbeck Park.
3 Southwell; Newark; Misterton; Everton.
4 Owthorpe; Thorney; Cotgrave.

Chrysanthemum segetum L. *Corn Marigold*

Native. Arable fields on light soils. Abundant before spraying and still fairly frequent. All Divs.

First Record: C. Deering, *Cat. Stirp.* 1738.

1 Annesley, the only record for this division.

Chrysanthemum Leucanthemum L. *Ox-eye Daisy*

Native. Meadows and grassy places. Common. All Divs.

First Record: C. Deering, *Cat. Stirp.* 1738.

Chrysanthemum maximum Ram. *Shasta Daisy*

Alien. Common on rubbish dumps and around houses.

Chrysanthemum uliginosum Pers.

Alien. Naturalised in a damp hedge bottom at Caythorpe (3). Occasionally on rubbish dumps.

Chrysanthemum Parthenium (L.) Bernh. *Feverfew*

Denizen. Commonly naturalised on old walls and near houses. Common on rubbish dumps. All Divs.

First Record: C. Deering, *Cat. Stirp.* 1738.

Matricaria inodora L. *Scentless Mayweed*

Native. Arable fields and waste places. Common. All Divs.

First Record: C. Deering, *Cat. Stirp.* 1738.

Matricaria Chamomilla L. *Wild Chamomile*

Native. Arable fields on light soils. All Divs. Common except on the heavy clays of Divs. 3 and 4. A typical plant of the Trent Valley.

First Record: C. Deering, *Cat. Stirp.* 1738.

Matricaria matricarioides (Less.) Porter. *Pineapple Weed*

Alien. Denizen. Farmyards, waste places, arable land. Common. All Divs.

First Record: J. W. Carr *MS. Flora*, no date or locality.

Matricaria decipiens C. Koch.

Rare. Alien. Div. 3.

Only Record: A. R. Horwood, "*Aliens from Notts.*" in *B.E.C. Rept.* 1915. "Trent Meadows."

Tanacetum vulgare L. *Tansy*

Native. Roadsides, round villages, waste places. Common, especially in the Trent Valley. Rare in Div. 4. All Divs.

First Record: C. Deering, *Cat. Stirp.* 1738.

4 On the Lincoln Road from Newark, *Ordoyno*; Langford; South Scarle†, *Carr MS.*

var. *crispum* is found occasionally on rubbish dumps and waste places.

Artemisia Absinthum L. *Wormwood*

Native. Waste places, road and path sides. Common, especially on the Trent side. Rare in 4. All Divs.

First Record: C. Deering, *Cat. Stirp.* 1738. "Grows plentifully all over most villages about Nottingham."

4 Willoughby-on-Wolds; Cropwell Bishop; Bunny.

Artemisia vulgaris L. *Mugwort*

Native. Roadsides and waste places. Very common. All Divs.

First Record: C. Deering, *Cat. Stirp.* 1738.

Tussilago farfara L. *Coltsfoot*

Native. Roadsides and waste places. Very common. All Divs.

First Record: C. Deering, *Cat. Stirp.* 1738.

Petasites hybridus (L.) Gaertn. *Butterbur*

Native. River and canal sides. Frequent. All Divs.

First Record: C. Deering, *Cat. Stirp.* 1738, both male and female, (*P. major, floribus pediculis longis insidentibus*).

The following records are arranged (within the divisions) according to watercourses.

1 Erewash Valley; Chiefly M. The F. occurs round an isolated pond at E. Kirkby.
Leen Valley; Lenton Mill F., *Deering*; Hempshill Hall M.
Meden Valley; Newbound Mill M.; Skegby village F.
Maun Valley; Mansfield, *Ordoyno.*
2 Leen Valley; Bestwood F.; Annesley F.
Trent Valley; Bramcote M.
Chesterfield Canal F., very common.
Meden Valley; Thoresby Lake M.
Maun Valley; Clipstone M.; Cavendish Lodge M.; Mansfield Woodhouse M.
Ryton Valley; Blyth M; Hodsock M.; Osberton F. very common; Hodsock, by the river F.
Poulter Valley; Carburton M.; Elkesley M.
Idle Valley; Retford; Misson.
3 Trent Valley; Radcliffe-on-Trent, *Gilbert*; Trentside from Sturton, north to county boundary, both M. and F. in abundance; Beckside at Eakring M.; Hill top by waterworks, East Markham M; stream side, Weston M.
Greet Valley; Southwell Silk Mill F†, *Ordoyno*; The M. is frequent by the Greet and its tributary from Graves Lane.
Doverbeck; Hoveringham F.; Caythorpe Mill F.
Chesterfield Canal; Clarborough F.; Gringley F.
4 Alverton, stream by railway F.

Petasites albus (L.) Gaertn.

Alien. Denizen. Only Record; Osberton Park by R. Ryton. Div. 2.

Petasites fragans (Vill.) C. Presl. *Winter Heliotrope*

Alien. Frequently naturalised near gardens. Divs. 2, 3.

First Record; River Bank, Newark Castle 1949.

1 Welbeck.
2 Abundant on Nottingham Castle Rock.
3 Newark; Carlton-on-Trent; N. Wheatley; W. Stockwith; Gonalston; Hawton; Saundby; Flintham.

Doronicum Pardalianches L. *Leopard's Bane*

Alien. Denizen. Naturalised in shady places. Rather rare. Divs. 1, 2.

First Record: G. Howitt, *Notts. Fl.* 1839.

1 Westwood Dumble, Bagthorpe, *Carr MS.*; Oldcoates.
2 Roadside by Rainworth Lodge†; Berry Hill, Mansfield; Bramcote, *G. Howitt*; Cockglade, Edwinstowe; Osberton estate in several places; Carlton-in-Lindrick.

Doronicum plantagineum L. *Leopard's Bane*

Alien. Naturalised in ornamental Woods at Oldcoates. Div. 1.

Senecio fluviatalis Wallr. *Broadleaved Ragwort*

Rare alien. Div. 1.

Only Record: G. Howitt *Notts. Fl.* 1839, "Banks of Greasley Reservoir."

Senecio aquaticus Hill. *Marsh Ragwort*

Native. Damp meadows. Frequent except in Div. 4. All Divs.

First Record: C. Deering, *Cat. Stirp.* 1738.

4 Kinoulton; Rempstone.

Senecio Jacobaea L. *Ragwort*

Native. Meadows, waste places, heathland. Very common. All Divs.

First Record: C. Deering, *Cat. Stirp.* 1738.

Senecio erucifolius L. *Hoary Ragwort*

Native. Meadows and grassy places on basic soils. Frequent except in Div. 2. All Divs.

First Record: C. Deering, *Cat. Stirp.* 1738.

2 Clipstone, as a casual; Babworth, canal side.

Senecio squalidus L. *Oxford Ragwort*

Alien. Denizen. Waste places, road and rail sides, pit dumps, etc. Now in almost every parish in the county. All Divs.

First Record: Trowell, 1940, Butcher.

S. squalidus x viscosus: Nottingham Dump 1957.

S. squalidus x vulgaris: Farndon 1955 et seq.

Senecio viscosus L. *Sticky Groundsel*

Denizen. Railway sidings, waste ground. Common, except in Div 4. All Divs.

First Record: G. Howitt, *Notts. Fl.* 1839, "Nottingham 1836." Still rare in 1930, *Carr MS.*

4 Railway lines at Normanton-on-Soar and Stanton-on-Wolds.

Senecio sylvaticus L. *Wood Groundsel*

Native. Heaths and sandy woods. Very common in Div. 2 and frequent on the coal measures in Div. 1, and the light drift soils and gravels in Divs. 3 and 4.

First Record: C. Deering, *Cat. Stirp.* 1738.

Senecio vulgaris L. *Groundsel*

Native. Arable land, gardens etc. Very common. All Divs.

First Record: C. Deering, *Cat. Stirp.* 1738.

var *radiatus* Koch. 2 Wollaton Park; Retford Dump.
3 Nottingham Dump.

Calendula officinalis L. *Pot marigold*

Alien. Frequent as a garden escape and on rubbish dumps.

Echinops Ritro L. var. *tenuifolius* *Globe Thistle*

Alien. Sometimes established in hedge bottoms and common on rubbish dumps.

Echinops commutatus Juratzka.

Alien. A large patch is established on the roadside outside Wedding Drive Lodge, Welbeck. Div. 2.

Carlina vulgaris L. *Carline Thistle*

Native. Dry banks and grassland on basic soils. Widespread. All Divs.

First Record: C. Deering, *Cat. Stirp.* 1738.

1 Greasley; Annesley†; Kirkby Grives†; Sookholme; Hills and Holes, Warsop†; *Carr MS.*

2 Nottingham Lings to Bobbers Mill, *Deering*; Mansfield Forest; Between Thoresby and Rufford, *Ordoyno*; Bulwell Heath, *Gilbert*; Clipstone; Edwinstowe; Barrow Hills, Everton†, *Carr MS.*; Ratcher Hill, Mansfield.

3 Colwick, *Deering*; Eaton Wood, *Mrs. Sandwith*; Kneesall; Lowdham; Kersall; Oxton; Kirklington.

4 Clipstone; Gotham; Balderton; Coddington; Cotgrave.

Arctium Lappa L. *Great Burdock*

Native. Damp woods and willow holts. Frequent. All Divs.

First Record: C. Deering, *Cat. Stirp.* 1738.

Arctium vulgare (Hill) A. H. Evans. *Burdock*

Native. Roadsides, scrub, waste places. Common. All Divs.

Arctium minus (Hill) Bernh. *Lesser Burdock*

Native. Hedgesides and woodland borders. Rather frequent especially in Divs. 1 and 2. All Divs.

First Record: J. W. Carr, *Tr. Nott. Nats.* 1903.

Carduus nutans L. *Musk Thistle*

Native. Meadows, roadsides, waste places. Common on light soils, especially the Bunter and in the Trent Valley.

First Record: C. Deering, *Cat. Stirp.* 1738.

Carduus crispus L. *Welted Thistle*

Native. Hedges and waste ground. Common on the clays on Divs. 3 and 4 less so elsewhere. All Divs.

First Record: C. Deering, *Cat. Stirp.* 1738.

Carduus acanthoides L. *Welted Thistle*

A rare casual. Div. 3.

Only Record: Besthorpe Gravel Pit 1958, det. W. A. Sledge.

Carduus tenuiflorus Curt. *Slender Thistle*

Casual. Rare. Div. 3.

First Record: G. Howitt, *Notts. Fl.* 1839.

3 Nottingham meadows and several places about Clifton, *G. Howitt*; East Stoke, *Leather*; Stoke Bardolph, *Williams*; South Nottingham or Beeston (Sq. 43/53) *Bailey, B.S.B.I. Maps Scheme.*

Cirsium eriophorum (L.) Scop. *Woolly Thistle*

Native. Rough meadows and scrub on basic soils. Rare. Now chiefly in and near Div. 4. Divs. 1, 3, 4.

First Record: R. Pulteney, *Phil. Trans.* 1756.

1 Broxtowe; Between Bulwell and Nuthall, *Jowett.*
3 Normanton; Kirklington; Debdon (i.e. Debdale) Hill, Caunton; Between Southwell and Thurgarton, *Ordoyno*; Walkeringham, *Miller*; Bunny Park; Beacon Hill, Newark.
4 Cotgrave Wolds†, *Pulteney*; Owthorpe†; Clipstone Wolds†; Colston Bassett; East Leake; Balderton, *Carr MS.*; Widmerpool; Cropwell Bishop; Wysall.

Cirsium vulgare (Savi) Ten. *Spear Thistle*

Native. Meadows, roadsides, waste places. Very common. All Divs.

First Record: C. Deering, *Cat. Stirp.* 1738.

Cirsium acaule (L.) Scop. *Stemless Thistle*

Native. Rough meadows and banks on basic soils. Uncommon. All Divs.

First Record: T. Ordoyno, *Fl. Nott.* 1807.

1 Warsop, *Carr MS.*
2 Between Budby and Ollerton, *Ordoyno*; Bulwell Forest, *Carr MS.*
3 Between Darlton and Great Markham, *Ordoyno*; Plumtree; West Leake; Fiskerton; Halloughton, *Carr MS.*; Lowdham; Southwell; Gonalston; Granby; Averham.
4 Barnby, *Fisher*; East Leake; Hickling; Langford Moor, *Carr MS.*; Barnstone; Gotham Hills; Balderton; Cropwell Butler; Normanton-on-Soar.

Cirsium dissectum (L.) Hill *Meadow Thistle*

Native. Meadows on fen peat. Very rare and decreasing. Divs. 1, 2, 3.

First Record: T. Jowett, *Bot. Cals.* 1826.

1 Harworth Carr.
2 Abundant in marshy fields east and west of Misson, *Mrs. Sandwith.* Still common there until about 1950, but now decreased by re-seeding; Everton meadows.
3 Clifton meadows (near Nottingham), *Jowett.*

Cirsium arvense (L.) Scop. *Creeping Thistle*

Native. Meadows, arable land, waste ground. Very common. All Divs.

First Record: C. Deering, *Cat. Stirp.* 1738.

var *mite* Wimm. and Grab.

3 Canal side Nottingham, det. W. A. Sledge; Field near the Gate Inn, Misterton.

var *setosum* C. A. Mey.

3 Newark Wharfs, *Fisher.*
4 Coddington Mill, det. W. A. Sledge.

Cirsium palustre (L.) Scop. *Marsh Thistle*

Native. Damp meadows. Common. All Divs.

First Record: C. Deering, *Cat. Stirp.* 1738.

Onopordon Acanthium L. *Scotch Thistle*

Denizen or perhaps native. Roadsides, railway banks. Has apparently decreased, Deering and Ordoyno considered it common. Divs. 2, 3, 4.

First Record: C. Deering, *Cat. Stirp.* 1738.

2 Nottingham Castle Rock; Barrow Hills, Everton, in quantity. *Carr MS.*; Norwith Hill, Misson†; *Mrs. Sandwith*; Harworth,
3 Many places about Nottingham, *Deering*, *G. Howitt*; Ratcliffe-on-Soar; Holme by Newark, *Carr MS.*; Southwell, *Chalk*; Beckingham, *A. Lowe*; Farndon; Sutton-on-Trent; East Bridgeford; Besthorpe Gravel Pit.
4 Harby.

Silybum Marianum (L.) Gaertn. *Milk Thistle*

Alien. Denizen. Waste places and borders of fields. Very rare now. Divs. 2, 3.

2 Chapel Bar; Nottingham Park and Castle Rock, *Deering*; Blidworth, *Ordoyno*; Frequent on sandy ground near Nottingham, *G. Howitt*; Ollerton, *Friend*; Clipstone, roadside to Edwinstowe, *Carr MS.*
3 Newark, *Ordoyno.*

Serratula tinctoria L. *Saw-wort*

Native. Damp grassland on basic soils. Local. All Divs.

First Record: C. Deering, *Cat. Stirp.* 1738.

1 Frequent.
2 Radford Lings, *Deering.*
3 Roe Wood, Winkburn†; Ossington; West Drayton; Eaton† and Gamston† Woods, *Carr MS.* Kneesall; Eakring; Calverton.
4 Plumtree and Clipstone Wolds; Stanton-on-Wolds†; Widmerpool; Upper Broughton; West Leake, *Carr MS.*; East Leake; Normanton-on-Wolds, *Williams.*

Centaurea nigra L. *Knapweed*

Native. Grassland. Very common. All Divs.

First Record: C. Deering, *Cat. Stirp.* 1738.

Centaurea nemoralis Jord. *Lesser Knapweed*

Native. Grassland. Divs. 3, 4. Records of this species have been determined by E. M. Marsden-Jones. Probably commoner than the records suggest.

3 Newark; Nottingham; Spalford.
4 Coddington; Barnstone; Balderton.

Centaurea Cyanus L. *Cornflower*

Native. Arable fields, freshly disturbed roadsides, on sand. Now rare. Divs. 2, 3, 4.

First Record: C. Deering, *Cat. Stirp.* 1738.

Modern Records:
2 Fields at Misson; Harworth (building site); Budby (roadside); Edwinstowe; Carlton-in-Lindrick, a lot on arable land.
3 North Clifton; Misterton; Girton; Langford, all on arable land; Beckingham; South Muskham; Walkeringham, on roadsides.
4 Fields at Wigsley.

Centaurea Scabiosa L. *Greater Knapweed*

Native. Roadsides and rough grassland. Frequent except in Div. 3. All Divs.

First Record: C. Deering, *Cat. Stirp.* 1738.

3 Colwick, *Deering*; Southwell railway bridge; Besthorpe; North Clifton; Collingham. Apparently absent from the Marls.

Centaurea Calcitrapa L.

A rare alien. Div. 1.

Only Record: H. Fisher, Herb. Grantham Museum 1908, Old Basford.

Centaurea montana L.

Alien. Frequent on rubbish dumps.

2 Hedge bottom, Carlton-in-Lindrick.

Centaurea Solstitialis L. *St. Barnaby's Thistle*

Alien. Casual. Arable land, often among lucerne, and in waste places. Rare. Divs. 3, 4.

First Record: H. Fisher, *Rept. Brit. Ass.* 1893.

3 Newark, *Fisher*; Lucerne field, Fiskerton; Lucerne field, Spalford.
4 Farmyard at Cotham.

Centaurea melitensis L. *Maltese Star Thistle*

A rare alien. Casual. Div. 3.

Only Record: H. Fisher, *Rept. Brit. Ass.* 1893, Newark.

Centaurea diluta Ait.

A rare alien. Casual. Div. 3.

Only Record: Nottingham Dump, a lot 1958, some plants 1961 and 1962.

Cnicus benedictus L. *Blessed Thistle*

A rare alien. Casual. Divs. 2, 3.

First Record: C. Deering, *Cat. Stirp.* 1738, "I have several times met with some plants of it on Dunghills, but suspect them to come from gardens, tho' near a Mile distant from the Town."

3 Nottingham (or 2), *Deering*; Garden weed, Newark.

Carthamus lanatus L. *Distaff Thistle*

A rare alien. Casual. Div. 3.

Only Record: Parnham's Mill Yard Newark 1951 et seq.

Cichorium Intybus L. *Chicory*

Denizen. Road and field sides, especially on sand. Frequent in Divs. 2 and 3, less so elsewhere.

First Record: J. W. Carr, *Victoria County History* 1906.

1 Church Warsop; Felley; Bulwell.
2 and 3 Frequent.
4 Stanton-on-Wolds†; Owthorpe, *Carr MS.*

Cichorium Endivia L. *Endive*

Alien. A relic of cultivation. Div. 3.

Only Record: Girton, in a potato field 1953.

Arnoseris minima (L.) Schweigg and Koerte. *Swine's Succory*

Native. Sandy fields. Very rare. Divs. 2, 3.

First Record: J. W. Carr, *Tr. Nott. Nats.* 1903.

2 Barrow Hills, Everton†, *Carr MS.*; Pusto Hill, Everton; Finningley.
3 Gorse Common, West Drayton, *Carr MS.*

Lapsana communis L. *Nipplewort*

Native. Gardens, hedgesides, waste places. Very common. All Divs.

First Record: C. Deering, *Cat. Stirp.* 1738.

Picris echiodes L. *Bristly Ox tongue*

Native. Roadsides, arable fields, especially on clay. Local. All Divs.

First Record: C. Deering, *Cat Stirp.* 1738.

1 Radford (or 2), *Deering*; Roadside to Strelley, *Gilbert.*
2 Lucerne field at Bilsthorpe.
3 Widely distributed, but not common.
4 Common.

Picris hieraciodes L. *Hawkweed Ox tongue*

Native. Banks and rough grassland on basic soils. Local. Divs. 1, 3, 4.

First Record: T. Jowett, *Bot. Cals.* 1826.

1 Wollaton; Bulwell Hall; Bilborough, *Jowett*; Kirkby; Strelley, *Gilbert*; Carlton-in-Lindrick, *Carr MS.*; Pleasley Vale, *Butcher.*
3 and 4. Rather frequent.

Crepis paludosa (L.) Moench. *Marsh Hawksbeard*

Native. Marshes. Very rare. Div. 1.

First Record: G. Howitt, *Notts. Fl.* 1839.

1 Between Annesley and Annesley Woodhouse, *G. Howitt*; By the border stream Newbound Mill, Teversall, in some quantity; in meadows by the Meden south of Newbound Mill, *Carr MS.*

Crepis biennis L. *Rough Hawksbeard*

Denizen. Roadsides and meadows. Local, has apparently increased recently. Divs. 1, 3, 4.

First Record: T. Ordoyno, *Fl. Nott.* 1807, J. W. Carr thought this erroneous. J. W. Carr *Tr. Nott. Nats.* 1903.

1 Styrrup; Bulwell.
3 Halam, *Ordoyno*; Hockerton, *Carr* 1903; Between Southwell and Thurgarton 1950†, *Butcher*; Grassthorpe; Misterton; Clarborough; Weston; Kersal; Ossington; Egmanton; Dunham; Granby.
4 West Leake Hills, *Williams*; Kilvington; Normanton-on-Soar.

Crepis capillaris (L.) Wallr. *Smooth Hawksbeard*

Native. Roadsides, grassland, waste places. Very common. All Divs.

First Record: T. Ordoyno, *Fl. Nott.* 1807.

Crepis taraxacifolia Thuill. *Beaked Hawksbeard*

Denizen. Roadsides, waste places. Increasing. All Divs.

First Record: H. Fisher, *Rept. Brit. Ass.* 1893.

1 Near Balloon Houses, Wollaton, *Butcher*; Bilborough.
2 Hesley.
3 Common.
4 Balderton, *Fisher*; Barnby.

Crepis setosa Haller. f. *Bristly Hawksbeard*

A rare alien. Casual.

Only Record: H. Fisher, *Rept. Brit. Ass.* 1893.

Hieracium Pilosella L. *Mouse ear Hawkweed*

Native. Banks and grassland. Very common. All Divs.

First Record: C. Deering, *Cat. Stirp.* 1738.

Hieracium brunneocroceum Pugsl. *Orange Hawkweed*

Alien Denizen. Occurs occasionally as a garden escape on roadsides near villages. Divs. 2, 3, 4.

First Record: Roadsides at Farndon 1950.

In Nottinghamshire Hawkweeds occur mainly in Divs. 1 and 2. In Div. 1 there are many artificial habitats, pit dumps, railway banks and sidings in the industrial areas, where Hawkweeds are sometimes dominant. They also occur in limestone quarries and on roadsides. In Div. 2 the industrial habitats are similar. There are also sand pits and natural woodland habitats. Except for natural occurrences (chiefly of *H. umbellatum* and *H. Bladonii*) on the sands and gravels, Hawkweeds are rare in Divs. 3 and 4 and practically confined to the banks of railways and roads. Our thanks are due to P. D. Sell and C. West for their help. More work is needed on the critical species.

Hieracium murorum L. Sens. lat. is recorded by T. Ordoyno 1807, and by G. Howitt (as *H. sylvatica*) 1839, as frequent.

Hieracium pulmonariodes Vill.

Alien. Denizen. Rare. Div. 2.

Only Record: *B.E.C. Rept.* 19 . Nottingham Castle Walls. Still there and on rocks and walls in Nottingham Park in fair quantity.

Hieracium vulgatum Fr. *Common Hawkweed*

Native. Road and railway sides, rocks, waste ground. Probably frequent in Divs. 1 and 2. Divs. 1, 2, 3.

First Record: Herb. Carr at Wollaton Hall, det. W. R. Linton 1894.

1 Linby; Awsworth, *Herb. Carr*; Trowell; Teversall; Hills and Holes, Warsop; Langwith.
2 Rocks at Bulwell; Near Bestwood Colliery; Calverton; Mansfield Woodhouse, *Carr MS.*; Sandpit at Styrrup.
3 Edingley Hill, *Herb. Carr*; Oxton Hills, *Fisher*, det. *Pugsley*; Roadside, Hockerton; Railway bank, Woodthorpe.

Hieracium maculatum Sm. *Spotted Hawkweed*

Denizen. Railway banks and waste gound. Local. Divs. 1, 2.

First Record: Abundant on railway banks at Pleasley Vale 1952 det. P. D. Sell.

1 Pleasley Vale; Quarries at Mansfield Woodhouse; Railway banks, Langold.
2 Clipstone; Railway bank, Warsop.

Hieracium diaphnoides Lindeb.

Native. Banks and waste ground. Widely distributed. Divs. 1, 2, 3.

First Record: Railway bank by the plaster works at Gotham 1952, det. P. D. Sell.

1 Cossall; Cresswell Crags.
2 Styrrup; Welbeck; Clipstone pit dump.
3 Gotham.

Hieracium anglorum (Ley.) Pugsl.

Native. Rare. Div. 2.

Only Record: H. Fisher in H. W. Pugsley, *Prod. Brit. Hier.* 1948, Rainworth. Probably collected *c.*1900.

Hieracium strumosum (Linton) Ley.

Native. Banks and quarries. Rare. Divs. 1, 3.

First Record: J. W. Carr MS. *c.*1920-30, teste H. W. Pugsley. Repeated in H. W. Pugsley, *Prod. Brit. Hier.* 1948.

1 Cresswell Crags Quarry.
3 Oxton Hill, *Carr MS.*

Hieracium Lachenalii C.C. Gmel.

Native. Roadsides, walls, banks. Widely distributed. Divs. 1, 2, 3.

First Record: J. W. Carr, *Tr. Nott. Nats.* 1904.

1 Lane at Linby, *Carr MS.*; Shireoaks; Market Warsop.
2 Annesley, *Carr MS.*; Hesley Hall on walls.
3 Southwell, *Fisher in Pugsley*; Oxton Hill, *Carr MS.*; Sutton Bonington.

Hieracium tridentatum Fr.

Only Record: H. Fisher in Carr, *Nat. Hist. Notts.* 1893 and specimen in Herb. Wollaton Hall, Rufford Forest by Inkersall. Div. 2.

Hieracium eboracense Pugsl.

Native. Banks. Rare. Divs. 2, 3.

First Record: H. Fisher in H. W. Pugsley *Prod. Brit. Hier.* 1948, probably collected *c.*1900.

2 Blyth, *Fisher.*
3 Roadside, Edingley Hill.

Hieracium Latobrigorum (Zahn) Roffey.

Native. Rare. Div. 2.

Only Record: R. W. Butcher in Carr's MS. *c.*1950, near Newstead Park Gates.

Hieracium umbellatum L. *Narrow leaved Hawkweed*

Native. Heaths, sandy woods and fields. Locally common. All Divs.

First Record: T. Ordoyno, *Fl. Nott.* 1809.

1 Wollaton.
2 Frequent.
3 Balderton; Bothamsall; West Drayton; Gamston by Retford, *Carr MS.*; Spalford; Girton; Nottingham, Trentside.
4 Frequent on the gravels east of the Trent.

var *coronopifolium* Bernh.

First Record: H. Fisher in H. W. Pugsley, *Prod. Brit. Hier.* 1948, probably collected *c.*1900.

2 Stapleford Hill; Ranskill.
3 Collingham, *Fisher.*
4 Barnby-in-the-Willows.

Hieracium sabaudum L. sens. lat. is recorded by T. Ordoyno 1807, and by G. Howitt as frequent, and H. boreale Fr. is recorded by J. W. Carr.

Hieracium Bladonii Pugsl.

Native. Heaths, sandy woods, disturbed ground. Local. Divs. 2, 3, 4.

First Record; H. Fisher in H. W. Pugsley, *Prod. Brit. Hier.* 1948. Probably collected about 1900.

2 Bulwell Forest; Calverton; Newstead; Finningley, *Butcher*; Ranskill.
3 Collingham, *Fisher*; Bingham; Halam Water Works.
4 Coddington† to Barnby†, *Fisher*; Turf Moor, Brough; Wigsley.

Hieracium perpropinquum (Zahn.) Pugsl.

Native. Div. 3.

Only Record: H. Fisher in H. W. Pugsley, *Prod. Brit. Hier.* 1948, Newark. Probably collected about 1900.

Hieracium vagum Jord.

Native. Railway banks, pit dumps, woods and roadsides. Common in Divs. 1 and 2, less so in Divs. 3 and 4 where it occurs chiefly on the gravels east of the Trent and on a few railway banks.

Hypochaeris radicata L. *Longrooted Cat's Ear*

Native. Grassland. Very common. All Divs.

First Record: C. Deering, *Cat. Stirp.* 1738.

Hypochaeris glabra L. *Smooth Cat's Ear*

Native. Grassland and arable on light sand. Uncommon. Div. 2, 3, 4.

First Record: T. Ordoyno, *Fl. Nott.* 1807.

2 Oxton Forest, *Ordoyno*; Between Worksop and Clumber, *Roffey*; Barrow Hills, Everton†, *Carr MS.*; Finningley, *Brown*; Carlton-in-Lindrick; Pusto Hill, Everton; Osberton.
3 Newark, *Fisher*; Wigsley†, *Carr MS.*; Besthorpe; Girton; North and South Collingham; Spalford; South Clifton; Gringley.
4 Langford Moor; Thorney; Wigsley.

Leontodon hispidus L. *Rough Hawkbit*

Native. Grassland, banks and rough ground. Common on calcareous soils in 1, 3 and 4, less frequent in 2.

First Record: C. Deering, *Cat. Stirp.* 1738.

Leontodon autumnalis L. *Autumnal Hawkbit*

Native. Grassland and lawns. Common and widespread. All Divs.

First Record: C. Deering, *Cat. Stirp.* 1738.

var *sordidus* Bab.

3 Mapperley Brickyard, *Carr MS.*

Leontodon Leysseri (Wallr.) Beck.

Native. Grassland and lawns. Common, except on the more acid sands of Div. 2.

First Record: T. Ordoyno, *Fl. Nott.* 1807.

Taraxacum officinale Weber. *Common Dandelion*

Native. Roadsides, grass land, waste places. Very common. All Divs.

First Record: C. Deering, *Cat. Stirp.* 1738.

Taraxacum palustre DC. *Marsh Dandelion*

Native. Bogs. Very rare. Div. 2.

Only Record: T. Jowett, *Bot. Cals.* 1826, "Bogs between Bulwell and Papplewick Forest."

Taraxacum laevigatum DC. *Sand Dandelion*

Native. Grassland on light soils. Common in suitable localities. Divs. 1, 2, 3.

First Record: C. Deering, *Cat. Stirp.* 1738.

1 Church Warsop; Welbeck.
2 Common.
3 Common on the gravels and blown sand.

Lactuca virosa L. *Wild Lettuce*

Native. Waste ground and bank sides. Uncommon. Divs. 2, 3, 4.

First Record: C. Deering, *Cat. Stirp.* 1738.

2 Nottingham Park, *Deering*; Between Blyth and Bawtry, *Ordoyno*.
3 Frequent on waste ground.
4 Between Coddington and Beckingham, *Ordoyno*; Alverton; Cotham, *Carr MS.*; R. Devon Side, Staunton.

Lactuca serriola L. *Prickly Lettuce*

Denizen. Waste places and river banks. Less common than the last. Divs. 3, 4.

First Record: Waste ground, Newark, 1949.

3 Frequent on waste ground in the Trent Valley.
4 Brough; Kilvington; Cotham.

(**Lactuca saligna** L.
Extinct or error. Div. 3.

First Record: R. Pulteney *Phil. Trans.* 1756.

3 In a hollow way at Carleton two miles from Nottingham, *Pulteney*; Near Bingham, *Crabbe*.)

Lactuca sativa L. *Garden Lettuce*
Alien. Common on rubbish dumps. All Divs.

Lactuca muralis (L.) Gaertn. *Wall Lettuce*
Native. Walls, rocks and dry banks. Local. All Divs.
First Record: C. Deering, *Cat. Stirp.* 1738.

1 Common.
2 Sparken Hill, Worksop, *Roffey*; Berry Hill, Mansfield†; Carlton-in-Lindrick, *Carr MS.*; Hesley Hall, *Gibbons*; Wollaton Park; Thoresby Park.
3 Halam Hill; Edingley Hill†; Epperstone Park†, *Ordoyno*; Lambley Dumble; Oxton; Westhorpe, Southwell; Laxton; Averham Churchyard†, *Carr MS.*
4 Stanford-on-Soar, *Carr MS.*

(**Sonchus palustris** L. *Marsh Sowthistle*
Native. Extinct or error. Div. 3.

First Record: C. Deering, *Cat. Stirp.* 1738. "Several Places about Nottingham."
3 Edingley Moor, *Ordoyno*; Edingley Mill Dam, *G. Howitt.* G. Howitt was usually reliable.)

Sonchus arvensis L. *Corn Sowthistle*
Native. Arable fields, waste places. Very common. All Divs.

First Record: T. Ordoyno, *Fl. Nott.* 1807.

Sonchus asper L. *Prickly Sowthistle*
Native. Cultivated and waste ground. Very common. All Divs.

First Record: C. Deering, *Cat. Stirp.* 1738.

Sonchus oleraceus L. *Common Sowthistle*
Native. Cultivated and waste ground. Very common. All Divs.

First Record: C. Deering, *Cat. Stirp.* 1738.

Tragopogon pratensis L. *Goat's Beard*
Native. Meadows and roadsides. Common. All Divs.

First Record: C. Deering, *Cat. Stirp.* 1738.

ssp. *minor* (Mill.) Wahlemb. is the common Notts. plant.

ssp. *pratensis.*

1 Pleasley Vale, *Carr MS.*
3 Clifton Hill, *G. Howitt.*

CAMPANULACEAE

Lobelia Erinus L. *Garden Lobelia*

Alien. Casual. Occurs on rubbish dumps. All Divs.

Jasione montana L. *Sheep's Bit*

Native. Sandy places, often on disturbed ground. Uncommon. Div. 2, 3.

First Record: C. Deering, *Cat. Stirp.* 1738.

2 Modern Records: Pusto Hill, Everton†, *Brown*; Harwell Hills, Everton; Bloom's Gorse, Rufford; Ranskill; Manton Wood; by Chequer House Station, Babworth.

3 Lincoln road side, Langford; Muskham, *Ordoyno*; Gravel pit at South Collingham, *Carr MS.*; Girton; Besthorpe; South Clifton. All these records except Muskham are on the blown sand.

Campanula glomerata L. *Clustered Bellflower*

Native. Calcareous grassland. Very rare. Divs. 1, 3.

First Record: C. Deering, *Cat. Stirp.* 1738.

1 Mansfield, *Deering*, *G. Howitt*; Trowell Moor, *Jowett*; Annesley, *G. Howitt*; Strelley, *Gilbert*; Teversall; Hills and Holes, Warsop†, *Carr MS.*

2 (Radford Hollows, *Dugdale*. An unlikely situation, and probably a mistranslation of Deering's Record for *C. Rapunculus*.)

3 Near West Leake, *Nichols*; Newark and Averham Meadows, plentifully, *Ordoyno*; Common in meadows at Holme, Winthorpe and elsewhere about Newark; Cromwell, common in meadows by the Trent, *Carr MS.* We have never been lucky in the Trent meadows, though they are not all ploughed.

Campanula latifolia L. *Giant Bellflower*

Native. Woods and hedges on strong land. Locally common. All Divs.

First Record: T. Ordoyno, *Fl. Nott.* 1807.

1 Frequent.
2 Bothamsall; Hodsock; Osberton.
3 Frequent.
4 Rempstone; Broadholme, *Carr MS.*; Cotham.

Campanula Trachelium L. *Nettle leaved Bell Flower*

Native. Woods on limestone. Rare. Divs. 1, (3), 4.

First Record: C. Deering, *Cat. Stirp.* 1738, probably in error for *C. latifolia*. G. Howitt, *Fl. Notts.* 1839.

1 Pleasley Wood, *G. Howitt*, *Carr MS.*; Sookholme, *Roffey*; Cuckney Hay Wood† and Boon Hills Wood†, Nether Langwith, *Carr MS.*; Woods at Warsop.
3 (Colwick Wood, etc., *Deering*.) Occurs occasionally as a garden escape.
4 Woods near West Leake on the Lias, *G. Howitt*.

Campanula Rapunculoides L. *Creeping Bell Flower*

Alien. Woods and railway banks, roadsides. Uncommon. All Divs.

First Record: C. Deering, *Cat. Stirp*. 1738.

1 Wollaton Lane, *Gilbert*; Railway bank, Bulwell.
2 Budby, *Brown*; Clipstone.
3 A rather frequent escape.
4 A lot in a plantation at Barnby; Railway banks at Normanton-on-Soar.

Campanula rotundifolia L. *Harebell*

Native. Grassland. Common. All Divs.

First Record: C. Deering, *Cat. Stirp*. 1738, p. 7 of the supplement.

Campanula Rapunculus L. *Rampion*

Alien. Extinct or error. Divs. 2, 4.

First Record: C. Deering, *Cat. Stirp*. 1738. Later botanists have thought he meant *C. rotundifolia*, but he records this separately in his Addenda, so there seems no reason to doubt his *C. Rapunculus*.

2 Radford Hollows, *Deering*.
4 In a plantation at Coddington, *Ordoyno*, per *Mr. Jacob Ordoyno*.

Campanula patula L. *Spreading Bellflower*

Native. Woods. Very rare. Div. 3.

Only Record: T. Jowett, *Bot. Cals*. 1826 "Among underwood in Wellow Park". Gathered in the same locality by Mrs. Collinson of Laxton Vicarage who sent specimens to Nottingham Nat. Hist. Mus. in 1916.

Specularia hybrida (L.) DC. *Venus' Looking Glass*

Native. Cornfields on calcareous soils. Rare. Divs. 1, 4.

First Record: J. Carter, *A Visit to Sherwood Forest* 1875.

1 Near Mansfield, *Carter*.
4 West Leake, *Carr* 1905; Kilvington†; Owthorpe† *Carr* 1909; Colston Basset.

ERICACEAE

Vaccinium Myrtillus L. *Bilberry*

Native. Heaths and sandy woods. Formerly frequent in Div. 2, but now decreasing. Rare elsewhere. Divs. 1, 2, 3.

First Record: H. Moll, *A New Description of England* 1724.

1 Aldercarr Wood, Newstead; Warsop.
2 Nottingham Lings; Newstead Park, *Deering*; Mansfield Forest†, *Ordoyno*; Bulwell Forest; Papplewick; In the woods of Birklands and Bilhaugh as well as on the open Forest, *Jowett*; Blidworth†; Fountain Dale; Lindhurst; Mansfield Woodhouse, *Carr MS.*; Thieves' Wood; Rainworth; East Kirkby.
3 Near Wigsley Wood, *Cole*; A little in Wigsley Wood.

Vaccinium Vitis-idaea L. *Cow-berry*

Native. Bogs. Very rare or extinct. Div. 2.

First Record: T. Jowett, *Bot. Cals.* 1826.

2 In Bogs on the Rainworth, particularly near Fountain Dale; Papplewick Forest, *Jowett*; Near Mansfield, *Carter*.

Vaccinium Oxycoccus L. *Cranberry*

Native. Bogs. Probably extinct. Div. 2.

Only Record: T. Ordoyno, *Fl. Nott.* 1807, "Oxton Bogs." Last seen there by H. Fisher about the end of the last century.

Calluna vulgaris (L.) Hull *Ling*

Native. Sandy woods and heaths. Local. All Divs.

First Record: C. Deering, *Cat. Stirp.* 1738.

1 Teversall; Kimberley; Trowell, all on the coal measures.
2 Common.
3 Bothamsall; West Drayton†; Gamston by Retford†; Wigsley Wood†, *Carr MS.*; Spalford; Thorney and Girton on the blown sand; Misterton.
4 Langford Moor†; Thorney†; Harby; Wigsley†, *Carr MS.*; Brough; Barnby; Coddington; Clipstone and Cotgrave Wolds.

var *pubescens* Hull. is commonly found with the type.

Erica cinerea L. *Bell Heather*

Native. Heaths and sandy woods. Local. Divs. 2, 3, 4.

First Record: C. Deering, *Cat. Stirp.* 1738.

2 Frequent.
3 Bothamsall, *Carr MS.*; Thorney; Wigsley.
4 Langford Moor†; Harby; Thorney†; Wigsley, *Carr MS.*; Turf Moor, Brough.

Erica Tetralix L. *Cross leaved Heather*

Native. Wet heaths. The least common species. Divs. 2, 3, 4.

First Record: *Gough's Camden* II 1789, probably copying an ambiguous record of Deering.

2 Still frequent, but decreasing with the falling water table.
3 Bothamsall; Gamston by Retford; Wigsley Wood, *Carr MS.*; Misterton.
4 Coddington Moor, *Ordoyno*; Langford Moor†; Harby; Wigsley, *Carr MS.*

Erica vagans L. (with pink and white flowers) and **Menziesia polifolia** D. Don were reported by H. Creed, in a correspondence in J. C. Loudon's *Magazine of Natural History*, etc. growing on Sherwood Forest. He had specimens. They might have been part of an ornamental planting in the Dukeries. Div. 2.

Rhododendron ponticum L.

Alien. Denizen. Commonly naturalised in woods particularly in Div. 2 and on the gravels east of the Trent. All Divs.

Pyrola minor L. *Common Wintergreen*

Native. Very rare or extinct. Div. 2.

Only Record: G. Howitt, *Notts. Fl.* 1839, "Found by Mr. J. Thompson in a wood near the Welbeck Toll Bar."

MONOTROPACEAE

Monotropa Hypopitys (L.) Dr. *Yellow Bird's Nest*

Native. Woods on sand. Very rare. Div. 2.

First Record: *Cat. Salt* Herb. Sheffield, *c.*1800.

2 Wood near Everton, *Salt*; Thoresby Park in an oak plantation by the Perlethorpe road, *Jowett*; In plantations of sweet chestnut near the Lodge at the Worksop to Ollerton entrance to Clumber Park, in considerable quantity; One or two plants in Birklands, near Robin Hood's Larder Oak, *Carr MS.*; Thoresby Park, near the Clumber Greyhound Lodge, under beech; Clumber Park in beech mast under Yew, near the south edge of the Lake.

PRIMULACEAE

Hottonia palustris L. *Water Violet*

Native. Drains and ponds, on light soil and peat. Local. Divs. 2, 3, 4.

First Record: C. Deering, *Cat. Stirp.* 1738.

2 Nottingham Park, *Deering*; Lenton, *Jowett*; Harworth; Scaftworth†; Misson†; Finningley†, *Carr MS.*; Hesley; Lound; Everton; Mattersey.
3 About Newark† and Kelham, *Ordoyno*; Nottingham Meadows; Clifton; Wilford, *Jowett*; Ratcliffe, *Gilbert*; North Muskham; Cottam; Saundby; Hayton; Gringley, *Carr MS.*; Misterton; Spalford; Besthorpe; Rolleston; Wigsley.
4 Wigsley; Thorney; Harby; Owthorpe.

Primula vulgaris Huds. *Primrose*

Native. Woods and sometimes in hedges. Frequent in Divs. 1 and 3, less so in Div. 2 and rare in Div. 4.

First Record: C. Deering, *Cat. Stirp.* 1738.

4 Widmerpool; Gotham; South Scarle; Wigsley, *Carr MS.*; Thorney.

Primula veris L. *Cowslip*

Native. Meadows and roadsides. Decreasing, but still common except in Div. 2, where it grows chiefly on the alluvial soils. All Divs.

First Record: C. Deering, *Cat. Stirp.* 1738.

Primula x variabilis Goupil (P. *veris x vulgaris*) *Oxlip*

Native. Open woodland. Uncommon. All Divs.

First Record: T. Ordoyno, *Fl. Nott.* 1807, as *P. elatior*.

1 Bulwell, *Jowett*; Eastwood; Greasley, *G. Howitt*; Broxtowe, *Gilbert*; Linby, *Carr MS.*
3 Oxton; Elston; Hockerton; Marnham; Tuxford; Caunton.

Cyclamen hederifolium Ait.

Alien. Divs. 3 or 4.

Only Record: Turner and Dillwyn, *Bot. Guide* 1805 "At Langar near the seat of Earl Howe, plentifully, but yet doubtful as a native," per Rev. G. Crabbe on the authority of Mr. Gregory. Ordoyno (1807) records it from the same locality.

The plant appears to have been exterminated.

Lysimachia thrysiflora Ait.

H. C. Watson *Top. Bot.* per Berkeley MS. There is no other record of this plant for Notts.

Lysimachia vulgaris L. *Yellow Loosestrife*

Native. Damp places and drain sides on peat and sand. Frequent on the Carrs and light alluvium, rare elsewhere. Divs. 2, 3, 4.

First Record: T. Ordoyno, *Fl. Nott.* 1807.

2 Farnsfield, *G. Howitt*; Harworth, *Mrs. Sandwith*; Budby, by the Bridge; Misson; Everton Carr†, *Carr MS.*; Finningley; Scaftworth; Scrooby; Gringley; Tiln; Ordsall; Rainworth; Mattersey.
3 Between Collingham and Cromwell; Flintham Wood, *Ordoyno*; Lenton, *G. Howitt*; Sutton Bonington; South Leverton; Saundby; Walkeringham, *Carr MS.*; Besthorpe; Girton; South Clifton; Spalford; Gringley.
4 Wigsley Wood in quantity†; Thorney†, *Carr.*

Lysimachia Nummularia L. *Creeping Jenny*

Native. Damp meadows and hedge bottoms. Common in the Trent Valley and frequent elsewhere. All Divs.

First Record: C. Deering, *Cat. Stirp.* 1738.

Lysimachia nemorum L. *Yellow Pimpernel*

Native. Damp woods. Locally frequent. All Divs.

First Record: C. Deering, *Cat. Stirp.* 1738.

1 Frequent.
2 Oxton, *Carr MS.*; Newstead; Annesley; Rufford; Hodsock; Osberton.
3 Frequent.
4 West Leake Hills; Stanton, *Carr MS.*; Widmerpool.

Lysimachia ciliata L.

A rare alien, on dumps. Div. 3.

First Record: Newark 1958.

Anagallis tenella (L.) Murr. *Bog Pimpernel*

Native. Bogs and marshy ground, often near calcareous streams.

Rare and decreasing. All Divs.

First Record: C. Deering, *Cat. Stirp.* 1738.

1 White Moor Close, Radford, *Deering*; Pleasley; Selston; Bulwell, *Jowett*; Worksop Manor, *Bohler*; Haggonfields, *Friend*; Newbound Mill, Teversall; Sookholme Moor†; Hills and Holes, Warsop; Shireoaks Park†, *Carr MS.*
2 Oxton Bottoms†, *Ordoyno*; Sherwood Forest; Bleak Hills, Mansfield; Papplewick Forest, *Jowett*; Between Idle Stop and Misson, *Miller*; Harworth, *Mrs. Sandwith*; Burns Green, Warsop, *Carr MS.*
3 Quonce Close, Newark; Gamston Moor; Halam Beck; Edingley Moor, *Ordoyno*; Wellow, *Friend.*
4 Coddington Carr Grounds, *Ordoyno.*

Anagallis arvensis L. *Scarlet Pimpernel*

Native. Arable land. Common. All Divs.

First Record: C. Deering, *Cat. Stirp.* 1738.

Anagallis foemina Mill. *Blue Pimpernel*

Native. Cornfields. Very rare. Divs. 1, 3, 4.

First Record: G. Howitt, *Notts. Fl.* 1839.

1 Sutton-in-Ashfield, sent by *E. Wright*, *Carr MS.*

3 Clifton, *G. Howitt*, per *Wolley*; Kingston-on-Soar, *Thornley*; Newark, *Fisher.*

4 Cornfields at Widmerpool, seeds from this plant cultivated in my garden for several years showed no variation in flower colour, *Carr MS.*; Owthorpe, a lot in a field of roots 1962.

Samolus Valerandi L. *Brookweed*

Native. Sides of peaty drains and calcareous streams. Very local. All Divs.

First Record: T. Ordoyno *Fl. Nott.* 1809.

1 Quarries at Shireoaks, Haggonfields and Lady Lee, Worksop, *Carr MS.*; Shireoaks Park.

2 Misson†; Gringley Carr†, *Miller*; Finningley†, *Carr MS.*; Everton Carr.

3 Southwell Parks; Ladywood, Weston, *Ordoyno*; Morton, *Jowett*; Gotham Cottage Moor, *G. Howitt*; Devon bank at Newark, casual; Misterton Carr.

4 Broadholme, *Carr MS.*

OLEACEAE

Syringa vulgaris L. *Lilac*

Alien. Frequently naturalised in hedges. All Divs.

Fraxinus excelsior L. *Ash*

Native. Hedges and woods. Common. In the Trent Valley the commonest hedgerow tree. All Divs.

First Record: C. Deering, *Cat. Stirp.* 1738.

Ligustrum vulgare L. *Privet*

Native. Hedges and scrubland. Common, but less so in Div. 2. All Divs.

First Record: C. Deering, *Cat. Stirp.* 1738.

Ligustrum ovalifolium Hassk. *Oval leafed Privet*

Alien. Naturalised in hedges, chiefly near villages. All Divs.

APOCYNACEAE

Vinca major L. *Greater Periwinkle*

Alien. Denizen. Woods, railway banks, hedges. Uncommon. All Divs.

First Record: T. Ordoyno, *Fl. Nott.* 1807.

1 Cresswell Crags†, *Carr MS.*
2 Ordsall; Ranskill; Finningley; Hesley.
3 Kirklington, *Ordoyno*; Halam; North Wheatley.
4 Rempstone.

Vinca minor L. *Lesser Periwinkle*

Denizen. Frequently planted and well naturalised in woodland. Uncommon. All Divs.

First Record: T. Ordoyno, *Fl. Nott.* 1807.

1 King's Mill, Mansfield; Bulwell Hall Woods, a lot.
2 Ranby Hall Wood; Hodsock.
3 Edingley Hill; Halam, *Ordoyno*; Clifton Woods, *Jowett*; near Newark†, *Fisher*; Grove; Toton.
4 Rempstone, *Carr MS.*

LOGANIACEAE

Buddleia Davidii Franch. *Buddleia*

Alien. Frequently naturalised on walls; and in waste places in towns. Divs. 1, 2, 3.

GENTIANACEAE

Blackstonia perfoliata (L.) Huds. *Yellow Wort*

Native. Dry calcareous banks and pastures. Local. Divs. 1, 3, 4.

First Record: C. Deering, *Cat. Stirp.* 1738.

1 Frequent.
3 Formerly frequent (see *Ordoyno*, *Carr*, etc.); Modern Records: Lowdham, *Evans*; Kersal; Halam; Eaton; Gamston-by-Retford; Everton; Clarborough.
4 Stanton-on-Wolds†; Gotham†; West Leake; Beacon Hill, Newark, *Carr MS.*; Coddington; Balderton.

Centaurium minus Moench. *Common Centaury*

Native. Rough meadow banks and open woodland. Rather frequent in all Divs.

First Record: C. Deering, *Cat. Stirp.* 1738.

(Gentiana Pneumonanthe L. *Marsh Gentian*

Native. Turf Bogs. Extinct. Divs. 3, 4.

First Record: T. Ordoyno, *Fl. Nott.* 1809.

3 "We have received specimens gathered in Houghton Park near Tuxford," *Jowett.*
4 On Langford and Stapleford (Lincs.) Moors, abundantly, *Ordoyno*; Gone from Langford Moor by Prof. Carr's time (1900).)

Gentiana Amarella L. *Autumn Gentian*

Native. Dry calcareous pastures. Formerly frequent in 1 (see G. Howitt), now uncommon everywhere. Divs. 1, 3, 4.

First Record: R. Pulteney, *Phil. Trans.* 1756.

1 Kirkby-in-Ashfield, *Kaye*; About Mansfield, *Ordoyno*; Hucknall; Bulwell, *Jowett*; Shireoaks, *Friend*; Annesley†; Teversall; Sookholme; Cresswell Crags†, *Carr MS.*; Hills and Holes, Warsop, *Butcher*; Skegby.
3 Kirklington Temple, *Ordoyno*; Mapperley Hills, *Jowett*; About Walkeringham, *Miller*; Walesby, *Friend*; Markham Clinton; Welham; Gamston by Retford†, *Carr MS.*; Hare Hills, Kersal.
4 East Leake, *Pulteney*, *Carr*; Costock; New Wood, Widmerpool, *Carr MS.*; Cotgrave Wolds; Coddington; Clipstone.

Gentiana campestris agg. *Field Gentian*

Native. Calcareous pastures. Very rare. Divs. 1, 2, 3.

First Record: T. Ordoyno, *Fl. Nott.* 1807.

1 Near Mansfield; Near Newstead, *G. Howitt.*
2 Lime Avenue, Clumber, *Roffey.*
3 Between Markham Moor and Great Markham, *Ordoyno.*

Gentiana baltica (Murb.) H. Sm.

Native. Dry limestone banks. Very rare. Div. 1.

Only Record: J. W. Carr, *Tr. Nott. Nats.* 1904, Annesley, on the Magnesian Limestone.

Menyanthes trifoliata L. *Buckbean*

Native. Bogs and pools. Very rare and rapidly decreasing. Divs. 1, 2, 3.

First Record: C. Deering, *Cat. Stirp.* 1738.

1 Basford Scottum, *Deering*; Boggy ground in the course of the Leen; Kirkby Hardwick, *Jowett*; Sutton-in-Ashfield and near Sutton Junction Station, *Carr MS.*; Shireoaks Park, *Brown*; Nuthall Lake, a lot.

2 Nottingham Park, *Deering*; Oxton Bottoms, *Ordoyno*; Ollerton; Farnsfield; Bulwell Forest, *Jowett*; Wilton near Worksop, *Friend*; Harworth; Dyke West of Misson, *Mrs. Sandwith*; Between Newington and Misson 1930; Burn's Green, Warsop, *Carr MS.*; Barrier Bank, Scaftworth.
3 Edingley Moor; Pond near Oxton Toll Bar, *Ordoyno*; Swamps between Bothamsall and Walesby, *Friend*; Small wood at Eaton, a fair quantity.

Nymphoides peltatum (Gmel.) O. Kuntze. *Fringed Water Lily*

?Denizen. Lakes. Very rare. Div. 1.

Only Record: T. Jowett, *Bot. Cals.* 1826, Welbeck Lakes. Repeated by G. Howitt 1839. Doubtless introduced.

POLEMONIACEAE

Gilia capitata Sims. *Queen Anne's Thimble Flower*

Alien. A rare casual. Div. 3.

Only Record: H. Fisher, *Rept. Brit. Ass.* 1893, Newark Wharfs.

Polemonium caeruleum L. *Jacob's Ladder*

A relic of cultivation. Rare. Divs. 1, 3.

1 Park Hall, Mansfield Woodhouse.
3 Nottingham Dump.

BORAGINACEAE

Cynoglossum officinale L. *Hound's Tongue*

Native. Dry grassland, often on disturbed ground. Local. All Divs.

First Record: C. Deering, *Cat. Stirp.* 1738.

1 Banks of the Erewash, near Ilkeston, *Jowett*; About Mansfield, *G. Howitt*; Trowell, *Gilbert*.
2 Wollaton Park Walls, *Deering*; Thoresby Park†, *Bohler*; Budby†; Edwinstowe, *Carr MS.*
3 About Collingham, *Ordoyno*; Colwick Park, *Sidebotham*; Thrumpton†; West Leake†, *Carr MS.*; Cropwell Bishop; Stanford-on-Soar.
4 Plumtree; Cropwell Bishop†; Owthorpe†; Gotham Hills†; Elton; Langar; Stonepit Plantation, Staunton, *Carr MS.*; Normanton-on-Soar.

(**Cynoglossum germanicum** Jacq. *Green Hound's Tongue*

Native. Extinct or error. Div. 2.

Only Record: J. Bohler, White's *Worksop and the Dukeries*, Thoresby Park.)

Asperugo procumbens L. *Madwort*

Alien. A rare casual. Div. 3.

Only Record: H. Fisher, *Brit. Ass. Rept.* 1893, Newark.

Symphytum officinale L. *Comfrey*

Native. Damp hedge bottoms, willow holts and river sides. Locally very frequent. Has apparently increased recently, see G. Howitt and J. W. Carr MS.

First Record: C. Deering, *Cat. Stirp.* 1738.

1 On the banks of the Erewash near Ilkeston, *Jowett*; Bulwell.
2 Lenton, *Jowett*; Blyth; Scaftworth; Misson.
3 Very common in the Trent Valley and occasionally in tributary valleys and around springs.
4 Coddington; Owthorpe; Broadholme.

Symphytum x uplandicum Nyman.

S. asperum Lepech. x *S. officinale* L.

This very variable hybrid appears to be widespread over the county in hedge bottoms, woods, and road and canal sides. Specimens from Clipstone and Farndon have been determined by A. E. Wade and T. G. Tutin. Flower colour ranges from sky blue to dingy purple. Divs. 1, 2, 3.

First Record: R. W. Butcher, Fosse Way, near Syerston, *c.*1940.

Symphytum orientale L.

Alien. A rare casual. Div. 3.

Only Record: By the Devon side at Newark July 1953 et seq.

Anchusa sempervirens L. *Green Alkanet*

Denizen. Hedgebanks and woodlands, near houses. Uncommon. Divs. 1, 2, 3.

First Record: T. Jowett, *Bot. Cals.* 1826.

1 Near the stone quarries at Mansfield, *Jowett* per *G. Howitt*; Trowell.
2 Ollerton, *G. Howitt*; On the edge of the Forest at Edwinstowe, *Carr MS.*; Stapleford; Gleadthorpe Screed, dominant over an acre of woodland; Bilby.
3 Old quarry at Colwick, *G. Howitt*; Collingham, *Bradley*; Lowdham; Epperstone; Bingham; Upton; Kelham; Nottingham Dump.

Anchusa officinalis L.

Only Record: H. Fisher *Rept. Brit. Ass.* 1893.

Borago officinalis L. *Borage*

Alien. Casual. Not seen since 1839. (*G. Howitt*). Divs. 1, 2, 3.

First Record: C. Deering, *Cat. Stirp.* 1738.

1 Kirkby Churchyard: Aspley, *G. Howitt.*
2 Near Nottingham Gallows . . . also beyond Chapple Bar, *Deering.*
3 Walls and amongst rubbish at Newark, *Ordoyno.*

Lycopsis arvensis L. *Bugloss*

Native. Arable fields. Common on light soils. All Divs.

First Record: C. Deering, *Cat. Stirp.* 1738.

1 Kimberley.
2 Very common.
3 and 4 Common on the river gravels and drift soils.

Myosotis palustris L. *Water Forget-me-not*

Native. River and stream sides. Very common. All Divs.

First Record: C. Deering, *Cat. Stirp.* 1738.

Myosotis secunda Murr. (*M. repens* Hook.) *Water Forget-me-not*

There has been confusion between this species and the next in Notts. G. Howitt and T. Jowett contradict each other, J. W. Carr changed his mind between 1904 (*Tr. Nott. Nats.*) and writing his MS. Flora. In his MS. he considers *M. caespitosa* the common species.

Only Record: G. Howitt, *Notts. Fl.* 1839: "In turf bogs; not frequent, Pleasley (Div. 1); Rainworth and Oxton Bogs (Div. 2)."

A not unlikely plant to find in the vanished 'turf bogs' growing with *Drosera* etc.

Myosotis caespitosa K.F. Schultz *Water Forget-me-not*

Native. Damp places and drain sides on sand and peat. Locally frequent. All Divs.

First Record: T. Jowett, *Bot. Cals.* 1826, G. Howitt said this was *M. secunda.* A. Gilbert, *Bot. for Beginners* 1880.

1 Langold Lake, *Mrs. Sandwith*; Teversall; Warsop; Strelley; *Carr MS.*; Cossall; Jacksdale; Shireoaks.
2 Frequent.
3 Frequent except on the marls.
4 Balderton.

Myosotis sylvatica Ehrh. *Wood Forget-me-not*

Native. Damp woodland. Locally frequent. Divs. 1, 2, 3.

First Record: C. Deering, *Cat. Stirp.* 1738.

1 Greasley; Shireoaks; Annesley; Teversall; Carlton-in-Lindrick.
2 Oxton Bogs†; Haughton Decoy, *Carr MS.*; Newstead; White water Bridge, Ollerton.
3 In many of the strong woodlands, often dominant in large patches.

Myosotis arvensis (L.) Hill *Field Forget-me-not*

Native. Fields, hedges, woods. Common. All Divs.

First Record: C. Deering, *Cat. Stirp.* 1738.

var. *silvestris* Schlecht. is common in woodland in Divs. 1 and 3.

First Record: T. Jowett, *Bot. Cals.* 1826.

Myosotis hispida Schlecht. *Early Forget-me-not*

Native. Open communities on sandy soils. Locally frequent. All Divs.

First Record: G. Howitt, *Notts. Fl.* 1839.

1 Church Warsop.
2 Frequent on the Forest.
3 Sconce Hills, Newark; Balderton, *Fisher*; North Muskham, *Carr MS.*; Besthorpe; South Clifton; Girton; Wigsley.
4 Langford Moor, *Butcher.*

Myosotis versicolor Sm. *Yellow and Blue Forget-me-not*

Native. Path and field sides, heaths, banks. More widespread than the last species. All Divs.

First Record: C. Deering, *Cat. Stirp.* 1738.

1 Carr MS., No locality.
2 Common.
3 Frequent on the blown sand, sporadic elsewhere.
4 Langford; Gotham; Clipstone; West Leake.

Lithospermum officinale L. *Gromwell*

Native. Wood verges and hedges. Rare. All Divs.

First Record: C. Deering, *Cat. Stirp.* 1738.

1 Between Broxtowe and Wigley Woods, *Ordoyno*; Bulwell (or 2), *Jowett*; Between Nuthall and Basford, *G. Howitt*; Haggonfields, Worksop, *Roffey*; Scratta Wood, Shireoaks, *Brown*, still there 1962.
2 Between Radford Field and Bobber's Mill, *Deering*; By Drury's Dam and Bleak Hills, Mansfield, *G. Howitt.*
3 Near Southwell; Halam Beck, *Ordoyno*; Sneinton Wood, *G. Howitt*; Walkeringham, *Miller*; Whip Ridding, Kirklington†; Clarborough, *Carr MS.*; Little Gringley; Saundby; Newark Dump.
4 Plumtree; Clipstone Wolds†, *Carr MS.*

Lithospermum arvense L. *Corn Gromwell*

Native. Arable fields, especially in beans, on clay or basic soils. Locally frequent. Divs. 1, 3, 4.

First Record: C. Deering, *Cat. Stirp.* 1738.

1 Rather frequent, *G. Howitt.* No modern records.
3 Before selective spraying it was frequent on the marls and river gravels.
4 Beacon Fields, Newark, *Ordoyno*; Staunton; Flawborough; Kinoulton; Cotham.

Echium vulgare L. *Viper's Bugloss*

Native. Sandy fields and waste ground. Uncommon. Divs. 1, 2, 3.

First Record: C. Deering, *Cat. Stirp.* 1738.

1 Rather common about the shafts of old coal mines, *Jowett*; Frequent, *G. Howitt.* No modern records.
2 Formerly rather frequent. Modern Records; Barrow and Pusto Hills, Everton, in great quantity; Walesby; Railway bank at Babworth.
3 Spalford Warrens; Besthorpe; Girton; Newark; Misterton.

CONVOLVULACEAE

Calystegia sepium (L.) Roem. and Schultz. *Great Bindweed*

Native. Damp hedgerows, woods, willow holts, waste ground. Very common. All Divs.

First Record: C. Deering, *Cat. Stirp.* 1738.

A pink flowered form found at Elkesley (Div. 2), Upton and Caunton, (Div. 3) was submitted to R. K. Brummitt, who considered it only a pink flowered form of the type.

Calystegia silvatica (Kit.) Griseb.

Alien. Denizen. Hedges and waste ground near houses. Frequent throughout the county. All Divs.

First Record: *B.S.B.I. Year Book* 1953, Report of meeting at Bawtry; "Harworth, hedge on Bawtry road." Div. 2.

Calystegia pulchra Brummitt and Heywood.

Denizen. Hedges near houses. Rare. Divs. 2, 3, 4.

2 Scaftworth, a lot on the by-pass and in the village; Everton, near an empty cottage on Pusto Hill. "Both these plants appear to be intermediate between *C. pulchra* and *C. silvatica.* They are the only such plants that have come to my notice." R. K. Brummitt.
3 Canal side, West Bridgford; Queen's Road, Newark.
4 Barnby-in-the-Willows.

Convolvulus arvensis L. *Corn Bindweed*

Native. Arable fields, roadsides, waste places. Very common. All Divs.

First Record: C. Deering, *Cat. Stirp.* 1738.

Cuscuta epithymum (L.) Murr. *Lesser Dodder*

Very rare or extinct. Div. 3.

Only Record: T. Ordoyno, *Fl. Nott.* 1807, Southwell. He does not mention the host plant.

ssp *Trifolii* Bab.; J. W. Carr, *Tr. Nott. Nats.* 1904. On Lucerne at Kingston-on-Soar, per Rev. A. Thornley; On clover at Hayton per Mrs. Collinson. Specimens seen. Div. 3.

Cuscuta europea L. *Large Dodder*

Only Record: J. Carter, *A visit to Sherwood Forest* 1875, 'Near Mansfield.'

SOLANACEAE

Lycopersicum esculentum Mill. *Tomatoe*

Alien. A common casual on dumps, sewage farms and the Trent bank. All Divs.

Solanum Dulcamara L. *Woody Nightshade*

Native. Wet woods, hedgerows, waste places. Very common. All Divs.

First Record: C. Deering, *Cat. Stirp.* 1738.

var. *tomentosum* Koch. is frequent on waste ground, dumps and car parks in Newark, Div. 3.

Solanum nigrum L. *Black Nightshade*

Native. Arable land, waste ground, gardens. Frequent except in Div. 1. All Divs.

First Record: C. Deering, *Cat. Stirp.* 1738.

1 Bulwell Dump.

Solanum miniatum Bernh.

Alien. A rare casual. Div. 3.

Only Record: Weed in a garden on the Fosse Road, Farndon 1961.

Solanum sarrachoides Sendtn.

Alien. A rare casual. Div. 3.

Only Record: A lot in a carrot field at Spalford 1960, det. N.Y. Sandwith.

Solanum tuberosum L. *Potato*

Alien. Casual. Frequent on dumps and as a relic of cultivation.

Nicandra physaloides (L.) Gaertn. *Schoo-fly*

Alien. A rare casual.

3 Cut-Through Lane, Beeston, *Mrs. Bulley*; Persistent garden weed at Farndon.

Lycium chinense Mill. *Duke of Argyll's Tea Plant*

Alien. Denizen. Hedges near houses. Uncommon. Divs. 1, 2, 4.

First Record: J. W. Carr, *Victoria County History* 1906.

1 Sutton-in-Ashfield, *Carr MS.*
2 Ollerton; Everton†, (still round Barrow Hills); Finningley, *Carr MS.*
4 Kinoulton.

Lycium halimifolium Mill.

Alien. Denizen. Hedges near houses. The commoner species. Distributed throughout the county. All Divs.

First Record: Newark 1953.

Atropa Belladonna L. *Deadly Nightshade*

Denizen. Around old buildings and quarries. Rare. Divs. 1, 2, 3.

First Record: C. Deering, *Cat. Stirp.* 1738.

1 About Mansfield, *Deering*, *Jones*; Shireoaks Quarry, *Friend*; Nuthall Temple.
2 Cuckney Church Close, *G. Howitt*; Nottingham Park†, *Williams.*
3 Foot of Clifton Hill, *Deering*, *Butcher*; Smith Street, Newark, *Newark Herald*; Dunkirk Meadows, Nottingham.

Datura Stramonium L. *Thorn Apple*

Alien. Casual. Waste places and gardens, rubbish dumps. Divs. 1, 2, 3.

First Record: C. Deering, *Cat. Stirp.* 1738.

1 Rubbish Tips, Worksop, *Friend.*
2 Dunghills, about Nottingham (or 3), *Deering*; Bilsthorpe, *Newark Advertiser* 1960.
3 Mapperley, *Gilbert*; Southwell, *Carr MS.* and 1960; Stoke Sewage Farm, *Stone* 1957; Newark; Bleasby; Wellow; South Collingham; Flintham; East Bridgeford; Elston; Muskham, *Newark Advertiser* 1960; Nottingham Dump; Farndon, 1960.

Hyoscyamus niger L. *Henbane*

Native. Waste ground and rough clay slopes. Formerly common (see G. Howitt) now rare. All Divs.

First Record: C. Deering, *Cat. Stirp.* 1738.

1 Lady Lee Quarry, Worksop, *Friend.*
2 Basford, *Deering.*
3 Southwell; Newark†, *Ordoyno*; Walkeringham, *Miller*, *Carr*; By railway under Colwick Wood; Ratcliffe-on-Soar, *Carr MS.*; South Clifton Hill, a lot, six feet high.
4 Clipstone Wolds.

Petunia axillaris

Alien. Not uncommon on rubbish dumps.

SCROPHULARIACEAE

Verbascum Phlomoides L.

Alien. Denizen. Dry woodland, roadsides. Divs. 2, 3. Establishing itself in quantity, particularly on the Forest.

First Record: Kirklington 1950. This plant was a bit of a hybrid.

2 Colonising young forestry at Carburton in quantity; Blidworth; Welbeck Park in several places; Newstead, roadside.
3 Kirklington; Nottingham Dump.

Verbascum Thapsus L. *Great Mullein*

Native. Quarries, open woodland, waste places, railway banks. Very frequent in Div. 1, less so in Divs. 2, and 3, rare in Div. 4.

First Record: C. Deering, *Cat. Stirp.* 1738.

4 Owthorpe.

Verbascum virgatum Stokes. *Twiggy Mullein*

Denizen or casual. Arable fields and gardens. Rare. Divs. 2, 3, 4.

First Record: J. Bohler in White's *Worksop and the Dukeries* 1875.

2 Edwinstowe; Clumber Park, *Bohler.*
3 A garden weed at Farndon for sixty years, Parnham's Mill yard, Newark 1951 et seq.
4 Field side at Brough 1951 et seq.

Verbascum pulverulentum Vill. *Hoary Mullein*

Extinct. Div. 2.

First Record: *Gibson's Camden* 1695. J. Ray *Synopsis* Ed. 3 1724.

2 Wollaton Hall and Park Walls, *Ray*, *Deering*; Walls in High Pavement and Sheep Lane, Nottingham, *Deering.*

Verbascum Lychnites L. *White Mullein*

Extinct. Div. 3.

Only Record: T. Martyn, in *Botanist's Guide* 1805 "Clifton Hill."

Verbascum nigrum L. *Dark Mullein*

Native. Hedges, dry woods. Rare. Divs. 1, 2, 3.

First Record: T. Ordoyno, *Fl. Nott.* 1807.

1 Annesley, *G. Howitt* per *Eddison.*

2 Plantations at Rufford; Wollaton; Near Mansfield; upon the Forest by Clipstone Water, *Ordoyno*; Ollerton, *G. Howitt*; In a hedge on the Edwinstowe side of Clipstone Village, *Carr* 1904; Welbeck Park.

3 Barton-in-Fabis (garden escape).

Linaria vulgaris Mill. *Common Toadflax*

Native. Hedges and rough grassland. Common. All Divs.

First Record: C. Deering, *Cat. Stirp.* 1738.

Linaria purpurea (L.) Mill. *Purple Toadflax*

Alien. Rather frequent on rubbish dumps.

Linaria repens (L.) Mill. *Pale Toadflax*

Denizen. On dumps and near houses. Not common. Div. 3.

3 Farndon village; Southwell dump; Gringley.

Linaria minor (L.) Desf. *Lesser Toadflax*

Colonist. Cornfields, railway lines and waste places. On every railway line in the county. Ordoyno, Howitt and Carr record it as a rare cornfield weed. We have seldom seen it in this habitat.

First Record: T. Ordoyno, *Fl. Nott.* 1807.

Linaria maroccana Hook.f.

Alien. Casual. Rare. Div. 3.

3 Wigsley Wood 1958; Nottingham Dump 1958.

Linaria spuria (L.) Mill. *Fluellen*

Native. Cornfields on clay. Rare except on the Lias, and decreasing. Divs. 3, 4.

First Record: C. Deering, *Cat. Stirp.* 1738.

3 Clifton Hill (by Nottingham), *Deering*; Balderton.

4 West Leake†; *G. Howitt*; Owthorpe†; Colston Bassett†; Widmerpool†; Hickling; Alverton†; Kilvington; Orston†; Staunton†; Elton; Granby; Cotham†; Balderton†, *Carr MS.*; Flawborough.

Linaria Elatine (L.) Mill. *Small Fluellen*

Native. Cornfields on clay. More frequent than the last. Divs. 1, 3, 4.

First Record: T. Jowett, *Bot. Cals.* 1826.

1 Bulwell; Hucknall; Mansfield, *Jowett*; Nether Langwith, *Carr MS.*; Nuthall.
3 Thurgarton; Halloughton, *Jowett*; Southwell, *Carr MS.*; Lowdham; Winkburn; Balderton.
4 West Leake; Stanton-on-Wolds; Orston; Owthorpe†; Widmerpool; Kinoulton†; Hickling†; Colston Bassett; Thorpe-in-the-Glebe; Balderton†, *Carr MS.*; Langford; Collingham; Cotham; Bunny; Harby.

Linaria Cymbalaria (L.) Mill. *Ivy leaved Toadflax*

Alien. Denizen. Naturalised on walls. Common in Divs. 1 and 3, less so in 2 and 4. G. Howitt, 1839, considered it rare.

First Record: T. Ordoyno, *Fl. Nott.* 1807.

2 Mansfield; Annesley.
4 Rempstone; Granby.

Antirrhinum majus L. *Snapdragon*

Alien. Denizen. Old walls and a frequent casual on dumps. Uncommon. Divs. 2, 3.

First Record: T. Ordoyno, *Fl. Nott.* 1807.

2 Worksop Priory; Walls at Mansfield.
3 Walls of the Friars at Newark†, *Ordoyno*; Newark Castle.

Antirrhinum Orontium L. *Corn Snapdragon*

Native or casual. Cornfields. Very rare. Divs. 2, 3, 4.

First Record: J. Bohler, White's *Worksop and the Dukeries* 1875.

2 Dry soils in many parts, *Bohler*. Possibly an error for *Linaria minor*.
3 Casual among corn at Newark, *Fisher*.
4 Casual among corn at Barnby, *Fisher*.

Antirrhinum Asarina L.

Alien. Naturalised on sandstone rock above Broadmarsh, Nottingham†, *Mrs. Bulley* 1952 et seq. Div. 2.

Scrophularia vernalis L. *Yellow Figwort*

Rare Alien. Denizen. Shrubberies. Div. 1.

Only Record: J. W. Carr MS. On a wooded knoll near the Hall in Wollaton Park 1910. Still there in a good quantity 1950 et seq.

Scrophularia aquatica L. *Water Figwort*

Native. River, canal and pond sides. Common. All Divs.

First Record: C. Deering, *Cat. Stirp.* 1738.

Scrophularia nodosa L. *Figwort*

Native. Moist woods. Common, less so in Div. 2. All Divs.

First Record: C. Deering, *Cat. Stirp.* 1738.

Mimulus guttatus DC. *Monkey Flower*

Alien. Denizen. Streamsides. Uncommon. J. W. Carr (MS.) said it was spreading rapidly in the North, but it seems to have received a check, perhaps through river pollution. Divs. 1, 2, 3.

First Record: J. W. Carr, *Tr. Nott. Nats.* 1904.

1 Creswell Crags, *Carr* 1904; Church Warsop; Nether Langwith.
2 Cuckney Mill; By the River Maun at White Water Bridge, Ollerton, Haughton and Bothamsall; Clumber Lake†, *Carr MS.*; Clayworth.
3 Meden, West Drayton; Rolleston, one plant by Trent, 1950; Parnham's Mill, Newark; Everton.

Mimulus moschatus Lindl. *Musk*

Alien. Denizen. Div. 2.

Only Record: G. S. Bailey *B.S.B.I. Maps Scheme* 1958, "Prolific weed in shrubberies at Wollaton Park."

Limosella aquatica L. *Mudwort*

Native. Probably extinct. Div. 3.

Only Record: T. Ordoyno, *Fl. Nott.* 1807, "Gravel pits near Kirklington Mill."

Digitalis purpurea L. *Foxglove*

Native. Woods and hedges on light soils. Locally common. All Divs.

First Record: C. Deering, *Cat. Stirp.* 1738.

1 Common on the coal measures.
2 Common.
3 In woods near the boundary with Div. 2 and established in some woods near country houses. Apparently native at Lady Masham's Cover, Farndon, on gravel.
4 Langford; Coddington†, *Butcher*; Thorney, all on gravel soils.

Veronica officinalis L.

Native. Heathland, old pasture and open woodland. Common on the light soils in Divs. 1 and 2. In the highly cultivated areas of Div. 3 it persists mainly on woodland rides, and in Div. 4 occurs on the drift soils. All Divs.

First Record: T. Ordoyno, *Fl. Nott.* 1807.

Veronica Chamaedrys L. *Germander Speedwell*

Native. Hedgebanks and grassy places. Common. All Divs.

First Record: C. Deering, *Cat. Stirp.* 1738.

Veronica montana L. *Wood Speedwell*

Native. Moist woods. Common in Divs. 1 and 3, chiefly near streams in Div. 2, absent from Div. 4.

First Record: T. Jowett, *Bot. Cals.* 1826.

Veronica scutellata L. *Marsh Speedwell*

Native. Bogs and marshes. Uncommon. All Divs.

First Record: T. Ordoyno, *Fl. Nott.* 1807.

1 Papplewick Mill, *Ordoyno*; Bulwell, *Jowett*; Kirkby Hardwick, *Hurt*.
2 Oxton; Farnsfield Carr, *Ordoyno*; Ollerton; Finningley; Harworth; Misson†, *Carr MS.*; Haughton Decoy; Scaftworth; Annesley; Osberton.
3 Edingley Moor, *Ordoyno*; Between Fiskerton and Farndon, *Jowett*; Farndon; Besthorpe.
4 Coddington Moor, *Ordoyno*; Wysall, *Carr MS.*

Veronica Beccabunga L. *Brooklime*

Native. Streams, ponds and marshes. Common. All Divs.

First Record: C. Deering, *Cat. Stirp.* 1738.

Veronica catenata Pennel. *Water Speedwell*

Native. Marshes and stream sides. This is the common species in Notts. though it has not previously been distinguished from *V. Anagallis-aquatica* L. Locally common. All Divs.

First Record: C. Deering, *Cat. Stirp.* 1738, as *V. Anagallis-aquatica*. Modern Records of segregate:

1 Kirkby; Styrrup.
2 Misson; Everton; Mattersey; Rufford.
3 Common, especially in the Trent Valley.
4 Widmerpool; Granby; Harby; Kilvington; Thorney; Barnby.

Veronica serpyllifolia L. *Thyme leaved Speedwell*

Native. Walls, lawns and sandy ground. Common. All Divs.

First Record: C. Deering, *Cat. Stirp.* 1738.

Veronica arvensis L. *Wall Speedwell*

Native. Walls, and bare ground, heaths. Common, especially on the Forest. All Divs.

First Record: C. Deering, *Cat. Stirp.* 1738.

Veronica triphyllos L. *Fingered Speedwell*

J. W. Carr, *Tr. Nott. Nats.* 1904, writes: "There is one specimen of this species in the Herbarium at Nottingham Natural History Museum, gathered at Barrow Hills, Everton. No date or collector's name are given, but the specimen is probably fifty or sixty years old." Div. 2.

Veronica persica Poir. *Buxbaum's Speedwell*

Alien. Colonist. Arable fields, gardens and waste places. Very common. All Divs.

First Record: H. Fisher, *Rept. Brit. Ass.* 1893 "Now common." It was not known to G. Howitt.

Veronica polita Fries. *Grey Speedwell*

Alien. Colonist. Gardens. We have not found this common, contrary to the experience of earlier botanists. Divs. 1, 2, 3.

Early Records: G. Howitt, *Notts. Fl.* 1839, "Common near Nottingham, perhaps not rare throughout the county." J. W. Carr MS., "Generally distributed throughout the county and probably commoner than the next." R. G. Williams MS., "Common round Nottingham."

1 Victoria County History.
2 A few plants in a field in Welbeck Park, with *Coronopus didymus*.
3 One plant in a nursery garden at Southwell; An occasional garden weed at Farndon (sometimes in carrots); Nottingham Dump.

Veronica agrestis L. *Field Speedwell*

Native. Gardens and arable fields, possibly preferring light land. Now uncommon. All Divs.

First Record: C. Deering, *Cat. Stirp.* 1738. G. Howitt (1839) regards it as common.

1 Watnall.
2 Field weed at Everton; Field weed at Osberton; Field weed at Scaftworth.
3 A pest in Farndon gardens; Eaton; Stockwith; Walkeringham.
4 Balderton; Cotham.

Veronica hederifolia L. *Ivy leaved Speedwell*

Native. Bare dry ground, arable land. Very common. All Divs.

First Record: C. Deering, *Cat. Stirp.* 1738.

Veronica filiformis Sm.

Alien. Denizen. Increasingly naturalised on roadsides, in lawns etc., but not yet common. Divs. 1, 3.

First Record: Laneside, Farndon 1940.

1 Garden Weed, Welbeck.
3 Farndon; Garden weed, Orston; Roadside, Thrumpton; Epperstone; Garden weed, Langar Hall.

Euphrasia brevipila Burnat and Gremli. *Eyebright*

Native. Rare. Divs. 1 or 2.

Only Record: J. W. Carr, *Tr. Nott. Nats.* 1904, "Common about Annesley."

Euphrasia nemorosa (Pers.) H. Mart. emend. Löhr. *Eyebright*

Native. Roadsides, heaths, dry banks, woodland rides. This is the common species in Notts. and generally distributed in all Divisions.

First Record: C. Deering, *Cat. Stirp.* 1738. The aggregate species. J. W. Carr MS. 1908, segregate.

var *collina* Pugsl. is very frequent.

Euphrasia Pseudo Kerneri Pugsl. *Eyebright*

Native. Rare. Divs. 3 or 4.

Only Record: J. W. Carr *Tr. Nott. Nats.* 1905 "West Leake Hills, Common."

Euphrasia anglica Pugsl. *Eyebright*

Native. Rare. Div. 2.

Only Records: J. W. Carr MS., Rufford Park, facing the Abbey 1907; Near the Buck Gates, Thoresby Park 1907, det. H. W. Pugsley.

(**Bartsia viscosa** L. is recorded for V.C. 56 in the *Comital Flora.*)

Bartsia Odontites Huds. *Red Bartsia*

Native. Farm roads, arable land. Common, especially on the heavy clays of Divs. 3 and 4, least common in Div. 2. All Divs.

First Record: C. Deering, *Cat. Stirp.* 1738.

Pedicularis palustris L. *Red Rattle*

Native. Bogs. Now very rare, G. Howitt considered it frequent. Divs. 1, 2, 3.

First Record: C. Deering, *Cat. Stirp.* 1738.

1 (Basford) Scottum; Radford Field; White Moor Close, *Deering*; Newbound Mill, Teversall, *Carr MS.*
2 Oxton Bottoms, Ordoyno; Bulwell Forest, *Carr MS.*; Lyndhurst Heath, *Hopkinson*; Below the Barrier Bank, Scaftworth.
3 Edingley Moor, *Ordoyno*; Moor Lane, Calverton; Bothamsall; Everton Carr, *Carr MS.*

Pedicularis sylvatica L. *Lousewort*

Native. Old pastures, woodland rides. Formerly frequent, see G. Howitt and J. W. Carr, now rather rare. All Divs.

First Record: C. Deering, *Cat. Stirp.* 1738.

Modern Records:
1 Teversal; Church Warsop.
2 Meadow at Chequer Farm, Osberton.
3 Manzer Gorse, Eakring; Mather Wood, Caunton; Park Springs, Winkburn; Epperstone; Oxton.
4 Only Record: Coddington and Langford Moors, *Ordoyno.*

Rhinanthus minor Ehrh. *Yellow Rattle*

Native. Meadows, roadsides and grassy places. Common. All Divs.

First Record: C. Deering, *Cat. Stirp.* 1738.

Rhinanthus major Ehr. *Great Yellow Rattle*

Native. Rare. Div. 4.

Only Record: G. Howitt, *Notts. Fl.* 1839: "Lane leading to Stapleford Moor."

Melampyrum cristatum L. *Crested Cow Wheat*

Native. Woodland verges, on basic Keuper Marl. Very rare. Div. 3.

Only Record: J. W. Carr, *Tr. Nott. Nats.* 1905. "In a wood near Retford, found by the Rev. J. Roffey and shown me by Mr. Lidster."

The exact station on the edge of Eaton Wood has probably been destroyed by road works, but the plant might still be found nearby.

Melampyrum pratense L. *Common Cow Wheat*

Native. Woods on light soil. Rare and decreasing. Divs. 2, 3, 4.

First Record: C. Deering, *Cat. Stirp.* 1738.

2 "Opposite my Lord Biron's Park in the road to Mansfield," *Deering*; Harlow Wood; Combes Wood, Farnsfield; Bulwell, *Jowett*; Clumber Wood, *Roffey*; Ollerton, by side of road to Proteus Lodge and in the adjoining plantation, *Carr MS.*
3 Epperstone Thickets, *Ordoyno*; Wigsley Wood, *Carr MS.*; Wellow Park, *Jones.*
4 Thorney Brown Wood, *Carr MS.*; Hedges of Drinsey Nook Lane and in the Rings, Thorney in some quantity.

OROBANCHACEAE

Orobanche Rapum-Genistae Thuill. *Great Broomrape*

Native. Sandy heaths. Very rare. Divs. 2, 3.

First Record: C. Deering, *Cat. Stirp.* 1738.

2 Among the gorse about Mansfield, *Deering* per *Wright*; Thoresby, *Ordoyno*; Whinney Lane, near Ollerton, *G. Howitt*; Harwell Hill, Everton, *Miller;* In a sandy warren east of Harworth, *Mrs. Sandwith*; In a rough field on the north side of Barrow Hill, *Carr MS.*

3 Manzer Gorse, (Eakring), *Ordoyno*; Harts Well, Farnsfield, *G. Howitt.*

Orobanche alba Steph. is recorded in the *Victoria County History*, **O. purpurea** Jacq. for V.C. 56 in the *Comital Flora.* The records were based on a specimen collected by J. K. Miller on Barrow Hills, Everton, and named by him *O. elatior.* We have submitted the specimen (now in the Lincoln Museum) to Mr. N. Y. Sandwith who identified it as *O. Rapum-Genistae.*

Orobanche minor Sm. *Lesser Broomrape*

Casual. Roadsides, waste places, newly seeded fields. Rare. Divs. 1, 3, 4.

First Record: H. Fisher in J. W. Carr's MS.

1 Bulwell old pit dump.

3 Hawton, *Fisher*; Farndon in new seeds: Newark, Kelham Road side where the corner was cut off, 1951 to 54.

4 Coddington, *Fisher*; Kilvington, a lot in new seeds.

Lathraea Squamaria L. *Toothwort*

Native. Woods and hedgebanks, parasitic on sycamore, elm, yew, thorn and hazel. Local. Divs. 1, 2, 3.

First Record: MS. note in C. Deering's own interleaved copy of his *Cat. Stirp.* "Kirkby Grives." See Jowett, *Bot. Cals.* It is still at the Grives.

1 Frequent.

2 Near Oxton Stews†, *Ordoyno*; Birklands, *Bohler* 1875.

3 In the garden of Wm. Sherbrooke, esq. at Oxton, *Ordoyno*; Epperstone Park; Laxton camp; Bevercotes Park†; Wellow Park†, *Carr MS.*; Oxton Dumble.

J. W. Carr discovered, with some acumen, that G. Howitt's records for this species really refer to *Melampyrum pratense.*

LENTIBULARIACEAE

Utricularia vulgaris agg. *Bladderwort*

Native. Pools and drains. Very rare. Now practically confined to the Carrs. Divs. 2, 3.

First Record: T. Ordoyno, *Fl. Nott.* 1807.

2 Bleak Hills, Mansfield, *Howitt*; Near Park Drain Station, Misson†, *Carr MS.*; and in other parts of Misson parish.
3 Kirklington Mill; Thurgarton Priory Lake; Muskham Fleet, *Ordoyno*; Misterton in several places; Gringley Carr.

Our plant is probably *U. vulgaris* L. but it never flowers.

Utricularia minor L. *Lesser Bladderwort*

Native. Drains and bogs on peat. Very rare. Divs. 2, 3.

First Record: T. Ordoyno, *Fl. Nott.* 1807.

2 Drain on Misson Bombing Range 1952, sp. Herb. R. C. L. Howitt.
3 Edingley Moor, *Ordoyno.*

Pinguicula vulgaris L. *Butterwort*

Native. Bogs and marshes. Formerly rather common (see G. Howitt), now probably extinct. Divs. 1, 2, 3.

First Record: C. Deering, *Cat. Stirp.* 1738.

1 Basford Scottum; White Moor Close, *Deering*; Park Hall, *Jowett*; Around Newbound Mill, Teversall; Sookholme Moor, *Carr MS.*
2 Oxton Stews, *Ordoyno*; Ollerton; Bulwell; Papplewick, *Jowett*; Burns Green, Warsop, *Carr MS.*
3 Halam Beck; Edingley Moor, *Ordoyno*; Epperstone; Kirklington; Clifton (by Nottingham), *Jowett.*

VERBENACEAE

Verbena officinalis L. *Vervain*

Native. Waysides. Very rare. Divs. 1, 2, 3.

First Record: C. Deering, *Cat. Stirp.* 1738.

1 Kirkby-in-Ashfield, *Kaye*; Near Mansfield, *Hurt.*
2 Bobber's Mill; Calverton, *Deering*; Budby, *Ordoyno*; Nottingham Forest, *G. Howitt.*
3 West Leake, *Pulteney MS.*; Southwell; Halam; Edingley; Kirklington; Maplebeck Churchyard, *Ordoyno*; Near North Wheatley Rectory, *Carr MS.*; One plant by the Trent at Beeston, *Williams.*

LABIATAE

Mentha rotundifolia L.

'Round-leaved Mints' are rare in the county. All material submitted by us to Mr. R. A. Graham has been *M. x niliaca.*

Old Records for *M. rotundifolia.*

1 Mansfield, *Deering*; Beauvale Abbey, *Jowett.*
2 Frequent, *Bohler* 1875.

Mentha x niliaca Juss. (*longifolia x rotundifolia*)

Denizen. Roadsides and waste places. Rare. Divs. 1, 2, 3.

First Record: J. W. Carr, *Tr. Nott. Nats.* 1904. (as *M. alopecuriodes* Hull.)

1 Cossall Marsh; Wollaton.
2 Clipstone, *Carr;* Finningley.
3 Wilford Dump; Dunkirk Meadows, Nottingham.

Mentha longifolia (L.) Huds. *Horse Mint*

Probably native by streamsides. Casual elsewhere. Uncommon. Divs. 1, 2, 3.

First Record: C. Deering, *Cat. Stirp.* 1738.

1 Mr. Petty's Mill Yard, Radford, *Deering*; Mansfield Bath, *Ordoyno*; Carr Banks, Mansfield, *Jowett*; Beauvale Abbey, *G. Howitt.*
2 Near the Bridge at Church Warsop, *Carr MS.*
3 Greet Bridge, Southwell; Newark Bridge; Thurgarton Hill, *Ordoyno*; Maplebeck, wet roadside; Newark (casual); Graves Lane, Edingley, in quantity near the stream in old pasture land. This plant is "Near the form which may possibly be native." R. Graham.

Mentha spicata L. *Spearmint*

Casual. Roadsides and dumps. Uncommon. Divs. 1, 3.

First Record: H. C. Watson, *New Botanist's Guide* 1835, per Cooper's Cat.

1 Cossall; Bulwell.
2 Budby.
3 Rather frequent.

Mentha x piperita L. (*aquatica x spicata*) *Peppermint*

Denizen. Streamsides. Rare and decreasing. Divs. 1, 2, 3.

First Record: C. Deering, *Cat. Stirp.* 1738.

1 Selston; Nether Langwith, *Carr MS.*; Bagthorpe.
2 By the Meden at Church Warsop, *Carr MS.*; Robin Dam, Rufford.
3 St. Anne's Well, *Deering*; Southwell Water Mill, *Ordoyno*; Bleasby, *Jowett*; Bothamsall.

var *hirsuta* (Fraser) Graham: Kersal, Div. 3.

Mentha aquatica L. *Water Mint*

Native. River and canal sides, marshes. Common. All Divs.

First Record: C. Deering, *Cat. Stirp.* 1738.

var *hirsuta* Huds. Kersal. Div. 3.

Mentha x verticillata L. (*aquatica x arvensis*) *Whorled Mint*

Native. Marshy places. Rare or overlooked. Divs. 2, 3, 4.

First Record: R. W. Butcher in Carr MS. as *M. sativa* L.

2 Boughton; Park Drain, Misson, *Butcher*.
3 West Bridgford; Holme Pierrepont, *Williams*; Farndon Holt.
4 Hickling, canal side.

Mentha x Smithiana Graham (*aquatica x arvensis x spicata*)

Native. Marshy places. Rare. Divs. 2, 3, 4.

First Record: T. Jowett, *Bot. Cals.* 1826.

2 Finningley, *Carr* 1903.
3 Bleasby, *Jowett*.
4 Owthorpe, canal side.

Mentha arvensis L. *Corn Mint*

Native. Arable fields, waysides, damp ground. Common. All Divs.

First Record: C. Deering, *Cat. Stirp.* 1738.

Mentha x gentilis L. (*arvensis x spicata*)

Denizen. Marshy places. Rare. Divs. 1, 3.

First Record: T. Ordoyno, *Fl. Nott.* 1807.

1 Mansfield, *Ordoyno*.
3 Newark; Southwell, *Ordoyno*; Adbolton.

Mentha Pulegium L. *Pennyroyal*

Native. Marshy places. Probably extinct. Divs. 2, 3.

2 H. Friend in Sisson's *Beauties of the Sherwood Forest*, no locality.
3 Gunthorpe Lordship; Wellow Green, *Deering*; Kirklington Mill, *Ordoyno*.

We would like to record our debt to the late R. A. Graham to whom nearly every critical specimen was submitted.

Lycopus europaeus L. *Gipsywort*

Native. River, canal and drain sides. Very common. All Divs.

First Record: C. Deering, *Cat. Stirp.* 1738.

Origanum vulgare L. *Sweet Marjoram*

Native. Banks on calcareous soil. Uncommon. All Divs.

First Record: C. Deering, *Cat. Stirp.* 1738.

1 Formerly frequent, see *G. Howitt*; Modern records: Mansfield Woodhouse; Nuthall; Watnall; Bulwell; Warsop.
2 Roadside near the Vicarage, Harworth, *Mrs. Sandwith.*
3 Colwick Hills, *Deering*; Between Newark and Balderton, *Ordoyno*; Carlton (by Nottingham); Burton Joyce; Clarborough; Little Gringley†; Eaton†, *Carr MS.*; Gamston by Retford; Sutton-on-Trent, (escape).
4 Coddington, *Ordoyno*; Normanton-on-Wolds.

Thymus Drucei Ronn. *Wild Thyme*

Native. Dry banks and pastures. Now rather rare. All Divs.

First Record: C. Deering, *Cat. Stirp.* 1738.

1 Kirkby-in-Ashfield†; Skegby; Teversall; Mansfield; Warsop†; Sookholme, *Carr MS.*; Pleasley Vale; Annesley.
2 Modern Records: Papplewick; Budby Forest; Walesby; Thoresby Park; Carlton-in-Lindrick; Osberton.
3 Normanton by Southwell; Edingley Moor, *Ordoyno*; Little Gringley; Clarborough, *Carr MS.* Kneesall; Oxton.
4 Gotham.

Thymus Pulegioides L.

Native. Pastures. Div. 4.

Only Record: West Leake Hills 1950, det. R. W. Butcher.

Calamintha ascendens Jord. *Common Calamint*

Native. Banks and fields. Very rare. Divs. 1, 2, 3.

First Record: C. Deering, *Cat. Stirp.* 1738.

1 About Basford, *Deering.*
2 Papplewick; Harlow Wood, *G. Howitt*; Bawtry road side, Harworth, *Mrs. Sandwith.*
3 North Collingham; Between North and South Muskham, *Ordoyno*; Morton, *G. Howitt*; Bank by the footpath to Averham Church, *Carr MS.*, still there 1952.

Calamintha Nepeta (L.) Savi. *Lesser Calamint*

Native. Extinct. Div. 4.

Only Record: T. Ordoyno, *Fl. Nott.* 1807, Fields about Coddington.

Calamintha Acinos (L.) Scheele. *Basil Thyme*

Native. Dry banks. Rather rare. All Divs.

First Record: C. Deering, *Cat. Stirp.* 1738.

1 Bulwell Lime Kilns, *Ordoyno*; 'Common', *G. Howitt*; Near Sellers Wood, Bulwell; Bulwell Wood Hall, Hucknall; Warsop†, *Carr MS.*
2 Bury (Berry) Hills, Mansfield, *Deering*; Blidworth, *Ordoyno*; Barrow Hills, Everton†, *Miller*; Bulwell Heath, *Gilbert.*
4 Gotham Hills; Normanton-on-Soar.

Clinopodium vulgare L. *Wild Basil*

Native. Hedgebanks and rough grassland, chiefly on strong land. Frequent except in Div. 2. All Divs.

2 Between Oxton and Calverton; Between Retford and Worksop, *Ordoyno*; Harworth; Osberton.

Melissa officinalis L. *Balm*

Alien. Denizen. Div. 4.

Only Record: R. G. Williams MS., *c.*1943. Hedges near the Lime Kiln Inn, Cropwell Bishop†.

Salvia horminoides Pourr. *Wild Clary*

Native. Roadsides and waste ground. Now very rare. Divs. 2, 3.

First Record: C. Deering, *Cat. Stirp.* 1738.

2 Nottingham Castle, *Deering*, *Carr MS.*; Hollow Way leading to Radford Road, *Deering*; About Mansfield, *Hurt*; Barrow Hills, Everton, *Carr MS.*
3 Spring House, Newark, *Ordoyno*; Between Gringley and Beckingham, *Miller*; Sconce Hills, Newark, *Fisher*; North Wheatley, *Carr MS.*; Cow Lane, Newark, *Leather*; Smith's Woodyard, Newark.

Salvia sylvestris L.

Alien. A rare casual. Div. 3.

Only Record: H. Fisher, *Brit. Ass. Rept.* 1893, Newark Wharfs.

Salvia Horminum L.

Alien. Rare. Div. 1.

Only Records: Goulding's list of Sir Richard Kaye's Plants in *Trans. Lincs. and Notts. Archi.-Soc.* 1923. Kaye received a specimen from Kirkby-in-Ashfield in 1782. Goulding does not question the identification and records that the plant occurred on waste ground at Welbeck from 1916 annually. We have so far found no *Salvias* at Welbeck.

Salvia reflexa Horn.

Alien. Rare casual. Div. 3.

Only Record: Nottingham Dump 1958.

Nepeta Cataria L. *Cat Mint*

Native. Hedge banks. Very rare. All Divs.

First Record: C. Deering, *Cat. Stirp.* 1738.

1 Welbeck, *Kaye*; Mansfield Bath, *Ordoyno*; Basford, *G. Howitt*; Hills and Holes, Warsop, *Carr MS.*
2 Nottingham, *Deering*; Between Cuckney and Warsop, *Ordoyno*; Between Blyth and Barnby Moor, and by the Bawtry Road, Blyth, *Mrs. Sandwith*; Bawtry Road, Harworth†, *Carr MS.*
3 Between Newark and Hawton, *Ordoyno*; Hayton, one plant, *Brown*; Ratcliffe road, Kingston-on-Soar; Flawborough, *Carr MS.*
4 Cotgrave Gorse and Long Plantation, *Carr MS.*

Glechoma hederacea L. *Ground Ivy*

Native. Hedges, roadsides, woods, waste ground. Very common. All Divs.

First Record: C. Deering, *Cat. Stirp.* 1738.

Scutellaria galericulata L. *Skull-cap*

Native. River and canal sides. Common. All Divs.

First Record: T. Ordoyno, *Fl. Nott.* 1807.

Scutellaria minor Huds. *Lesser Skull-cap*

Native. Probably extinct. Div. 3.

Only Record: George Miller (son of J. K. M.) in a letter to E. A. Woodruffe Peacock, "*Scutellaria minor* grows plentifully on the bank of the Chesterfield Canal at Walkeringham."

This would have been a possible locality.

Prunella vulgaris L. *Self-heal*

Native. Meadows, roadsides, waste places. Very common. All Divs.

First Record: C. Deering, *Cat. Stirp.* 1738.

Sideritis montana L.

Alien. A rare casual. Div. 3.

Only Record: A. R. Horwood, *B.E.C. Rept.* 1915, Kingston-on-Soar.

Marrubium vulgare L. *White Horehound*

?Native. Roadsides, around dwellings. Very rare or extinct. Divs. 1, 2, 3.

First Record: C. Deering, *Cat. Stirp.* 1738.

1 Basford, *Deering*; Bulwell stone pits, *Ordoyno*.
2 Nottingham Castle Rock, *Deering*; Between Blidworth and Kirkby; Between Worksop and Ollerton, *Ordoyno*; Farnsfield. *G. Howitt*.
3 Between Redhill and Calverton, *Deering*.

Stachys sylvatica L. *Hedge Woundwort*

Native. Hedgesides, woods, waste places. Very common. All Divs.

First Record: C. Deering, *Cat. Stirp*. 1738.

Stachys palustris L. *Marsh Woundwort*

Native. River and canal sides, marshes. Frequent in Divs. 1, 2, 3 but absent from 4.

First Record: C. Deering, *Cat. Stirp*. 1738.

Stachys x ambigua Sm. (*palustris x sylvatica*)

3 Canal bank, Drakeholes, Wiseton, *Carr MS*.

Stachys arvensis L. *Field Woundwort*

Native. Sandy arable fields. Uncommon. All Divs.

First Record, T. Ordoyno, *Fl. Nott*. 1807.

1 Frequent in the coal district, *G. Howitt*; Trowell; Nether Langwith, *Carr MS.*; Carlton-in-Lindrick.
2 Bulwell, *Jowett*; Farnsfield; Welbeck; Bilsthorpe; Osberton estate.
3 Farnsfield Brick Kilns, *Ordoyno*; Trentside, Nottingham†, *Gilbert*; Ossington; West Drayton; Misterton, *Carr MS.*; Colwick, *Brooks*; Besthorpe; Lowdham; Stoke; Thorney.
4 Coddington, *Ordoyno*; Owthorpe; Alverton, *Carr MS.*; Cotham; Harby.

Stachys officinalis (L.) Trev. *Betony*

Native. Heathy pastures and open woodland. Frequent, especially on the coal measures. All Divs.

First Record: C. Deering, *Cat. Stirp*. 1738.

Galeopsis speciosa Mill. *Large Hemp Nettle*

Native. Arable fields, especially on peat. Formerly rather frequent (see G. Howitt), now chiefly found on the Carrs. All Divs.

First Record: C. Merrett, *Pinax* 1667.

1 Harworth Carr.
2 Between Scrooby and Sherwood Forest, *Merrett*; Mansfield, *Deering*; Farnsfield, *Ordoyno*; Gringley Carr†; Everton Carr†; Misson†, *Miller*; Harworth; Between Hesley Hall and Limpool, *Mrs. Sandwith*.

3 Langford; North Wheatley; Misterton†, *Carr MS.*; Farndon; Stockwith; South Collingham; Spalford; Colwick.
4 Barnby; Balderton; Coddington, *Ordoyno*; Wigsley.

Galeopsis Tetrahit agg. *Common Hemp Nettle*

Native. Fields and waste places. Very common. All Divs.

First Record: C. Deering, *Cat. Stirp.* 1738.

Galeopsis dubia Leers. *Downy Hemp Nettle*

Native. Arable fields. Very rare or extinct. Divs. 2, 3, 4.

First Record: W. Hudson, *Fl. Anglica* 1762.

2 Farnsfield, *Ordoyno*; Near Annesley, *Eddison*; Oxton Forest, *G. Howitt*; Kirkby, *Gilbert*; Everton Carr 1918, *Mrs. Sandwith.*
3 Near Newark, *Hudson.*
4 Balderton; Barnby; Coddington, *Ordoyno.*

Galeopsis angustifolia Ehrh. *Narrow leafed Hemp Nettle*

Native. Arable fields on clay or peat. Local and now rare. Divs. 3, 4.

First Record: G. Howitt, *Notts. Fl.* 1839.

3 Walesby.
4 West Leake, *G. Howitt, Carr*; East Leake; Owthorpe†; Colston Bassett; Granby; Orston; Alverton, *Carr MS.*; Staunton; Kilvington; Cropwell Bishop; Coddington.

Leonurus Cardiaca L. *Motherwort*

Alien. Casual or Denizen. Waste places and near gardens. Rare. Divs. 1, 2, 3.

1 Basford; Broxtowe, *Deering*; Between Tickhill and Worksop, *Hudson* (*Smith Engl. Fl. III*); Mansfield, *Ordoyno*; Greasley, *G. Howitt.*
2 Lenton, *Deering*; Clipstone, 1896 and 1905, *Carr MS.*
3 Three Mile House between Newark and Lincoln, *Ordoyno*; Nottingham Dump 1958.

Lamium album L. *White Deadnettle*

Native. Roadsides and waste places. Common. All Divs.

First Record: C. Deering, *Cat. Stirp.* 1738, "Very common about Hedges and Banks."

Lamium maculatum L. *Spotted Deadnettle*

Alien. Occasionally naturalised by roadsides. Divs. 1, 4.

First Record: Rempstone 1954 et seq., Stanford road side.

1 Pleasley Vale.
4 Rempstone.

Lamium purpureum L. *Red Deadnettle*

Native. Roadsides, arable and waste land. Very common. All Divs.

First Record: C. Deering, *Cat. Stirp*. 1738.

Lamium hybridum Vill. *Cut leaved Deadnettle*

Native. Arable land on light soils. Locally frequent, especially on the Carrs. Divs. 2, 3.

First Record: G. Howitt, *Notts. Fl.* 1839, Appendix.

2 Misson; Ranskill.
3 Frequent in the Trent Valley, especially in the North.

Lamium amplexicaule L. *Henbit*

Native. Arable land. Frequent on the light soils of Divs. 2, 3, 4, rare in Div. 1.

First Record: C. Deering, *Cat. Stirp*. 1738.

1 Bulwell, *Carr MS., Butcher.*

Lamium Galeobdolon Crantz. *Yellow Archangel*

Native. Woods and shady banks. Locally common. Divs. 1, 2, 3.

First Record: C. Deering, *Cat. Stirp*. 1738.

1 and 3 Common.
2 Annesley, *Carr MS.*; Newstead.

Ballota nigra L. *Black Horehound*

Native. Hedges and waste ground. Common. All Divs.

First Record: C. Deering, *Cat. Stirp*. 1738.

Teucrium Scorodonia L. *Wood Sage*

Native. Bushy places on light soil. Locally common. All Divs.

First Record: C. Deering, *Cat. Stirp*. 1738.

1 Frequent on the coal measures.
2 Common.
3 Bothamsall; West Drayton, *Carr MS.*; Wigsley.
4 Common on the gravels east of the Trent.

Teucrium Chamaedrys L.

Only Record: H. C. Watson *N.B.G.* 1835, from Cooper's Catalogue with specimen.

Ajuga reptans L. *Bugle*

Native. Moist woods and pastures. Common, but less so in Div. 2. All Divs.

First Record: C. Deering, *Cat. Stirp*. 1738.

PLANTAGINACEAE

Plantago indica L.

Alien. A rare casual. Div. 3.

First Record: A. R. Horwood, *B.E.C. Rept.* 1915.

3 Kingston-on-Soar, *Horwood*; Nottingham Dump 1960, 1962.

Plantago Coronopus L. *Buck's Horn Plantain*

Native. Heaths and gravelly paths. Locally frequent. All Divs.

First Record: C. Deering, *Cat. Stirp.* 1738.

1 Hills and Holes quarry, Warsop.
2 Common.
3 Kelham; North Muskham; Cromwell; Eaton, *Carr MS.*; Rolleston; Besthorpe; North Clifton; Spalford; Girton.
4 Turf Moor near Brough.

Plantago lanceolata L. *Ribwort*

Native. Grassland and banks. Very common. All Divs.

First Record: C. Deering, *Cat. Stirp.* 1738.

Plantago media L. *Hoary Plantain*

Native. Grassland on basic soils. Frequent except in Div. 2. All Divs.

First Record: C. Deering, *Cat. Stirp.* 1738.

2 Rainworth.

Plantago major L. *Greater Plantain*

Native. Roadsides, farmyards, grassland. Very common. All Divs.

First Record: C. Deering, *Cat. Stirp.* 1738.

Littorella uniflora (L.) Aschers. *Shoreweed*

Native. Gravelly margins of pools. Very rare. Divs. 1, 2.

First Record: G. Howitt, *Notts. Fl.* 1839.

1 Greasley Reservoir per *J. Percy, G. Howitt.* Still there.
2 Oxton Bogs, per *Mr. Valentine, G. Howitt.*

ILLECEBRACEAE

Herniaria glabra L. *Rupture Wort*

Native. Damp gravelly ground. Extinct. Div. 3.

Only Record: T. Ordoyno, *Fl. Nott.* 1807 "Quonce Close, Newark and Sandy closes thence towards Hawton."

J. W. Carr says Ordoyno meant *Aphanes arvensis*, which is mean. Sconce Close would be rather dry for *Herniaria* now, but must have been much damper in Ordoyno's day when it grew *Anagallis tenella* etc.

Herniaria hirsuta L.

Alien. A rare casual. Div. 3.

Only Record: H. Fisher, *Rept. Brit. Ass.* 1893. Included in list of aliens on wharfs, railway banks and river dredgings as very scarce.

Sceleranthus perennis L.

A rare casual Div. 3.

Only Record: H. Fisher *Rept. Brit. Ass.* 1893. Included in list of aliens on wharfs, railway banks and river dredgings as very scarce.

T. H. Cooper's record in the *New Botanist's Guide* 1835 is completely unsubstantiated.

Sceleranthus annuus L. *Annual Knawel*

Native. Sandy fields. Locally common. All Divs.

First Record: C. Deering, *Cat. Stirp.* 1738.

1 Trowell; Harworth.
2 Common.
3 and 4 Common on the blown sand and occasional on light land elsewhere.

var *biennis* Reuter. 2 Manton Forest, near Worksop, *Roffey*.

AMARANTHACEAE

Amaranthus retroflexus L.

Alien. A rare casual. Div. 3.

First Record: *Victoria County History* 1906, Div. 3 in square brackets.

3 Kingston-on-Soar, *Horwood*; Nottingham Dump.

(**Amaranthus Blitum** L. is recorded in the Victoria County History 1906 in square brackets.)

CHENOPODIACEAE

Chenopodium rubrum L. *Red Goosefoot*

Native. Farmyards, pit dumps and a weed on organic soils. Rather common. All Divs.

First Record: C. Deering, *Cat. Stirp.* 1738.

Chenopodium Bonus Henricus L. *Good King Henry*

Alien. Denizen. Roadsides near houses. Widespread and well-established, though not common. All Divs.

First Record: C. Deering, *Cat. Stirp*. 1738.

Chenopodium hybridum L. *Sowbane*

?Alien. Gardens and waste ground. Rare. Div. 3.

First Record: H. Fisher, *Tr. Nott. Nats*. 1904, 'Occurs as an alien about Newark.'

It still occurs as a weed in several Newark gardens, as Potterdyke, *Leather* 1936; Victoria Street 1951 et seq.

Chenopodium urbicum L. *Upright Goosefoot*

Alien. A rare casual. Div. 3.

Only Record: H. Fisher, *Tr. Nott. Nats*. 1904, 'Occurs as an alien about Newark.'

var *intermedium* Moq.

3 Kingston-on-Soar, *Carr* 1907; Stoke Bardolph Sewage Farm, *Williams*.

Chenopodium murale L. *Nettle Leaved Goosefoot*

?Native. Waste places. Rare. Divs. 1, 2, 3.

First Record: C. Deering, *Cat. Stirp*. 1738.

1 Canal Bridge, Woodend, Shireoaks; Lady Lee Quarry, Worksop, *Brown*.

2 Dunghills near Nottingham Gallows, *Deering*; Common in the vicinity of Nottingham (and 3?), *G. Howitt*.

3 Kingston-on-Soar, *Horwood*; Nottingham Dump 1958 et seq.; Weed in the gardens of Flintham Hall.

Chenopodium opulifolium Schrad.

Alien. Waste places. Rare. Div. 3.

First Record: H. Fisher, *Rept. Brit. Ass*. 1893.

3 Newark, *Fisher*; Nottingham Meadows, *Carr MS.*; Kingston-on-Soar, *Horwood*.

Chenopodium album L. *Fat Hen*

Native. Arable land and waste ground. Very common. All Divs.

First Record: C. Deering, *Cat. Stirp*. 1738.

Chenopodium ficifolium Sm. *Fig leaved Goosefoot*

Denizen or Native. Waste places and arable land. Local. Divs. 2, 3.

First Record: Misterton 1954.

2 Misson.
3 Common on the Trent banks and adjoining arable fields.

Chenopodium glaucum L.

A rare casual. Div. 2.

Only Record: J. W. Carr MS., "Abundant where manure was tipped in a green lane between Misson and Idle Stop."

Chenopodium Vulvaria L. *Stinking Goosefoot*

Native. Waste places. Rare. Divs. 2, 3.

First Record: C. Deering, *Cat. Stirp.* 1738.

2 Between Chapple Bar and the sandhills (Nottingham), *Deering*; Between Radford Forest and the Church, *Jowett.*
3 Halam, *Becher*; Nottingham Lammas Fields, *Jowett*; Kingston-on-Soar, *Horwood.*

Chenopodium polyspermum L. *Many seeded Goosefoot*

Native. Arable land, particularly on peat soils. Locally frequent. All Divs.

First Record: T. Jowett, *Bot. Cals.* 1826.

1 Eastwood; Radford, *Jowett*; Trowell; Welbeck.
2 Hesley, *Gibbons.*
3 'An alien at Newark', *Fisher*; Cottam; North Collingham; Balderton; Nottingham Dump; Farndon; Bunny.
4 Frequent.

Beta maritima L. *Sea Beet*

Extinct. Div. 2.

First Record: J. Sherard in *Dillenian Ed. of Ray's Synopsis* 1724.

2 "This does not only grow in maritime Places and Salt Marshes, but in divers Grounds about this Town, on several parts of Nottingham Common, by the Roadside from the Workhouse to the Forest etc.," *Deering.* Extinct by G. Howitt's time.

var. *Rapa* *Sugar Beet*

Occurs on road sides and headlands but does not persist.

Atriplex littoralis L. *Grass leaved Orache*

A rare casual. Div. 3.

First Record: H. Fisher, *Rept. Brit. Ass.* 1893.

3 About Newark, *Fisher*; Nottingham Dump 1960 and 61.

Atriplex patula L. *Common Orache*

Native. Arable land and waste places. Very common. All Divs.

First Record: C. Deering, *Cat. Stirp.* 1738.

var *bracteata* Westerld. is very common.

Atriplex hastata L.

Native. Arable land and waste ground. Very common. All Divs.

First Record: J. W. Carr, *Victoria County History* 1906.

Atriplex deltoidea Bab.

A rare casual. Div. 3.

Only Record: H. Fisher, Newark, in *Carr MS.*

Atriplex hortensis L. *Garden Orache*

Alien. Waste places. Rare. Divs. 3, 4.

First Record: Mill Gate Dump, Newark 1949.

3 Newark; Hawton; Farndon; Nottingham Dump.
4 Coddington.

The plant is usally var *rubra* (Crantz) Roth.

POLYGONACEAE

Polygonum Convolvulus L. *Black Bindweed*

Native. Arable land and waste places. Common. All Divs.

First Record: C. Deering, *Cat. Stirp.* 1738.

Polygonum Bistorta L. *Bistort*

Native. Damp meadows. Rather frequent. Divs. 1, 2, 3.

First Record: C. Deering, *Cat. Stirp.* 1738.

1 and 2 Rather frequent.
3 Wellow, *Friend*; Fields by the Dover Beck, Gonalston†; Caythorpe; Eakring, *Carr MS.*; Graves Lane, Edingley.

Polygonum amphibium L. *Amphibious Bistort*

Native. Still waters and damp places. Common, least so in Div. 4. All Divs.

First Record: C. Deering, *Cat. Stirp.* 1738.

var *terrestre* Leers. is as common as the type.

Polygonum lapathifolium L. *Pale Persicaria*

Native. Arable fields. Common. All Divs.

First Record: T. Jowett, *Bot. Cals.* 1826.

Polygonum Persicaria L. *Persicaria, Pig Grass*
Native. Arable fields and bare damp ground. Very common. All Divs.

First Record: C. Deering, *Cat. Stirp.* 1738.

Polygonum nodosum Pers.
Native. Arable fields. Distribution imperfectly known.

First Record: Misson 1955. Div. 2.

Polygonum Hydropiper L. *Waterpepper*
Native. Near ponds and in damp places. Common. All Divs.

First Record: C. Deering, *Cat. Stirp.* 1738.

Polygonum mite Schrank.
Native. Damp places. Rare. Divs. 2, 3.

First Record: Sp. in Lincoln Museum from Herb. Canon R. E. G. Cole.

2 Nottingham Church Cemetery, *Bohler*; Everton Carr, *Mrs. Sandwith*; Near R. Idle, Misson, *Brown*.
3 Willow Holts near Radcliffe-on-Trent, *Cole*. Osier Holt at Wilford; Beeston, *Carr* 1903 and 1909.

Polygonum minus Huds.
Native. Damp places. Rare. Divs. 2, 3.

First Record: C. Deering, *Cat. Stirp.* 1738.

2 Near the Idle at Misson†, *Brown*.
3 Sneinton field, *Deering*; Ditches between Nottingham and Lenton, *Jowett*.

Polygonum aviculare agg. *Knotgrass*
Native. Arable land and paths. Very common and resistant to spray. All Divs.

First Record: C. Deering, *Cat. Stirp.* 1738.

No work has been done on the segregate species.

Polygonum cuspidatum Sieb. and Zucc.
Alien. Roadsides and waste places. Well established and rather frequent. All Divs.

First Record: Roadside near Mattersey old bridge 1952.

Polygonum sachalinense Schmidt.
Alien. Damp ground and stream sides. Uncommon. Divs. 1, 2, 3.

First Record: Well established by the canal at Wiseton 1952.

1 Welbeck.
2 East Kirkby; Several places in Welbeck Park.
3 Wiseton.

Polygonum baldschuanicum Regel. *Russian Vine*

Alien. Waste places. Divs. 2, 3. Established in several places round Nottingham.

Fagopyrum esculentum Moenche. *Buckwheat*

Alien. Occurs as a casual when sown for game. Infrequent. Divs. 2, 3, 4.

First Record: C. Deering, *Cat. Stirp.* 1738. "Not commonly met with either wild or cultivated . . . sown on Clifton Hill."

2 Sir Richard Sutton's Temple on Sherwood Forest, *Ordoyno*; near Wollaton, *Jowett*; Blidworth; Clumber Park, *Carr MS.*
3 Clifton Hill, *Deering*; Wigsley.
4 Turf Moor, Brough.

Oxyria amaranthoides L.

A rare casual. Div. 3.

Only Record: A. R. Horwood, *B.E.C. Rept.* 1915, Trent Meadows.

Rumex hydrolapathum Huds. *Great Water Dock*

Native. Banks of canals, gravel pits, etc. Frequent except in Div. 4. All Divs.

First Record: C. Deering, *Cat. Stirp.* 1738.

4 Thorney† *Carr MS.*

Rumex crispus L. *Curled Dock*

Native. Damp grassland and waste places. Very common. All Divs.

First Record: C. Deering, *Cat. Stirp.* 1738.

Rumex obtusifolius L. *Broad leaved Dock*

Native. Roadsides, farmyards, waste places. Very common. All Divs.

First Record: C. Deering, *Cat. Stirp.* 1738.

Rumex sanguineus L. *Red veined Dock*

Native. Hedges and woods. Frequent. All Divs.

First Record: C. Deering, *Cat. Stirp.* 1738.

Rumex conglomeratus Murr. *Clustered Dock*

Native. Roadsides, meadows and waste places. Very common. All Divs.

First Record: C. Deering, *Cat. Stirp.* 1738.

Rumex pulcher L. *Fiddle Dock*

Native. Very rare. Div. 2.

Only Records: G. Howitt, *Notts. Fl.* 1839, "Nottingham Park and near Radford Church."

Rumex palustris Sm. *Marsh Dock*

Native. Damp bare ground. Local and less common than the next. Divs. 2, 3.

First Record: J. Salt, *List of Plants about Sheffield*, *c.*1800.

2 Everton Common, *Herb. Salt*; Warping Drain, Misson, *Carr* 1909. By the bridge at the end of Clumber Park, *Rose*.
3 Gringley Carr, *Miller*; Farndon; Stoke Bardolph Sewage Farm; Besthorpe Gravel Pit.

Rumex maritimus L. *Golden Dock*

Native. Bare ground, near ponds and gravel pits. Locally frequent, particularly in the tidal part of the Trent Valley. Divs. 1, 2, 3.

First Record: C. Deering, *Cat. Stirp.* 1738.

1 Moor Green; Martin's Pond, Wollaton; Jacksdale.
2 Wollaton Park, *Gilbert*; Misson.
3 By the Leen at Sneinton, *Deering*; Clifton (by Nottingham), *Jowett*; Gringley Carr, *Miller*; Collingham†, *D. Bradley*; Besthorpe; Littleborough; Dunham; Ragnall; Rolleston; Adbolton; Girton; Farndon.

Rumex Acetosa L. *Sorrel*

Native. Meadows and grassland. Very common. All Divs.

First Record: C. Deering, *Cat. Stirp.* 1738.

Rumex Acetosella L. *Sheep Sorrel*

Native. Sandy meadows and fields, heaths. Very common on all light lands. All Divs.

First Record: C. Deering, *Cat. Stirp.* 1738.

Rumex tenuifolia (Walh.) Löve.

Native. On the driest sands. Local. All Divs.

First Record: Heath behind Normanton Inn, Clumber, *R. W. Butcher* 1951.

1 Railway line at Styrupp.
2 Frequent.
3 Frequent on the blown sand.
4 Thorney; Coddington; Barnby.

THYMELAEACEAE

Daphne Laureola L. *Spurge Laurel*

Native. Woods on heavy soils. Locally common. Divs. 1, 3, 4.

First Record: C. Deering, *Cat. Stirp.* 1738.

1 Woods near Beauvale, *G. Howitt*; Shireoaks†, *Bohler.*
3 Frequent.
4 Langar†, *Crabbe*; Hedges at Owthorpe, *Jowett, Williams*; Colston Bassett; Staunton.

LORANTHACEAE

Viscum album L. *Mistletoe*

Native. Local. Divs. 2, 3.

First Record: C. Deering, *Cat. Stirp.* 1738.

2 Budby; Edwinstowe, *Friend*; Thoresby Park on old Thorns (now also on lime); Oldcotes, *Carr MS.*; Hesley on Populus, Hawthorn, Apple and *Crataegus crus-galli, Dallman*; Clumber Park on Thorn; Hodsock on thorn and *Robinia Pseud-Acacia.*
3 Thorney wood, Nottingham, *Deering*; Orchards at Halam, *Ordoyno*, (now on poplar); Bingham Road; Chilwell, *Gilbert*; Winkburn, everywhere, on thorn, lime, elm, poplar and crab; East Markham on poplar.

EUPHORBIACEAE

Euphorbia platyphyllos L. *Broad Spurge*

Native. Cornfields. Very rare. Div. 4.

Only Record: J. W. Carr, *Tr. Nott. Nats.* 1905. "Cornfields at West Leake."

Euphorbia Helioscopia L. *Sun Spurge*

Native. Arable land and waste places. Common. All Divs.

First Record: C. Deering, *Cat. Stirp.* 1738.

Euphorbia Amygdaloides L. *Wood Spurge*

Native. Woods. Extinct. Div. 3.

Only Record: C. Deering, *Cat. Stirp.* 1738, Colwick Wood.

Euphorbia virgata Walst. and Kit.

Alien. A rare casual. Div. 2.

Only Record: Rubbish Tip at Ranskill 1952.

Euphorbia Cyparissias L. var *major* Koch. *Cyprus Spurge*

A rare alien. Div. 1.

Only Record: Derelict ornamental woodland at Park Hall near Mansfield.

Euphorbia peplus L. *Petty Spurge*

Native. Arable land and waste places. Very common. All Divs.

First Record: C. Deering, *Cat. Stirp.* 1738.

Euphorbia exigua L. *Dwarf Spurge*

Native. Arable fields on basic and clay soils. Locally frequent. All Divs.

First Record: C. Deering, *Cat. Stirp.* 1738.

1 Between Mansfield and Pleasley, *Deering*; Frequent, *Carr*; Shireoaks; Watnall; Huthwaite; Nuthall.
2 Bramcote, *Butcher*.
3 and 4 Very frequent.

Euphorbia Lathyrus L. *Caper Spurge*

Alien. A persistent weed in old gardens.

First Record: *Victoria County History* 1906.

3 Upton Mill, *Leather*; Tolerated at Farndon for sixty years.

(**Buxus sempervirens** L. *Box*

This has been included in all Notts. lists since Deering, no localities are given. It is nowhere even naturalised.)

Mercuralis perennis L. *Dog's Mercury*

Native. Woods and hedges. Common, least so in Div. 2. All Divs.

First Record: C. Deering, *Cat. Stirp.* 1738.

Mercuralis annua L. *Annual Mercury*

Casual. Garden and field weed. Very rare or extinct. Div 3.

First Record: T. Ordoyno, *Fl. Nott.* 1807.

3 'In gardens; Newark; Southwell,' *Ordoyno*; Lammas Fields, Nottingham, *Jowett*.

ULMACEAE

The Elms are a muddlesome lot, most of them looking much the same, though very variable in habit. The lower branches are generally trimmed off, so to get reasonable specimens for identification it is usual to stand on the roof of the car and use ten foot tree pruners. Our thanks are due to Dr. Melville who has taken so much trouble with our specimens. In Notts. the interesting Elms grow mostly in the South and East. This area, contained in Divs. 3 and 4, borders the rich elm country of the Midland Shires. South of the Trent particularly in Div. 4, there is much woodland with a canopy of almost pure elm. These woods are mostly very dull, growing few of the rarer woodland plants found on the clays. The Bunter block has few elms except those planted round the Dukeries. It seems to form a barrier to the spread of species further North and West. We have few records from Div. 1. C. Deering (1738) thought it was to be doubted whether elms were "of the Natural Growth of these Parts" but seemed "to be Favourites with several Gentlemen in this Neighbourhood, who take Delight to plant them about their Lordships preferably to any other Trees."

Ulmus glabra Huds. *Wych Elm*

Native. Woods and hedges. Very common. All Divs.

First Record: C. Deering, *Cat. Stirp.* 1738.

Ulmus x elegantissima Horwood *U. glabra x Plotii.*

Native. Hedges and woods. Locally frequent. Divs. 2, 3, 4.

First Record: Owthorpe, May 1952, det. R. Melville.

2 Scrooby.
3 Averham; Kneesall; Spalford; Wiverton; Flintham; Caythorpe.
4 Owthorpe; Rempstone; Widmerpool; Upper Broughton.

Ulmus glabra x Plotii x Coritana

Only Record: Cottam. Div. 3, det. R. Melville.

Ulmus procera Salisb. *English Elm*

Denizen. Woods and hedges.

The older botanists, including Prof. Carr, considered this species common. This has definitely not been our experience. The lush trees one associates with this species are not at all typical of the Notts. countryside. All Divs.

First Record: C. Deering, *Cat. Stirp.* 1738.

Modern Records:
1 Welbeck.
2 Bramcote, *Butcher*; Lane behind Normanton Inn; Osberton.
3 Stanford-on-Soar, *Butcher*; Elston Towers.
4 Thorney.

Ulmus stricta (Ait.) Lindl. *Cornish Elm*

Frequently planted in parks and hedges

Ulmus Coritana Melville.

Native. Hedges. Rare. Div. 4.

Only Record: Hedges near the Honeybutts, Owthorpe 1959, "a variety towards var. *angustifolia*" det. R. Melville.

Ulmus x hollandica Mill. *U. coritana x glabra.* *Dutch Elm*

Native. Hedges. Uncommon. Div. 3.

Only Records: Farndon, by the Blue Bell 1955; East Bridgeford 1957.

Ulmus Coritana x Plotii

Native. Hedges. Uncommon. Divs. 3, 4.

First Record: Sutton Bonington 1955.

3 Sutton Bonington.
4 Hedges by Bellrock mine, Staunton; Upper Broughton.

Ulmus carpinifolia Gled. *Smooth leaved Elm*

Native. Plantations and Spinneys. Rare. Divs. 2, 3.

First Record: C. Deering, *Cat. Stirp.* 1738.

2 Bramcote, *Jowett*, "Now nearly extirpated with building and the Elm disease," *Butcher*; Red Hill (Arnold); Near Farnsfield, *G. Howitt.*
3 Roadside spinney, Flintham.

Ulmus x vegeta (Loud.) A. Ley *U. carpinifolia x glabra.*

Native. Hedges. Uncommon. Divs. 3, 4.

First Record: East Stoke, Fosse Road side 1953, det. R. Melville.

3 East Stoke.
4 Rempstone; Staunton.

Ulmus carpinifolia x Plotii x ? glabra

Only Record: Spinney on Fosse Road side, Flintham, 1957. Div. 3. det. R. Melville.

Ulmus Plotii Druce *Plot's Elm*

Native. Hedges. Frequent in Div. 3. Divs. 3, 4.

First Record: Fosse Road side, Farndon 1953, det. R. Melville.

3 Fosse Road side Farndon and Flintham; Southwell; Winthorpe; Girton; Granby; Hoveringham; Edingley.
4 Coddington.

URTICACEAE

Humulus Lupulus L. *Wild Hop*

Native, though formerly cultivated especially round Southwell. Damp hedges, woods and willow holts. Common. All Divs.

First Record: C. Deering, *Cat. Stirp.* 1738.

Cannabis sativa L. *Hemp*

A rare alien. Rubbish Dumps. Divs. 1, 3.

First Record: Kimberley Dump 1957.

1 Kimberley.
3 Nottingham Dump 1958 et seq.; Newark Dump 1960.

Ficus Carica L. *Fig Tree*

Alien. Waste places in towns, river and canal sides. Widespread. Divs. 1, 2, 3.

First Record: Canal side at Retford 1952.

Urtica dioica L. *Stinging Nettle*

Native. Hedges, woods, waste places. Very common. All Divs.

First Record: C. Deering, *Cat. Stirp*. 1738.

Urtica urens L. *Annual Nettle*

Native. Arable land and waste ground, especially on light soil. Common. All Divs.

First Record: C. Deering, *Cat. Stirp*. 1738.

Urtica pilulifera L. *Roman Nettle*

An evanescent species occuring in the imaginations of some botanists, and occasionally in the herbaria of the more horticulturally minded.

Parietaria diffusa Mert. and Koch. *Pellitory-of-the-Wall*

Native. Old walls and rocks. Locally frequent. Divs. 1, 2, 3.

First Record: C. Deering, *Cat. Stirp*. 1738.

1 Beauvale Priory; Cresswell Crags†, *Carr MS.*; Brinsley.
2 Nottingham Castle Rock†, *Deering*; Ordsall railway crossing; Blyth, *Carr MS.*; Worksop Priory.
3 Common, especially on skerry walls in the Trent Valley.

Helxine Solierolii Req.

Alien. This pestilential plant has been injudiciously introduced in many gardens, where it has become quite ineradicable.

MYRICACEAE

Myrica Gale L. *Bog Myrtle*

Native. Boggy woods. Very rare. Divs. 2, 3.

First Record: T. Ordoyno, *Fl. Nott*. 1807.

2 Sutton Wood, near Retford, *Ordoyno*, per *Dr. Mason*.
3 Wigsley Wood, *Cole*. Still persists in considerable quantity.

CUPULIFERAE

Betula pendula Roth. *Silver Birch*

Native. Woods and heaths on light soils. Common. All Divs.

First Record: C. Deering, *Cat. Stirp.* 1738.

Betula pubescens Ehrh.

Native. Damp woodland on light soils. Local. All Divs.

First Record: J. W. Carr, *Tr. Nott. Nats.* 1904.

1 Common on the Coal Measures.
2 Still occurs on the remaining damp areas on the Forest.
3 Spalford; Girton.
4 Langford Moor; Thorney.

Alnus glutinosa (L.) Gaertn. *Alder*

Native. Streamsides and wet woods. Common, less so in Div. 4.

First Record: C. Deering, *Cat. Stirp.* 1738.

Carpinus Betulus L. *Hornbeam*

Denizen. Planted in woods and near large houses. Not infrequent. Divs. 2, 3, 4.

First Record: C. Deering, *Cat. Stirp.* 1738, "This is rather a nursery than a common Tree, and is only raised by Gentlemen about their Seats."

2 The Dukeries; Nottingham Church Cemetery, *Bohler*; Hesley, *Gibbons*; In several woods on the Welbeck estate; Rufford; Many places on the Osberton estate.
3 Clifton (by Nottingham), *Gilbert*; Normanton-by-Southwell; Gonalston.
4 Rempstone; Brown Wood, Thorney.

Corylus Avellana L. *Hazel*

Native. Woods and hedges. Common, less so in Div. 2. All Divs.

First Record: C. Deering, *Cat. Stirp.* 1738.

Quercus Robur L. *Oak*

Native. Woods and hedges. Common. All Divs.

First Record: C. Deering, *Cat. Stirp.* 1738.

Quercus x intermedia Boenn. *Q. Robur x sessiliflora.*

Occurs where *Q. sessiliflora* is frequent. On the blown sand, the hybrid appears to be more frequent than *Q. sessiliflora.*

First Record: J. Sidebotham, *Phytol.* 1842.

Quercus sessiliflora Salisb. *Durmast Oak*

Native. Woods. Frequent on the Sherwood Forest, rare elsewhere. All Divs.

First Record: C. Deering, *Cat. Stirp.* 1738.

1 Welbeck.
2 J. Hopkinson, 1927, records a proportion of 35% *sessiliflora* 57·4% *robur* and 7·6% hybrids among oaks. Among younger 'semi-planted trees' in Birklands, 53% *sessiliflora*, 40% *robur*. These would still seem reasonable proportions on the Forest, though much old oak wood has now been replanted with conifers.
3 Clifton (by Nottingham) *G. Howitt.*
4 Thorney, *Posnet*; Wigsley.

Quercus Cerris L. *Turkey Oak*

Alien. Widely planted both as an ornamental and forestry tree. It regenerates freely. Frequent, especially in Div. 2. All Divs.

First Record: Regenerating freely on Coddington Moor 1950.

Quercus Ilex L. *Evergreen Oak*

Alien. Rarely planted, and only as an ornamental tree, most of the large estates have a few specimens.

Quercus rubra Duroi (non L.) *Red Oak*

Alien. Increasingly planted by both the Forestry Commission and private owners on light land, especially the Sherwood Forest. The plantations are still very young.

Castanea sativa Mill. *Sweet Chestnut*

Alien. Denizen. Woods and hedges. Formerly frequently planted, especially on light soils. Common on the Coal Measures of Div. 1 and in Div. 2; less so in Divs. 3 and 4. Some of the large estates have fine mature timber, and it regenerates freely (where the public are not too ravenous), but does not now appear to be so much planted for forestry. All Divs.

First Record: C. Deering, *Cat. Stirp.* 1738, "very commonly observed about Nottingham, there are some by the Engine House and in St. Peter's Church Yard."

Juglans regia L. *Walnut*

Alien. Planted near houses. Becoming rare owing to the value of its timber.

Fagus sylvatica L. *Beech*

Denizen. Woods, parks and hedges. Widely planted round country estates, especially on the Sherwood Forest. Recently the Forestry Commission have started planting large stands of beech in strong woodland that was previously oak, and both the Commission and the private owners favour beech as a broad leafed tree on the Forest. It regenerates freely. All Divs.

First Record: C. Deering, *Cat. Stirp*. 1738. "This Tree is almost a Stranger in these parts, and I have not observed any near this Town, except within Woollaton Garden Walls, but many large ones grow at Rufford in Sir George Saville's Park."

Salix Nottinghamshire is probably one of the best counties in England for Willows. The Trent Valley had at one time a thriving basket making industry and every riverside village had its willow holt. This industry suffered a set-back during the 1914-18 war owing to lack of labour, and never recovered, until now there are only a few osiers grown commercially in the county. At least three quarters of the holts have vanished or lie derelict. A few have been planted with poplar.

My holt at Farndon (11 acres) was last cut for basket willows in about 1925, after which it was let go derelict, a haunt for foxes, poaching cats and destructive children. We are now gradually clearing it, and replanting with poplar, Cricket-bat Willow and a collection of the more unusual native willow species and hybrids. It is one of the few places where *Salix Calodendron* has always grown.

Big Holt Stoke is now turned over to farm crops.

The holt at Brinkley, Southwell, was grubbed up and planted with poplar about 1954.

Attenborough Holt has turned into a gravel pit, but many interesting osiers still persist.

Bole and Burton Rounds, a scattered collection of small holts, are with one small exception now derelict, but with the trees still standing.

Lound Holt close to the Idle, one of the few holts outside the Trent Valley (about 6 acres), is now derelict but still contains an interesting collection of willows. It is the only holt in which we have seen *S. pentandra* cultivated as an osier, and one of the few with a stand of *S. basfordiana*. Here we first found *S. purpurea x triandra*.

Beckingham Holt, opposite Gainsborough, was kept in production up to the last war, and then closed down owing to labour shortage. This is the only holt in which we have seen *S. daphnoides*, and one of the few where *S. purpurea x triandra* does really well.

A few acres of willows, chiefly *S. viminalis*, are grown in fields at Cottam. Some of these are sent to Warrington to be made into large baskets coarse fishermen use, chiefly to sit on. Close by, a small holt by the railway, now derelict, contains *S. decipiens*. This beautiful tree also grows by streams and in small plantations all over the Osberton estate.

At one time willows were planted on the banks of the Trent to prevent erosion. There are many miles of willows, *S. viminalis* and *S. triandra*, on the tidal reaches. This procedure is now frowned on by the Trent River Board, who consider that the trees make an eddy, which removes the soil from behind the trees, allowing them to fall into the river. Thus the bank is eroded more quickly than if they had not been there.

Many small holts and corners of fields are planted with *S. fragilis*, pollarded and used originally for fencing. They are now often unkempt and partly blown down. On most of the larger estates there are a few acres given over to willows. These have been out of commission for many years and are now a refuge for foxes or a covert for pheasants, according to the outlook of the owner. The gravel pits which abound in the Trent Valley are quickly over-run with willows. These are mostly *S. cinerea* in its many shapes and forms, some *S. caprea* and *S. viminalis*, with a few hybrids.

With trees which have been cultivated for so long it is difficult to say which species are native. The holts of course are planted, also many rows of pollards, chiefly *S. fragilis* F. As willow is still used by farmers for fencing stakes, which easily root in moist soil, so you find astonishing hybrids miles from anywhere. These are not intentionally planted trees and in many places look native. Often well intentioned people, fishermen, bird watchers etc., push willow sticks into moist soil for obscure purposes. These always grow, and add to the confusion.

Bat Willow, *S. caerulea*, are grown in a few places in the county. Even with good management these often do not make the grade, though one or two fine stands have been marketed. Other than *S. caerulea* there is little outlet for willow timber; too small for the merchant, too explosive for firewood.

The soil of the Trent Valley is a sandy loam overlying river gravel, with a top soil of only two feet in many places. The PH Value is round about 7. Flooding is frequent and much of the land is termed wash land by the River Board.

Salix pentandra L. *Bay Willow*

Native on streamsides and in alder carr, particularly in the west of the county. It is planted for its ornamental value, and occasionally, as at Lound, as a basket willow.
Uncommon. All Divs.

First Record: T. Jowett's interleaved *Ordoyno* 1821.

1 Annesley Woodhouse; Sutton Dam, *G. Howitt*; Hills and Holes, Warsop M; Streamside Norwood, Teversall F.; Streamside, Sookholme.
2 Bank of the Leen between Nottingham and Lenton, *Jowett*; Oxton, *Sidebotham*; Nottingham Church Cemetery, *Bohler* 1866; Riverside below Worksop, *Bohler* 1875; Bestwood, *Carr MS.*; Wood at L Lake Rainworth, *Leather*; Conjure Alders, Bothamsall; Patmore Cover M.; Planted in Lings Wood, Scaftworth M.; Lound Willow Holt.
3 Streamside at Grave's Lane, Edingley; By the Maun, West Drayton.
4 Planted at Rempstone.

Salix fragilis agg. *Crack Willow*

First Record: T. Ordoyno, *Fl. Nott.* 1807.

var *fragilis*

3 A row of pollards by the Trent at Attenborough F.

var *Russelliana* (Sm.) Koch.

Native. Widely planted for fencing etc., but now neglected. Female only recorded. This is the common pollard willow in Notts. All Divs.

var *latifolia* Anders.

Planted? Rare. Divs. 1, 2, 3. Male only recorded.

1 In a small holt at Trowell, several pollards.
2 Budby Carr; Osberton Ash Holt.
3 Farndon.

Salix x cuspidata Schultz. *S. fragilis x pentandra.*

Planted? Rare.

1 Old quarry by the Maun at Mansfield M.
3 North Muskham railway bridge, two trees, M.

♂ **Salix decipiens** Hoffm. "White Dutch." *Varnished Willow*

Planted as a basket willow. Rare. Male only recorded.

First Record: T. Jowett, *Bot. Cals.* 1826, "Near Nottingham." Repeated by G. Howitt E.B. 1937.

2 Planted in willow holts and by streams all over the Osberton estate; Carlton-in-Lindrick.
3 A few trees in a willow holt by the railway at Cottam.

This tree is rather near *S. fragilis*, but not a hybrid between *fragilis* and *triandra* as some authorities have thought, and is best treated as a species.

Salix basfordiana Scaling. *Basford Willow*

This most ornamental tree first appeared as a seedling in the willow beds of Mr. William Scaling ("Ten years basket maker to her Majesty and the Royal Family") at Basford Notts, about 1870. Both male and female trees are recorded. Widely planted as an ornamental tree and grown by nurserymen for tying up parcels of trees. Recorded as an osier from:

2 Lound Holt M; Harworth.
3 Beckingham Holt M; Attenborough Holt and gravel pits F; Merryweather's Brinkley Nurseries, Southwell.

Salix sanguinea Scaling. "Belgian Reds". *Red Willow*

Introduced by Mr. William Scaling of Basford, Notts. from the Ardennes in 1863. Grown as an ornamental tree but less commonly than the last. Recorded as an osier from Beckingham Holt and occurs in Attenborough gravel pits. Div. 3. Notts. trees appear to be males. These two willows are mostly treated as varieties of *S. fragilis*, and may be hybrids between that species and *S. alba* var. *vitellina*, *S. basfordiana* being nearer *fragilis*; and *S. sanguinea*, from its habit and leaf characters, nearer *alba*.

Salix alba L. *White Willow*

Native. Hedges and streamsides. Widely planted for fencing etc., but now neglected. Common, but less so than *S. fragilis*. All Divs. First Record: C. Deering, *Cat. Stirp*. 1738.

var *regalis* Hort.

Planted in a few places, particularly the Dukeries. A few trees in a ballast pit by the Great North Line at Ranskill. Div. 2. Male only.

var *caerulea* (Sm.) Sm. *Cricket Bat Willow*

Grown in several places for its timber, especially in the Trent Valley. It is here at the northern limit of its commercial range, and while fine specimens have been seen, as at Thrumpton, most plantations are suffering from disease, frost or plain neglect. Female only, except for some rather strange trees planted by Newark Rowing Club. Divs. 2, 3, 4.

var *vitellina* (L.) Stokes. *Golden Willow*

First Record: G. Howitt, *Fl. Nott*. 1839, "In osier holts and moist hedges, common." E.B. 1389.

We have not been able to find this variety in the county. G. Howitt cannot have been confused with *S. basfordiana* which had not yet appeared. This is one of the toughest willows and was formerly used for tying by market gardeners and celery growers. Var *chrysostela* is grown ornamentally at Welbeck.

Salix chermesina Hartig. (*alba vitellina* var *britzensis* Späth.)

Planted as an ornamental tree but less commonly than *S. basfordiana.*

Salix x viridis Fries. *alba x fragilis.*

Native. Willow holts, hedges, gravel pits. Frequent, especially in the Trent Valley. All Divs.

First Record: T. Jowett, *Bot. Cals.* 1826.

Salix x chrysocoma Doell. (*alba vitellina x babylonica* L.)

The common Weeping Willow in this county. Planted in many places, especially the Dukeries.

Salix daphnoides Vill. *Violet Willow* "Violets"

Alien. Rare. Sometimes planted as an ornamental. Grown as a basket willow at Beckingham, Div. 3. Female.

Salix triandra L. *Almond-leafed Willow*

Native. Hedges, damp places, willow holts. Common in the Trent Valley, less so elsewhere. All Divs.

One of the commonest basket willows and found in every osier holt, it is a most variable species with many distinct varieties. Notts. willow growers favoured Black Maul, Pomeranian (imported by Mr. Scaling of Basford), Counsellor (chiefly in the south), Lincolnshire Dutch (especially round Gainsborough) and Black Holland.

var *concolor* Anders, and var *discolor* Anders. are both frequent.

var *Hoffmaniana* (Sm.) Bab. A small twiggy bush of little use to willow growers, occurs among the type.

var *amygdalina* L. "Whissenders" Grown in some willow holts chiefly in the northern part of the Trent Valley. Div. 3.

First Record: T. Jowett, *Bot. Cals.* 1826, Clifton (by Nottingham)†.

Salix x Hippophaefolia Thuill. *S. triandra x viminalis* 'Black Tops'

Hedges, willow holts, riversides. Local. Divs. 2, 3.

2 Lound Holt F.; Scaftworth M.; Misson F.; Finningley F.; Osberton M.;

3 Frequent.

Salix x Trevirani Sprengl. *S. triandra x viminalis.*

Only Record: H. Fisher, *Proc. Brit. Ass.* 1893, Newark M.

Salix undulata Ehrh. *S. triandra x viminalis?*

Frequent in willow holts in the Trent Valley and planted on the tidal reaches of the Trent bank. Rare elsewhere. Female only. Divs. 2, 3.

2 Scrooby, hedge in village.

Salix viminalis L. *Common Osier*

Native. Willow holts, damp hedges, gravel pits, swamps. Occurs in a variety of natural habitats and is the commonest osier in willow holts. 'Long Skein' and 'Brown Merrin' are grown in the Trent Valley. All Divs.

First Record: C. Deering, *Cat. Stirp.* 1738.

var *intricata* Leefe, with bifid stigmas occurs commonly with the type.

var *linarifolia* Wimmer occurs especially in the northern willow holts.

Salix x stipularis Sm. *S. viminalis x ?*

Native. Very rare. Divs. 2, 3.

2 Finningley gravel pits, det. Meikle.
3 Balderton gravel pits.

Salix petiolaris Sm. An American species recorded by T. Jowett for the saw yard in Colwick Park. Div. 3.

Salix purpurea sens. lat. *Purple Willow*

Doubtfully native. Willow holts, damp hedges and woods. Rather frequent, especially in the Trent Valley; 'Kecks' and 'Welsh' are grown.

var *Lambertiana* (Sm.) Koch.

The commonest variety of this species, both in willow holts and elsewhere. The female is rare. All Divs.

First Record: T. Jowett, *Bot. Cals.* 1826.

var *helix* Koch.

Found rarely in willow holts. Grown as 'Dicks' a fine basket willow, it was one of the first varieties to disappear from cultivation. A most distinctive plant breaking low into a twiggy bush even when it is allowed to grow freely without cutting. Male only. Divs. 2, 3, 4.

First Record: G. Howitt, *Notts. Fl.* 1839. E.B. 1343.

2 Lound Holt, a lot.
3 Brinkley Holt, Southwell; Big Holt, Thorpe; Herrod's Holt, North Collingham; Beeston; Bunny.
4 Rempstone Old Church Yard.

var *Woolgariana* Borrer, a robust form.

Only Record: Misson, a few trees in a hedge below the village. Div. 2.

var *pendula* Dippel. is grown round the lake at Scaftworth. Div. 2.

Salix x rubra Huds. *S. purpurea x viminalis.* *Green leafed Osier*

Willow holts, gravel pits, planted on the Trent bank in the tidal teach. Uncommon. There are two forms of the female, one with divaricate twigs and short stigma, the commoner with slender stigma and strict habit. Divs. 2, 3.

First Record: C. Deering, *Cat. Stirp.* 1738.

2 Lound Holt, F., both forms; Scrooby.
3 Wilford; Clifton, *Jowett*; West Drayton, *Butcher*; Brinkley Holt, Southwell M. and both types of F.; Besthorpe gravel pit F.; South Muskham; Attenborough gravel pit M. and F.; Bole Holts F.; Beckingham, river bank F.; Carlton-on-Trent Holt, M. and F.

Salix x Forbyana Sm. *S. purpurea x viminalis x ? cinerea.*

Willow Holts, hedges and damp places.

The female is common in the Trent Valley and frequent elsewhere. The male, previously unknown in Britain, was discovered at Attenborough by the river (Div. 3) in 1954, det. R. D. Meikle, and at Lound Willow Holt and by Rufford Lake, (Div. 2).

Salix purpurea x triandra

A few bushes of this rare hybrid were discovered in Lound Willow Holt, Div. 2, and named by R. D. Meikle. It was then found in quantity and fine condition at Beckingham Holt, Div. 3. An exactly similar bush is grown in the University of Bristol's experimental ground at Long Ashton, under the name of *S. Kirkii.* We have plants from all three sources in cultivation at Farndon. The bush is rather similar to *S. purpurea* var. *helix* in habit but more robust and with red twigs. The leafs reddish when young, approaching *S. triandra.* The flowers have the semi-conate filament typical of the hybrids of *S. purpurea.* Male only.

Salix Calodendron Wimmer. (*S. dasyclados* auct.)

Doubtfully native. Willow holts, riversides, by ponds.
A few plants in every willow holt and by many streams in the Trent Valley. Rare elsewhere. Female only. The Nottinghamshire plant is the same as those gown from cuttings kindly sent us by Mr. E. Swann from his type bushes at Holme-next-the-Sea. Divs. 3, 4.

First Record: T. Ordoyno, *Fl. Nott.* 1807, 'Thickets and wet places. G. Howitt, *Notts. Fl.* 1839, 'In moist situations, frequent.' As *S. acuminata* Sm.

3 Frequent.
4 Pond at Staunton; Kilvington.

Salix Caprea L. *Goat Willow*

Native. Woods and hedges, especially on clay, sometimes in gravel pits. Common, less so in Divs. 2 and 4. All Divs.

First Record: C. Deering, *Cat. Stirp.* 1738.

var *sphacelata* Sm.

Only Record: T. Jowett, *Bot. Cals.* 1826, "Bulwell Bogs", Div. 1 or 2.

Salix Caprea x cinerea occurs with the parents but not commonly—It often takes the form of a triple hybrid with *S. aurita.*

Salix x sericans Tausch. *S. Caprea x viminalis.*

Hedges and gravel pits. Frequent in Div. 3, less so elsewhere. The male is commoner than the female. Divs. 2, 3, 4.

First Record: Averham 1953. M.

2 Coxmoor near Kirkby; Finningley; Harworth; Bilby M.
3 Frequent on both clay and gravel. Female at Misterton.
4 Harby.

Salix cinerea sens. lat. *Common Sallow*

First Record: C. Deering, *Cat. Stirp.* 1738.

There is some confusion in this group. T. Jowett and G. Howitt record *S. cinerea* Sm. E.B. 1897 'rather common,' *S. aquatica* Sm. E.B. 1437 'Oxton Bogs,' *Jowett*, 'Not uncommon in many parts of the county', *G. Howitt*, *S. oleifolia* Sm. E.B. 1402 'Oxton Bogs,' *Jowett*. The present distribution appears to be as follows.

Salix cinerea L. var. *oleifolia* Gaud. (*S. atrocinerea* Brot.)

Native. Woods, hedges, gravel pits and all moist places. A very common willow especially on acid and sandy soils.

Salix cinerea L. (*S. aquatica* Sm.)

Native. Damp places in the Sherwood Forest. Rare or overlooked. Div. 2.

2 Marsh round Rufford Lake 1960 M. and F. det. R. D. Meikle; Thoresby Lake.

We are growing these plants, they may possibly turn into a form of *S. Caprea x cinerea* var. *oleifolia.*

Salix x geminata Forbes. *S. cinerea x viminalis.*

Hedges, gravel pits, moist ground. The commonest of the hybrids with *viminalis*. All Divs.

First Record: G. Howitt, *Notts. Fl.* 1839., as *S. Smithiana* Willd.

1 Nuthall; Shireoaks; Awsworth.
2 and 3 Very frequent.
4 Wysall; Rempstone.

Salix aurita L. *Eared Sallow*

Native. Damp acid ground. With the progressive drying out of the county this species has almost disappeared, and hybridised out with *S. cinerea*. Divs. 1, 2, 3.

First Record: C. Deering, *Cat. Stirp.* 1738, no locality.

1 Nuthall, *Jowett*.
2 Papplewick Forest; Bulwell (or 1), *Jowett*; Nottingham Forest, *Sidebotham*; Lindhurst Heath, *Hopkinson*; Laneside at Finningley. The only true bush we have seen in the county, it has now succumbed to road widening.
3 Morton Holt; Colwick, *G. Howitt*.

Salix aurita x cinerea.

Native. Moist heaths and hedges, gravel pits, woods. A very common and variable hybrid, some bushes coming quite close to true *aurita*. All Divs.

Salix x fruticosa Doell. *S. aurita x viminalis*.

Very rare. Div. 3.

Only Record: One tree in Besthorpe Old Brickyard, det. R. D. Meikle.

Salix nigricans Sm. var. *cotinifolia*.

Native. ?Extinct. Div. 2.

Only Record: G. Howitt, *Fl. Notts*. 1839, "On heaths and in woods; rare? Bulwell Forest, *Jowett*. Nr. Clipstone and Mansfield Woodhouse." E.B. 1810.

Salix repens sens. lat. *Creeping Willow*

Native. Moist heaths. Rare. Divs. 2, 3, 4.

First Record: C. Deering, *Cat. Stirp.* 1738.

2 Basford Scottum, *Deering*; Papplewick Forest, *Jowett*, *Carr*; Gravel pit, Sutton near Retford, *Carr*; Lyndhurst Heath, *Hopkinson*; Finningley gravel pits M.
3 Bothamsall, by the road to West Drayton opposite Lawn Covert; West Drayton; Gamston by Retford, *Carr MS.*; Spalford Warrens.
4 Lane leading to Stapleford Moors, *G. Howitt*. Still grows in fair quantity in this locality, i.e. Langford Moor, both male and female. Harby; Wigsley Wood, *Carr MS.*; Turf Moor, Collingham, M. and F.

Nottinghamshire material collected by us appears all to be the hybrid *S. argentea x repens*, often considered the common Creeping Willow inland. It is very variable, but the different forms, of leaf shape and habit, are quite inconstant in cultivation.

Salix argentea (Sm.) A. and G. Camus.

Native. Rare. Div. 4.

Only Record: Langford Moor 1951. Cuttings from this bush grown at Farndon have retained all the typical characters of the species.

(**Salix lapponum** L. var *pseudo glauca* is recorded by G. Howitt, *Fl. Notts.* 1839 as *S. glauca* E.B. 1810, following T. Jowett's (1826) record of *S. glauca.* Jowett's record is very ambiguous and this alpine species would not occur in Notts.)

Populus alba L. *White Poplar*

Alien. Occasionally planted in ornamental grounds.

First Record: C. Deering, *Cat. Stirp.* 1738. This record may refer to *P. canescens.*

Populus canescens Sm. *Grey Poplar*

Denizen. Moist woods and hedges. Frequent. All Divs.

First Record: G. Howitt, *Notts. Fl.* 1839.

Populus tremula L. *Aspen*

Native. Hedges and woods, especially on sand. Locally common. All Divs.

First Record: C. Deering, *Cat. Stirp.* 1738.

1 Shireoaks; Nether Langwith.
2 Wollaton Park, *Deering*; Ranby; Clumber; Rufford; Osberton.
3 Frequent.
4 Common on the gravels east of the Trent.

Populus nigra L. *Black Poplar*

Native or denizen. Rare. Distribution uncertain.

First Record: C. Deering, *Cat. Stirp.* 1738.

Populus italica (Duroi) Moench. *Lombardy Poplar*

Alien. Frequently planted as a specimen tree and in dreary rows.

Populus x serotina Hartig. *Black Italian Poplar*

Alien. Woods and hedges. Frequent and generally distributed. All Divs.

First Record: R. W. Butcher in Carr's MS. Flora, *c.*1950.

Populus x Eugenei Sim-Louis, *P. robusta* Schneid., *P. Wilsoni* Schneid. and other species, are being planted widely in moist woodland.

EMPETRACEAE

Empetrum nigrum L. *Crowberry*

Native. Bogs and damp heaths. Probably extinct. Div. 2.

First Record: T. Ordoyno, *Fl. Nott.* 1807.

2 Sherwood Forest, near Mansfield, *Ordoyno*; Fir plantation on the Derby Road, two miles from Mansfield; Rainworth; Oxton Forest, *Jowett*; Fountain Dale; Oxton Bogs, *G. Howitt*; Still at Oxton Bogs till 1920, when it was exterminated by gravel workings, *Carr MS.*

CERATOPHYLLACEAE

Ceratophyllum demersum L. *Hornwort*

Native. Ponds, canals and large drains. Common. All Divs.

First Record: T. Ordoyno, *Fl. Nott.* 1807.

Monocotyledones

HYDROCHARIDACEAE

Hydrocharis Morsus-Ranae L. *Frogbit*

Native. Ditches and pools. Uncommon. Divs. 2, 3.

First Record: C. Deering, *Cat. Stirp.* 1738.

2 Nottingham Park, *Deering*; Everton Carr†; Misson; Scaftworth†; Finningley, *Carr MS.*

3 Between Lenton and Beeston, *Deering*; Between Newark and Kelham, *Ordoyno*; Nottingham Meadows, *G. Howitt*; Beckingham, *Miller*; Mons Pool, Collingham, *Wooley*; Abundant about Newark; Averham; Cottam, *Carr MS.*; Spalford; Girton; South Clifton; Tolney Lane, Newark.

Stratiotes Aloides L. *Water Soldier*

Native. Still waters. Extinct. Divs. 1, 3.

First Record: G. Howitt, *Notts. Fl.* 1839. Ordoyno's record is for Lincolnshire.

1 Strelley Moat, *G. Howitt.*

3 Between Morton (Lincs.) and Walkeringham (Notts.), *Miller.*

There is also an unlocalised specimen in the herbarium of H. Bacon of Thurgarton.

Elodea canadensis Michx. *Canadian Water Weed*

Alien. Denizen, Rivers, canals, drains and ponds. Very common. All Divs.

First Record: J. Mitchell, *Bot. Gaz.* I 1849. In the Leen at Nottingham.

ORCHIDACEAE

Neottia Nidus Avis (L.) L. C. Rich. *Bird's Nest Orchid*

Native. Woods. Very rare. Divs. 1, 3.

First Record: T. Ordoyno, *Fl. Nott.* 1807.

1 Pleasley; Woods between Newstead and Linby, *G. Howitt.*
3 Epperstone Wood, per *Miss Sherbrooke*; Lound Wood, Eakring; Brockwood Hill Woods, Thurgarton, *Ordoyno*; Roe Wood, Winkburn; High Wood, Ossington, *Carr MS.*

Listera ovata (L.) R. Br. *Twayblade*

Native. Woods, meadows. Common except in Div. 2. All Divs.

First Record: C. Deering, *Cat. Stirp.* 1738.

2 Roadside by the entrance to Newstead Park; Birklands, Edwinstowe, *Carr MS.*

Spiranthes spiralis (L.) Chevall. *Ladies' Tresses*

Native. Calcareous grassland. Very rare. Divs. 2, 3.

First Record: J. Pulteney, *Phil. Trans. Vol.* 49. 1756.

2 Ten plants on a small gravel heap near Idle Stop, Misson, *Brown.*
3 East Leake, *Pulteney*; Colwick, *Gough's Camden* 1759 (probably *Pulteney*); One specimen in Kangaroo Close, Beckingham, *Miller.*

Cephalanthera Damasonium (Mill.) Druce. *White Helleborine*

Native. Woods. Very rare. Div. 1.

Only Record: G. Howitt, *Notts. Fl.* 1839, "Woods between Newstead and Linby.

Cephalanthera longifolia (Huds.) Fritsch. *Sword leaved Helleborine*

Native. Woods. Very rare. Div. 2.

Only Record: G. Howitt, *Notts. Fl.* 1839, "Woods near Welbeck, *Mr. J. Thompson.*"

Epipactis palustris (L.) Crantz. *Marsh Helleborine*

Native. Boggy meadows. Very rare or extinct. Divs. 1, 3, 4.

First Record: T. Ordoyno, *Fl. Nott.* 1807.

1 Bulwell Bogs, *Jowett*; Kirkby Hardwick; Mansfield Woodhouse; Near Newstead, *G. Howitt*; Marshy ground, near Newbound Mill, Teversall, in some quantity 1907 et seq., *Carr MS.*
3 Halam; Edingley Moor; Kirklington Mill, *Ordoyno*; Gamston Moor (by Nottingham), *Jowett.*
4 Coddington, *Ordoyno.*

Epipactis Helleborine (L.) Crantz. *Broad leafed Helleborine*

Native. Woods. Locally frequent. Divs. 1, 2, 3.

First Record: T. Ordoyno, *Fl. Nott.* 1807.

1 Welbeck; Carlton-in-Lindrick, *Friend*; Teversall; Aspley Wood, *Carr*; Trowell; Bramcote; Owday Wood, Carlton-in-Lindrick; Gateford.

2 Clumber Woods, *Roffey*; Cowlinshaw Plantation, Carlton-in-Lindrick.

3 Frequent.

Orchis ustulata L. *Burnt Orchid*

Native. Calcareous meadows. Probably extinct. Divs. 1, 3.

First Record: G. Crabbe in Nichol's *Hist. Liecs.* 1795.

1 Near Bulwell, *Jowett* (sp. in Herb. Jowett); Between Sutton-in-Ashfield and Kirkby Hardwick, *G. Howitt.*

3 Trentside beyond Bingham, *Crabbe*; Trentside between Nottingham and Southwell, *Crabbe* 1805; Near Halloughton Wood; Newark and Averham Meadows; Trentside between Hazleford and Nottingham, *Ordoyno.*

Orchis Morio L. *Green Winged Orchid*

Native. Meadows on basic soils. Formerly common (see G. Howitt), becoming rare. All Divs.

First Record: C. Deering, *Cat. Stirp.* 1738.

1 Linby; Kirkby, *Gilbert*; Shireoaks, *Roffey*; Strelley; Cossall; Greasley; Annesley: Selston, *Carr MS.*

2 Harworth, *Mrs. Sandwith*; Lindhurst near Mansfield, *Carr MS.*; Finningley.

3 'Frequent and locally abundant', *Carr MS.*

Modern Records: Treswell; Clifton by Nottingham; Bradmore; Upton; Farndon.

4 West Leake Hills; Stanton-on-Wolds; Colston Bassett; Hickling; Upper Broughton; Thorpe-in-the-Glebe, *Carr MS.*; Thorney.

Orchis latifolia sens. lat. *Marsh Orchid*

Native. Marshy meadows. Formerly frequent, (see G. Howitt) becoming rare. All Divs.

First Record: C. Deering, *Cat. Stirp.* 1738.

Orchis incarnata L. (*O. strictifolia* Opiz.) *Early Marsh Orchid*

Native. Bogs with basic waters. Very rare. Div. 1.

Only Record: Hills and Holes, Warsop, det. V. S. Summerhayes.

Mr. Summerhayes considers that J. W. Carr's records for *O. incarnata* in *Trans. Notts. Nats.* 1903 et seq and in his MS. Flora would "probably refer in the main to *O. praetermissa* at that date."

Orchis praetermissa Druce. *Marsh Orchid*

Native. Marshy meadows. The common marsh orchid of Notts., but becoming increasingly rare. Divs. 2, 3.

First Record: Southwell 1950, det. V. S. Summerhayes.

2 Misson; Serlby; Scrooby; Scaftworth; Harworth.
3 Southwell; Eakring; Ossington; Barton-in-Fabis.

O. praetermissa x Fuchsii 3 Southwell; Maplebeck.

Orchis maculata sens. lat. *Spotted Orchid*

Native. Woods, meadows and marshes.

First Record: C. Deering, *Cat. Stirp.* 1738.

The old records probably refer chiefly to *O. Fuchsii*, though *O. ericetorum* may well have been more common before the acid bogs were drained.

Orchis ericetorum E. F. Linton. *Heath Spotted Orchid*

Native. Very rare. Div. 4.

Only Record: A few plants in a marshy meadow at Stanton-on-Wolds. Det. V. S. Summerhayes. 1951.

Orchis Fuchsii Druce. *Spotted Orchid*

Native. Damp meadows and woods. Common, less so in Div. 2.

All Divs. Not previously distinguished.

Orchis mascula L. *Early Purple Orchid*

Native. Strong woodland. Locally common. Absent from Div. 2. Divs. 1, 3, 4.

First Record: C. Deering, *Cat. Stirp.* 1738.

Orchis pyramidalis L. *Pyramid Orchid*

Native. Calcareous meadows. Formerly frequent in 1 and 3 (see G. Howitt), becoming rare. Divs. 1, 3, 4.

First Record: C. Deering, *Cat. Stirp.* 1738.

Modern Records:
1 Shireoaks, *Brown*; Hills and Holes, Warsop; Creswell Crags.
3 Everton; Clarborough Tunnel; Little Gringley.
4 Coddington clay pits.

(**Orchis hircina** Crantz. *Lizard Orchid*

Recorded by Deering for Colwick and Clifton, probably in error for *Plantanthera chlorantha*.)

Ophrys apifera Huds. *Bee Orchid*

Native. Calcareous pastures. Rare and decreasing. Divs. 1, 3, 4.

First Record: C. Deering, *Cat. Stirp.* 1738.

1 Aspley Grounds, *Deering*; Bulwell Lime Quarries; Kirkby Hardwick; Mansfield quarries, *Ordoyno*; Bulwell Wood Hall, *Jowett, Carr*; Shireoaks quarry, *Friend*; Hills and Holes, Warsop†; Lady Lee, Worksop, *Carr MS.*; Kirkby-in-Ashfield; Styrrup.

3 Kirton, *Mrs. Collinson*; Gamston-by-Retford†, *Carr MS.*; Everton; Clarborough Tunnel.

4 About Leake, *Nichols, G. Howitt*; Blue Hill, Cropwell Bishop, *Carr MS.*; Beacon Hill, Newark; Cotgrave Wolds.

Ophrys insectifera L. *Fly Orchid*

Native. Fields and woods. Formerly frequent in Div. 1 (see G. Howitt) now very rare. Div. 1.

First Record: C. Deering, *Cat. Stirp.* 1738.

1 Aspley Grounds, *Deering*; Bulwell Quarries, *Ordoyno*; Linby Woods, *Jowett, Carr*; Pleasley Woods and fields, *Jowett*; Shireoaks, *Friend*; Kirkby Grives, *Carr MS.*; Trowell Moor, *L. C. Brown* 1959.

Habenaria conopsea (L.) Benth. *Fragrant Orchid*

Native. Damp calcareous meadows. Very rare. Divs. 1, 3.

First Record: C. Deering, *Cat. Stirp.* 1738.

1 About Aspley, *Deering*; Bulwell Hall, *Ordoyno*; Kirkby; Mansfield Woodhouse, *G. Howitt*; Hucknall Torkard; Newbound Mill, Teversall; Hills and Holes, Warsop†; Sookholme, *Carr MS.*

3 Near Kirklington Mill; By the bridge between Halloughton and Thurgarton; Gamston by Nottingham; Averham Meadows, *Ordoyno.*

Habenaria viridis (L.) R. Br. *Frog Orchid*

Native. Calcareous meadows. Very rare. Divs. 1, 3.

First Record: T. Ordoyno, *Fl. Nott.* 1807.

1 Wollaton; Watnall; Bulwell; Annesley, *G. Howitt*; Canal side between Wollaton and the Ilkeston road, *Gilbert*; Lady Lee, Worksop, *Friend*; Hucknall Torkard; Kirkby Grives, *Carr MS.*

3 Cotton Mill Meadow and Westhorpe Dumble, Southwell; Normanton-by-Southwell; Newark and Averham meadows; Oxton Hill, *Ordoyno*; Clifton meadows; By the old camp, Laxton; Jordan's Castle, Wellow; East Markham, *Carr MS.*

Platanthera chlorantha (Cust.) Rchb. *Butterfly Orchid*

Native. Strong woodland. Rare. Divs. 1, 3.

First Record: T. Ordoyno, *Fl. Nott.* 1807.

1 Pleasley; Beauvale; Brinsley; Bulwell; Aspley, *G. Howitt.*
3 'In most of the woods of the Clay District', *G. Howitt.*

Modern Records:
Hockerton Moor Wood; Lady Wood, Caunton; Eaton and Gamston Woods, plentifully; Broadwaters Wood, Ossington; Beverley Springs, Headon.

Platanthera bifolia (L.) L. C. Rich. *Lesser Butterfly Orchid*

Native. Probably extinct. Div. 3.

Only Record: T. Ordoyno, *Fl. Nott.* 1807 "Meadows and pastures; not common. Southwell; and in the meadows leading to Oxton Wood; also closes between Winkburn and Kirklington."

IRIDACEAE

Iris Pseudacorus L. *Yellow Flag*

Native. Marshes, pools, canal and river sides. Common. All Divs.

First Record: C. Deering, *Cat. Stirp.* 1738.

Iris foetidissima L. *Gladdon*

Native. Limestone woodland. Very rare. Div. 1.

Only Record: Dyscar Wood, Langold 1959. Two patches each consisting of several plants were found. They were not flowering, but were growing in undisturbed natural surroundings, with every appearance of being native.

Iris germanica L.

Alien. Frequent on rubbish dumps, and naturalised in Besthorpe Gravel Pits, Div. 3.

Crocus nudiflorus Sm. *Autumn Crocus*

Denizen. Formerly naturalised over large areas of Nottingham, Dunkirk and Wilford meadows. The habitats have been lost to development, mining subsidence, pit dumps, Wilford Power Station, Flood prevention schemes, and Nottingham City dump. Occasional plants still occur. Divs. 2, 3.

The Rev. J. T. Becher first discovered this to be a distinct species. It was admitted by Sir J. E. Smith *Engl. Bot.* vol. 7, table 491, the drawing being made from Becher's specimen. It must also have been described by Dr. M. Lister in a letter to Ray, whose answer

(1669) runs "*Crocus autumnalis pratensis* unless you mean *Colchicum*—I do not know." Deering mistook it for *Colchicum*. The specimen labelled *Colchicum* in his assistant, Mr. Tutin's, herbarium was, according to Jowett, *Crocus*. (see T. Jowett, *Bot. Cals.*, and his interleaved copy of Ordoyno).

Old Records:
Meadows between Nottingham and the Trent; On the road to St. Anne's Well, the third field on the left before you come to the Boycroft, *Becher*; Nottingham Meadows; Fields near St. Annes' Well; Nottingham Park; Fields between Fox Lane and Mapperley Hills, *G. Howitt*; "Numerous specimens in 1887 in a field at the Trent Bridge end of Arkwright Street now covered by buildings"; "It still grows in meadows by the Trent beyond Clifton Colliery," *Carr MS.*

Modern Records:
Trent Lane, Dunkirk, Three plants found by *Mr. Turton* of Kimberley 1950 and brought by him to a Nottingham Field Science Club meeting; Trent Lane, Dunkirk, *D. Darlison* 1952; Several plants behind Wilford 1958, *A. Johnson* and *J. Spencer*; Still abundant in one Trentside meadow between Nottingham and Newark.

Crocus vernus (L.) All. non Mill. *Spring Crocus*

Denizen. Formerly abundant with *C. nudiflorus* but now even more rare. Divs. 2, 3.

Old Records:
Above Fox Lane in the Clay Field, it grows also in Nottingham Meadows in several places on the right hand side of the Road going to Kings Meadow, *Deering*. It clothes several acres of the Nottingham Meadows between the Town and the Trent; On Bluebell Hill, about a mile to the north east of the Town; Between Larkdale and the Bowling Alley; half a mile to the north of Nottingham, *Jowett*; Still grows plentifully in Nottingham and Lenton meadows beyond Clifton Colliery, *Carr MS.*

Modern Records:
Dunkirk Meadows and Trent Lane, *Leather* 1933, *Darlison* 1951 and 1953; "one small patch" 1953, *Butcher*; Wilford Church Yard 1959. The garden form is occasionally found established, as on Mansfield Forest (Div. 2.).

Crocus aureus Sibth. *Yellow Crocus*

Alien. Occurs on road sides round villages.

Sisyrinchium augustifolium Mill. *Blue eyed Grass*

A rare alien. Div. 1.

Only Record: J. Brown 1950, several plants in an old Magnesian Limestone quarry at Lady Lee, Shireoaks.

Crocosmia x Crocosmiiflora (Lemoine) H.E. Br. *Montbretia*

Alien. Denizen. Frequent on dumps and occasionally established in damp places. Divs. 3, 4.

3 River bank below West Stockwith.
4 Ballast pits at Balderton, quite a lot.

AMARYLLIDACEAE

Narcissus Pseudo-Narcissus L. *Wild Daffodil*

Native. Woods and meadows. Rare. Divs. (2), 3.

First Record: T. Ordoyno, *Fl. Nott.* 1807.

The Daffodil has been widely planted in the Dukeries and on large estates, often in woods remote from the House. It appears to be native in the following localities.

3 In a close near Oxton Toll Bar, *Ordoyno*; Askham Closes, Near Tuxford, *Jowett*; Babbington Springs, Marnham, abundant in the north west corner of the Wood, 1907, *Carr MS.* Still abundant here in 1954. This wood has now been destroyed, a few plants still persist in the 'field.'

Galanthus nivalis L. *Snowdrop*

Denizen. Widely naturalised in woods near houses and on large estates. All Divs.

First Record: T. Ordoyno, *Fl. Nott.* 1807.

DIOSCOREACEAE

Tamus communis L. *Black Bryony*

Native. Hedges and woods. Very common. All Divs.

First Record: C. Deering, *Cat. Stirp.* 1738.

LILIACEAE

Ruscus aculeatus L. *Butcher's Broom*

Denizen. Sometimes planted in woods. Rare. Divs. 2, 3.

First Record: C. Deering, *Cat. Stirp.* 1738.

2 "In a Hedge going from the Backside towards . . . Radford, but not in a very thriving way, nor dare I affirm it to be of the Natural Growth of that Spot," *Deering*.
4 In a small plantation at Staunton, with other ornamental shrubs.

Asparagus officinalis L. ssp. *officinalis* *Garden Asparagus*

Denizen. Frequently found as an escape, in hedge bottoms and waste places.

Polygonatum multiflorum (L.) All. *Solomon's Seal*

Native. Limestone Woods. Very rare. Divs. 1, 2, 3.

First Record: J. Bohler, *Worksop and the Dukeries* 1875. (Jowett's record was in Derbyshire.)

1 Pleasley Vale, *Bohler*, *Friend*, *Fisher* and *Carr*. The last two definitely found it in Notts. (near the Upper Mill), we can only find it in Derbyshire; Broxtowe Woods, *Gilbert*; Banks Carr Wood, Styrrup, *Mrs. Sandwith*; Underwood, in various parts of a small wood near the school, having every appearance of being native; Wallingwells Wood, Carlton-in-Lindrick, native.
2 Stone Hills Wood, Sutton-in-Ashfield, several strong colonies, 1910, *Carr MS.*; Hodsock, perhaps native in several woods; Naturalised at Cockglade, Ollerton.
3 Plantations at Langford, *Carr MS.*; North Leverton (escape).

Polygonatum odoratum (Mill.) Druce. *Angular Solomon's Seal*
Denizen or Native. Woods. Very rare. Div. 1.
Only Record: Menagerie Wood, Worksop Manor, *Roffey*.

Convallaria majalis L. *Lily of the Valley*

Native. Woods, especially on sand. Rare. All Divs.

First Record: T. Ordoyno, *Fl. Nott.* 1807.

1 Pleasley Wood, *Bohler*, *Adams* (probably Derbys.).
2 Cockglade, Ollerton, *Ordoyno*. Still in great quantity near the former site of the house; Newstead; Bestwood; Stapleford (escape); Naturalised in Welbeck Park on a former camp site and near Drinking Pit Lane Lodge.
3 Abundant in Wigsley Wood†, *Carr MS.*; Naturalised in Balderton Ballast Pits; Toton (escape).
4 West Wood, Thorney; Plot Wood, Wigsley, originally planted by Miss Howard of Wigsley.

Hemerocallis flava L. *Day Lily*

Alien. Naturalised in derelict ornamental grounds at Cockglade, Ollerton. Div. 2.

Allium Scorodoprasm L. *Sand Leek*

Native or casual. Sandy places. Very rare. Div. 3.

Only Record: By the ballast pits at Barnby Moor 1955.

Allium vineale L. *Crow Garlic*

Native. Roadsides, meadows and open woodland. Locally common. Divs. 1, 2, 3.

First Record: C. Deering, *Cat. Stirp.* 1738.

1 Hills and Holes, Warsop; Harworth.
2 Larkdale, *Deering*; Nottingham Castle Rock, *Sidebotham*; Derby road, under Wollaton Park Wall, *Butcher*; Ranby; Harworth; Gleadthorpe.
3 Common in the Trent Valley; Westhorpe, Southwell, *Ordoyno*. Plants with bulbils and flowers and plants with bulbils only appear equally common in the Notts. communities.

Allium ursinium L. *Ramsons*

Native. Damp woods. Locally common. Divs. 1, 2, 3.

First Record: C. Deering, *Cat. Stirp.* 1738.

1 Often so rampant and odoriferous that it keeps the squeamish out of the woods.
2 Church Warsop, *Carr MS.*; Budby; Newstead; Blyth; Hodsock.
3 In most strong woods and dumbles.

Allium carinatum L.

Alien. Denizen. Roadsides and grassy places. Rare. Divs. 1, 4.

First Record: *Victoria County History* 1906 in brackets.

1 Hills and Holes, Warsop, a fair amount 1952.
4 Laneside at Alverton 1949, plentifully.

Allium oleraceum L. *Field Garlic*

Native. Road and path sides, grassy places. Uncommon. All Divs.

First Record: T. Jowett. *Bot. Cals.* 1826.

1 Between Nuthall and Bulwell†, *Jowett*; Mansfield; Mansfield Woodhouse†, *G. Howitt*; Skegby; Teversall; Sookholme†, *Carr MS.*; Lady Lee, Worksop.
2 On the sandstone round Nottingham, *G. Howitt*; Wollaton Park, *Williams*; Harworth.
3 Fiskerton†; Ordsall, *Carr MS.*; East Stoke, *Leather*; Besthorpe; Langford.

Allium paradoxum G. Don.

Alien. Naturalised in derelict ornamental ground at Cockglade, Ollerton. Div. 2.

Scilla non-scripta (L.) H. and L. *Wild Hyacinth*

Native. Woods, especially on light soils. Very common. All Divs.

First Record: C. Deering, *Cat. Stirp.* 1738.

Scilla hispanica Mill.

Alien. Frequently naturalised in ornamental woodland and a virulent garden weed.

Ornithogalum umbellatum L. *Star of Bethlehem*

Denizen. Fields and roadsides, especially on light soils. Rare. Divs. 1, 2, 3.

First Record: Revd. J. T. Becher in Ordoyno's *Fl. Nott.* 1807.

1 Fields between Kirkby and Kirkby Hardwick, *Becher*; Roadside Welbeck.
2 Larkdale, Nottingham and the Bowling Alley fields, *Jowett*; Fields at Bramcote, *Carr MS.*; Naturalised at Cockglade, Ollerton; Roadside, Carburton, plentifully.
3 Nottingham Meadows, *G. Howitt*; Between Walkeringham and Stockwith, *Miller*; About Wigsley Wood, *Cole*; Bank near the Church at Averham, *Carr MS.*; Naturalised at Balderton Ballast pit, and Farndon bottom lane.

Ornithogalum nutans L. *Drooping Star of Bethlehem*

Alien. Grassy places. Very rare. Divs. 3, 4.

First Record: J. E. Smith's *Eng. Fl.* II 1824, per Mr. Hadden.

3 Nottingham Meadows, *Hadden*; Nottingham Meadows on the left hand side of the road leading to Wilford Boat, *G. Howitt.*
4 Orchard at Staunton Hall.

Lilium pyrenaicum Gouan.

Alien. Casual. Div. 2.

Only Record: Canal side at Ranby 1954.

Tulipa sylvestris L. *Wild Tulip*

Alien. Denizen. Woods and meadows. Uncommon. It seldom flowers. Div. 3.

First Record: G. Howitt, *Notts. Fl.* 1839.

3 Nottingham Meadows, plentifully . . . but never flowers, *G. Howitt*; "Wild in the Churchyard and lawn at Fledborough", *Penrose*; Beeston Meadows; Thrumpton Meadows, *Victoria County History*; Winkburn Park†, *Leather*; Spinney behind Holme Pierrepont Hall; Elston Woods.

Gagea lutea (L.) Ker. Gawl. *Yellow Star of Bethlehem*

Native. Woods. Very rare. Divs. 1, 3.

First Record: G. Howitt, *Notts. Fl.* 1839, also a specimen in Herb. Jowett, given him by Howitt.

1 Pleasley Wood; Banks of the Erewash at Brinsley, *G. Howitt*; Wood above the Upper Mill, Pleasley; "fairly plentifully in the Park at Nuthall Temple, not flowering very freely (station now destroyed)," *Carr MS.*
3 Flintham Wood in considerable quantity, *Carr MS.* Still plentiful at Trent Hills, Flintham.

Colchicum autumnale L. *Meadow Saffron*

Native. Meadows. Uncommon and decreasing. Divs. 1, 2, 3.

First Record: W. Stukeley, *Itinarum Curiosum* 1724. Deering's record refers to *Crocus*, see above.

1 Mansfield, *Hurt*; Meadows by Steetley Quarry, *Bohler*.
2 *Victoria County History*.
3 About Brough, *Stukeley*; Newark and Holme meadows; Winkburn, *Ordoyno*; East Stoke†, *Fisher*; Kneesall†; East Markham, hilltop above Sibthorpe Place, *Carr MS*.

Narthecium ossifragum (L.) Huds. *Bog Asphodel*

Native. Extinct. Div. 4.

Only Record: T. Ordoyno, *Fl. Nott.* 1807, "Two plants were found on Coddington Moor, by Mr. Jacob Ordoyno."

Paris quadrifolia L. *Herb Paris*

Native. Moist woods on clay and limestone. Rather rare. Divs. 1, 2.

First Record: C. Deering, *Cat. Stirp.* 1738.

1 Aspley, *Deering, Jowett*; Kirkby Grives, MS. entry in *Deering's* own copy of his *Cat.* (see *Jowett*); Pleasley; Annesley and Beauvale Woods, *Jowett*; High Park, Greasley, *Gilbert*; Steetley, *Bohler*; Carlton-in-Lindrick, *Friend*; Scratta Wood, near Worksop, *Roffey*; Aldercar Wood and Jack O'Sherwood, Newstead; Quarry Banks, Linby; Watnall Coppice, *Carr MS.* We have not been able to find the plant in this Div. Many habitats have been destroyed or planted with conifers, but some of the woods are still suitable.
3 Formerly frequent.

Modern Records:
Several woods at Caunton; Egmanton Wood; Eaton and Gamston Woods; Winkburn; Bevercotes Park; Ossington; Southwell; Halloughton Wood.

JUNCACEAE

Juncus conglomeratus L.

Native. Damp heaths, acid pastures and woods. Common in Div. 2 and on the coal measures and frequent on drift soils and acid pockets in Divs. 3, 4. All Divs.

First Record: T. Ordoyno, *Fl. Nott.* 1807.

Juncus effusus L. *Soft Rush*

Native. Damp meadows, stream and drain sides. Common. All Divs.

First Record: C. Deering, *Cat. Stirp.* 1738.

Juncus inflexus L. *Hard Rush*

Native. Damp places especially on basic soils. Locally very common, less so in Div. 2. The dominant rush of Div. 4.

First Record: C. Deering, *Cat. Stirp.* 1738.

Juncus subnodulosus Schrank. *Blunt Flowered Rush*

Native. Damp places especially on peat. Locally frequent. Divs. 1, 2, 3.

First Record: T. Jowett, *Bot. Cals.* 1826.

1 Teversall; Sookholme; Scratta Wood, Shireoaks†, *Carr MS.*; Styrrup Carr, *Brown.*
2 The dominant rush on the Carrs; Bulwell Forest; Rainworth, *Carr MS.*; Ordsall.
3 Dominant on the Carrs and frequent in the Trent Valley; Southwell.

Juncus acutiflorus Hoffm. *Sharp Flowered Rush*

Native. Damp places on acid soils. Not common. All Divs.

First Record: T. Jowett, *Bot. Cals.* 1826, "In this county." G. Howitt considers it 'rather frequent' and does not give localities.

1 Greasley.
2 Lound; Thoresby; Misson.
3 Frequent on the blown sand; Manzer Gorse; Dunkirk Meadows; Eaton.
4 West Leake; Langford Moor.

Juncus articulatus L. *Jointed Rush*

Native. Marshes, streamsides, damp meadows. Very common. All Divs.

First Record: C. Deering, *Cat. Stirp.* 1738.

Juncus bulbosus L. *Bulbous Rush*

Native. Boggy meadows and drain sides. Locally frequent. All Divs.

First Record: T. Jowett, *Bot. Cals.* 1826.

1 Shireoaks Park; Gateford.
2 Common on the Carrs; Budby Forest; Osberton.
3 North Muskham; Misterton; Calverton; West Drayton; Wigsley.
4 Langford Moor.

Juncus squarrosus L. *Heath Rush*

Native. Damp heaths and heathy woods. Local. Divs. 2, 3, 4.

First Record: T. Jowett's interleaved Ordoyno 1821.

2 Locally frequent.
3 Spalford; Wigsley; West Drayton.
4 Langford Moor†, *Carr MS.*; Turf Moor, Brough; Barnby.

Juncus compressus Jacq. *Round fruited Rush*

Native. Damp grassy places, often colonising bare ground by gravel pits. Probably increasing. All Divs.

First Record: T. Ordoyno, *Fl. Nott.* 1807.

1 Hills and Holes, Warsop†, *Carr MS.*; Lady Lee, Worksop; Shireoaks Park; Mansfield; Carlton-in-Lindrick.
2 Oxton Bogs, *G. Howitt*; Thoresby Park.
3 Frequent on the alluvial soils.
4 Wet meadow at Granby.

Juncus bufonius L. *Toad Rush*

Native. Damp arable land and bare ground on light soils. Very common, especially in 2. All Divs.

First Record: C. Deering, *Cat. Stirp.* 1738.

Juncus tenuis Willd.

Alien. Div. 2.

Only Record: Garden weed at Bramcote 1948-53, *Butcher.*

Luzula sylvatica (Huds.) Gaud. *Great Wood Rush*

Native. Damp woods. Rare and a shy flowerer. Divs. 1, 3.

First Record: T. Ordoyno, *Fl. Nott.* 1807.

1 Felley Mill, *Jowett*; Woods between Annesley and Greasley, *G. Howitt*; Beauvale Woods, *Carr MS.*
3 Epperstone Wood, *Ordoyno*; Treswell Wood†, *Carr MS.*; Roselle Wood, Oxton.

Luzula pilosa (L.) Willd. *Hairy Woodrush*

Native. Woodland rides. Common, especially on lighter soils. All Divs.

First Record: T. Ordoyno, *Fl. Nott.* 1807.

Luzula multiflora (Retz.) Lej.

Native. Heaths and woods, especially on light soils. Locally frequent. All Divs.

First Record, T. Jowett, *Bot. Cals.* 1826.

1 Bulwell.
2 and 3 Frequent.
4 Bunny; Thorney†, *Carr MS.*; Owthorpe; Clipstone Wolds.

var. *congesta* DC. appears to be rather commoner than the type.

Luzula campestris (L.) DC. *Field Woodrush*

Native. Meadows, lawns etc. Very common. All Divs.

First Record: C. Deering, *Cat. Stirp.* 1738.

PALMACEAE

Phoenix dactylifera L. *Date Palm*

Alien. Seedlings are frequent on Nottingham Dump.

TYPHACEAE

Typha latifolia L. *Great Reed Mace*

Native. Canals, gravel pits, ponds. Very common. All Divs.

First Record: C. Deering, *Cat. Stirp.* 1738.

Typha angustifolia L.

Native. Drains and standing waters. Less common that the last. All Divs.

First Record: T. Jowett, *Bot. Cals.* 1826.

1 Wollaton†; Bulwell†, *Jowett*; Eastwood, *G. Howitt*; Teversall; Nuthall; Newthorpe.
2 Misson; Ranskill; Ordsall.
3 Frequent in the river valleys.
4 By the canal, Owthorpe, *Carr MS.*

Sparganium ramosum Huds. *Bur Reed*

Native. Rivers, ponds, canals, etc. Very common. All Divs.

First Record: C. Deering, *Cat. Stirp.* 1738.

Sparganium neglectum Beeby.

Native. Similar habitats to the last. Rare or overlooked. Divs. 1, 2.

First Record: R. G. Williams MS. 1940-45.

1 Wollaton Canal, *Williams.*
2 Misson, *B.S.B.I. expedition* 1952.

Sparganium simplex Huds. *Unbranched Bur Reed*

Native. Slow rivers and drains, canals. Common, but less so than *S. ramosum.* All Divs.

First Record: T. Ordoyno, *Fl. Nott.* 1807.

Sparganium angustifolium Michx. *Floating Bur Reed*

Native. Extinct. Divs. 1, 2, 3.

First Record: C. Merret, *Pinnax* 1666.

1 Ponds at Kirkby Hardwick, *Hurt.*
2 "On the east side of Scrooby, nigh a great wood where the foot way is cast up," *Merret*. This is still a very damp fen area, and would have been a likely habitat in 1666.
3 Trent Bridge, Nottingham, *Deering* (He does not record *S. simplex.*)

ARACEAE

(**Arum neglectum** (Towns.) Ridl.

C. Deering, *Cat. Stirp.* 1738 has this interesting record "*Arum aureis venis pulcherrimus obsitum*, Wake Robin with gold coloured Veins. This beautiful Leaf I saw in a Collection of Plants of Mrs. Collins . . . first found by Miss Stanhope of Bingham, plentifully growing in a Close called Felldyke between Bingham and Car Coulston, who transplanted it to their Gardens where it continues without degenerating.")

Arum maculatum L. *Lords and Ladies*

Native. Woods and hedge sides on strong land. Common except in Div. 2 where it is confined to woods on the fen peats and on the border with Div. 1. All Divs.

First Record: C. Deering, *Cat. Stirp.* 1738.

Acorus Calamus L. *Sweet Flag*

Alien. Denizen. Rivers, canals, lakes. Locally frequent. Divs. 1, 2, 3.

First Record: C. Deering, *Cat. Stirp.* 1738.

1 Banks of the R. Erewash near Eastwood, *G. Howitt*; Pond by Oldmoor Wood, Strelley, *Carr MS.*; Abundant all along the Nottingham Canal.
2 Papplewick Forest, *G. Howitt*; R. Ryton, Osberton, *Thornley*; Thoresby Lake; Arnot Hill Park (?planted).
3 Plentifully in the R. Soar in many Spots, *Deering*; R. Trent from Barton to Colwick, *G. Howitt*. It is still plentiful in the Soar, in the Trent it occurs sporadically down to Newark, but does not flower.

LEMNACEAE

Lemna minor L. *Lesser Duckweed*

Native. Ponds and standing waters. Very common. All Divs.

First Record: C. Deering, *Cat. Stirp.* 1738.

Lemna polyrhiza L. *Great Duckweed*

Native. Ponds and ditches. Decreasing. Divs. 2, 3, 4.

First Record: C. Deering, *Cat. Stirp.* 1738.

2 Lenton; Scaftworth; Misson†; Everton Carr, *Carr MS.*; Serlby; Scrooby.
3 Formerly frequent in the Trent Valley. It is still rather plentiful downstream of Newark, but has become rare upstream.
4 Thorney.

Lemna trisulca L. *Ivy leafed Duckweed*

Native. Ponds, canals, drains, etc. Common. All Divs.

First Record: C. Deering, *Cat. Stirp.* 1738.

Lemna gibba L. *Gibbous Duckweed*

Native. Ponds, canals and drains, rather tolerant of pollution. Locally common. All Divs.

First Record: T. Jowett, *Bot. Cals.* 1826.

1 Shireoaks; Bulwell.
2 Frequent, especially on the Carrs.
3 Common.
4 Frequent in the Grantham Canal; Broadholme.

ALISMACEAE

Alisma Plantago-aquatica L. *Water Plantain*

Native. Ponds, rivers and all waters. Very common. All Divs.

First Record: C. Deering, *Cat. Stirp.* 1738.

Alisma lanceolata With.

Native. Fen drains. Rare or overlooked. Divs. 2, 3.

First Record: *B.S.B.I. Year Book* 1953.

2 Drain in field at Misson, *B.S.B.I. expedition* 1952.
3 Misterton.

Alisma Ranunculoides L. *Lesser Water Plantain*

Native. Drains and pools on peat and limestone. Local. All Divs.

First Record: C. Deering, *Cat. Stirp.* 1738.

1 Pond at Hills and Holes, Warsop; Quarry near Haggonfields, Worksop, *Carr MS.*; Shireoaks Park.
2 Misson in several places†, *Carr MS.*; Gringley Carr; Tiln; Finningley; Everton Carr.
3 Clifton, *Deering*; Kirklington; Edingley Moor, *Ordoyno*; Morton, *G. Howitt*; Gringley Carr†, *Miller*; Misterton Carr and in drains towards the Trent.
4 Langford Moor, *Ordoyno*.

Sagittaria sagittifolia L. *Arrowhead*

Native. Slow rivers and drains, still waters. Common. All Divs.

First Record: C. Deering, *Cat. Stirp.* 1738.

Butomus umbellatus L. *Flowering Rush*

Native. Ponds, canals and river sides. Locally common. All Divs.

First Record: C. Deering, *Cat. Stirp.* 1738.

1 Common on the Nottingham Canal; Shireoaks.
2 Pool in Nottingham Park, *Deering*; Misson, *Mrs. Sandwith, Brown*; Lenton; Beeston; Canal at Retford† and Babworth, *Carr MS.*; Wiseton; Scaftworth.
3 Common in the river valleys.
4 Common on the Grantham Canal.

NAIADACEAE

Triglochin palustris L. *Arrowgrass*

Native. Swampy meadows. Frequent except in Div. 4. All Divs.

First Record: T. Ordoyno, *Fl. Nott.* 1807.

4 Rempstone Old Church Yard.

Scheuchzeria palustris L.

Native. Extinct or error. Peat Bogs.

Only Record: H. C. Watson, *Top. Bot.* 1883. The record in Watson's MS. is "In a marsh called the Car between Bawtry and Walkeringham north Nottinghamshire. Sent to me by the Rev. M. J. Berkeley." A. Bennett was unable to trace Berkeley's specimen in either Watson's, Winch's, Hooker's or the Brit. Mus. Herbaria (see Carr MS.). As the plant formerly grew at Thorne Moor nearby, the station is not impossible.

POTAMOGETON

The pondweeds of Nottinghamshire occur in four main types of habitat. The rivers are a dying asset, though formerly they must have grown many good species. *P. lucens* was common in G. Howitt's time and, as Deering records it from the Trent, it is probable that this was its headquarters. Howitt also describes *P. densus* as frequent. This may have grown in some of the smaller streams, besides the drains in Nottingham Meadows and possibly other meadows of the Trent Valley. This species is now almost confined to the Carrs, while there is only one recent record of *P. lucens.*

The Trent is now so highly polluted that there are no submerged higher plants, except stray pieces in broken water round weirs. The tributaries draining from the industrial and mining areas are in rather the same condition. Though the lakes on the great estates serve as settling tanks for coal slack on the Forest streams which run through them, pollution appears to be creeping downstream. *Ranunculus* species are dying out in the Meden below Thoresby, though *P. perfoliatus* and *P. crispus* still survive. These species also occur in some of the western tributaries of the Trent. On the Lias, the Devon and its tributaries have been subjected to deep dredging. This has destroyed the old gravel bottom, and produced a constant problem of silting up, and high banks which grow nothing but teasels. The occurence of *P. densus* at Granby makes one wonder what these formerly unexplored streams grew in the past.

The gravel pits follow the Trent Valley from the Derbyshire border down to Besthorpe. Northwards the great new pits are found chiefly on the gravels and sands of the Idle valley. All these pits are relatively new and only appear to have been colonized by the commoner species, *P. perfoliatus*, *crispus*, *natans* etc., though *P. coloratus* and *P. gramineus* are growing in pits at Misson. Their chief botanical interest is in the marginal plants, especially in the tidal part of the valley.

Nottinghamshire is well served by canals. The Grantham Canal is largely silted up, but still produces *P. x cooperi* in the neighbourhood of Nottingham. The Chesterfield Canal shares the general dullness of the area where it passes through the Forest, but is interesting elsewhere. *P. x Friesii* and *P. Lintoni* are its best pondweeds, there are also *Ranunculus Baudotii* and *Callitriche truncata* in quantity. The Nottingham Canal is excellent for pondweeds, with *P. praelongus*, *compressus*, *x Friesii* and *x salicifolius*. It feeds from Moor Green, an unpolluted reservoir on the junction of the permian and the coal measures.

By far the most interesting area is the Carr Lands of the Idle Valley below Retford. Gringley, Everton and Misterton Carrs, with the peat lands of Misson on the north bank of the Idle, are low lying areas with an elevation of about five to eighteen feet. The peat is intersected with the usual network of fen-land drains. They grow *P. praelongus*, *gramineus*, *coloratus*, *x nitens*, *x sparganifolius* and *densus*, which last occurs in drains in the peat of all parishes upstream to Tiln. The PH value of these drains is not high, most readings being about seven. *Gramineus* and *densus* are the commonest of the interesting species; *coloratus* and *praelongus* are rare, while *lucens* with its hybrids, so common in the Lincolnshire and Cambridgeshire Fens, is totally absent from this part of Nottinghamshire. On the other hand the water is not entirely acid, as in the old bogs of the Sherwood Forest, which, where they survive, produce *P. polygonifolius*.

Detailed records follow:—

Potamogeton natans L. *Broad leafed Pondweed*

Native. Still waters. Very common. All Divs.

First Record: C. Deering, *Cat. Stirp.* 1738.

Potamogeton polygonifolius Pourr.

Native. Drains and bogs on acid soils. Rare. Divs. 2, 3, 4.

First Record: Langford Moor, June 1952, det. G. Taylor and J. E. Dandy.

2 Hesley; Harworth; Clipstone Lake.
3 Spalford.
4 Langford Moor.

Potamogeton coloratus Hornem.

Native. Ponds and ditches with basic waters. Uncommon. Divs. 1, 2, 3.

First Record: J. W. Carr, *Tr. Nott. Nats.* 1904.

1 Magnesian limestone quarry at Worksop, *Carr*; Abundant in pools in Shireoaks Park; Drains on Styrrup Carr.
2 Drains at Misson.
3 Several ballast pits at Misterton; Drains on Gringley Carr.

Potamogeton lucens L. *Shining Pondweed*

Native. Ponds, rivers, canals. Rare and decreasing. Divs. 1, 2, 3.

First Record: C. Deering, *Cat. Stirp.* 1738.

1 Nottingham and Erewash Canals at Eastwood, *Carr MS.* The Erewash Canal is now very polluted. Repeated gatherings from the Nottingham Canal sent by us to Dr. Taylor and Mr. Dandy have all proved to be *P. x salicifolius*, so the parent appears to have been hybridized out.
2 Drain at Misson, *Carr MS.*
3 In the Trent, *Deering;* Common, *G. Howitt*; R. Soar at Kingston; R. Trent at Colwick, *Carr MS.*; Newark, *Fisher*; R. Idle at Gamston, *Butcher*; Mons Pool, Collingham.

Potamogeton x salicifolius Wolfg. *lucens x perfoliatus*

Native. Rare. Div. 1.

First Record: J. W. Carr MS. Flora.

1 'A piece mixed with a lot of *P. lucens* from the Nottingham Canal at Eastwood was so named with a slight element of doubt by A. Bennett," *Carr MS.*; Abundant in the Nottingham Canal at Eastwood, Trowell and Awsworth. See under last species.

Potamogeton gramineus L. *Various leafed Pondweed*

Native. Ponds and drains. Rare. Now confined to the Carrs. Divs. 2, 3.

First Record: G. Howitt, *Notts. Fl.* 1839.

2 Frequent in pools on the Forest, *G. Howitt*; Abundant in a dyke on Everton Carr†, *Mrs. Sandwith*; Wiseton Canal, *B.S.B.I. expedition* 1952; Misson in several places; Gringley Carr.
3 Gringley Carr; Misterton Carr.

Potamogeton x sparganifolius Laest. ex Fr. *gramineus x natans*

Only Record: Drain by Cross Lane, Gringley Carr 1955 et seq. det. Dr. G. Taylor and Mr. J. E. Dandy. Div. 3.

Potamogeton x nitens Weber. *gramineus x perfoliatus*

Native. Rare. Divs. 2, 3.

First Record: J. W. Carr, *Tr. Nott. Nats.* 1904 as *P. falcatus* Fryer. Mr. Dandy informs us that Carr's specimen can be attributed to this hybrid.

2 Near Park Drain Station, Misson†, *Carr*; By the lane leading to the Whin Cover, Finningley.
3 Gringley and Misterton Carrs.

(**Potamogeton alpinus** Balb. *Reddish Pondweed*

Extinct or error.

Only Record: H. C. Watson, *N.B.G.* on the authority of Cooper's marked catalogue, but with no specimen.)

Potamogeton praelongus Wulf. *Long Pondweed*

Native. Canals, rivers, drains on the Carrs. Rare. Divs. 1, 2, 3.

First Record: J. W. Carr, *Tr. Nott. Nats.* 1905.

1 Nottingham Canal at Wollaton (now filled in).
2 Near Park Drain Station, Misson, *Brown*; Drain on Everton Carr.
3 Beeston Canal at Lenton; R. Soar at Ratcliffe, *Carr*; Drains on Gringley and Misterton Carrs.

Potamogeton perfoliatus L. *Perfoliate Pondweed*

Native. Rivers, drains, ponds, etc. Very common. All Divs.

First Record: C. Deering, *Cat. Stirp.* 1738.

Potamogeton Friesii Rupr. *Flat-Stalked Pondweed*

Native. Canals and pools. Rather frequent. All Divs.

First Record: H. C. Watson *N.B.G.* 1844 on authority of T. H. Cooper's specimen.

1 Nottingham Canal at Eastwood, *Carr*; Still frequent throughout its length.
2 Chesterfield Canal at Drakeholes, Worksop and Retford; Scrooby; Misson.
3 Grantham Canal at Gamston and Cotgrave; Chesterfield Canal at Misterton, Hayton and Gringley; Mons Pool, Collingham.
4 Grantham Canal at Owthorpe and Kinoulton; Staunton.

Potamogeton pusillus L.

Native. Drains, gravel pits, slow streams. Fairly common except in 2. All Divs.

First Record: G. Howitt, *Notts. Fl.* 1839 (the aggregate species) Nottingham Canal at Cossall det. J. E. Dandy 1953. (segregate species).

2 Misson.

Potamogeton Berchtoldii Fieb.

Native. Drains, gravel pits, slow streams, with acid waters. Frequent in 2 less so elsewhere. Divs. 2, 3, 4.

First Record: J. Brown *c.*1950; Near Park Drain Station, Misson, det. Dr. G. Taylor.

2 Common.
3 Besthorpe.
4 In the R. Devon at Staunton.

Potamogeton trichoides Cham. and Schlecht. *Hairlike Pondweed*

Native. Still waters. Rare or overlooked. Divs. 1, 2.

First Record: Dr. G. Taylor.

3 Colwick Gravel Pit, det. G. Taylor.

Potamogeton compressus L. *Grass wrack Pondweed*

Native. Canals, deep pools, and rivers. Rare. All Divs.

First Record: G. Howitt, *Notts. Fl.* 1839.

1 Nottingham and Erewash Canals at Eastwood, *Carr MS.*; Nottingham Canal at Trowell, Bramcote, Eastwood and Awsworth.
2 Ditch in Lenton Lane, *G. Howitt*; Beeston Canal at Lenton, *Carr MS.*
3 R. Trent at Attenborough; R. Soar at Kingston; Grantham Canal, Cotgrave, *Carr MS.*; Oxbow at South Muskham.
4 Grantham Canal above Hickling Pool, a lot.

Potamogeton crispus L. *Curly Pondweed*

Native. Rivers, canals, still waters. Very common. All Divs.

First Record: C. Deering, *Cat. Stirp.* 1738.

Potamogeton x Cooperi (Fryer) Fryer. *P. crispus x perfoliatus*

Native. With the parents. Locally frequent. Divs. 2, 3.

First Record: J. W. Carr, *Tr. Nott. Nats.* 1904.

2 Chesterfield Canal at Retford; Drains on Gringley and Everton Carrs.

3 Grantham Canal at Gamston, *Carr*; Also at West Bridgford; Chesterfield Canal at Drakeholes, *Brown*; Drains on Misterton and Gringley Carrs; Static Water Tank at West Stockwith.

Potamogeton x Lintoni Fryer *P. crispus x Friesii*

Native. Drains and canals. Uncommon. Divs. 2, 3.

First Record: Chesterfield Canal at Misterton, June 1952.

2 Drains at Misson; Canal at Retford, Osberton and Manton.

3 Chesterfield Canal at Misterton; Drakeholes.

Potamogeton pectinatus L. *Fennel Pondweed*

Native. Rivers, Canals and still waters. Very common. All Divs.

First Record: T. Ordoyno, *Fl. Nott.* 1807.

var. *flabellatus* Bab. occurs commonly in swift waters.

var. *ungulatus* Hagstr. forma *subaequalis* Hagstr.

"River Leen, *Mitchell*, Herb. Upsala. The only European locality given for this form in Hagstrom's *Critical Researches on the Potamogeton* (Stockholm 1916). The collector was Dr. James Mitchell of Nottingham" (from J. W. Carr's MS.)

Potamogeton densus L. *Opposite leafed Pondweed*

Native. Drains, streams and ponds, often on peat. Very local. All Divs.

First Record: T. Ordoyno, *Fl. Nott.* 1807 (no locality).

1 Bulwell, *Gilbert*; Nether Langwith; Shireoaks Park, Worksop†, *Carr MS.*

2 Cuckney in the Mill Dam and the stream; Everton†, *Carr MS.*; R. Poulter, West Drayton, *Butcher*; Misson; Tiln; Scrooby; Scaftworth; Mattersey.

3 Nottingham Meadows, *Jowett*; Beeston, *Mason*; R. Whipling, Whatton, *Carr MS.*; Kirklington gravel ponds; Gringley Carr; Misterton; Stockwith.

4 Pond at Granby.

Zannichellia palustris L. *Horned Pondweed*

Native. Streams, ponds, canals, etc. Common, especially in Div. 2. All Divs.

First Record: T. Jowett, *Bot. Cals.* 1826.

CYPERACEAE

Eleocharis palustris (L.) R. Br. *Common Spike Rush*

Native. Marshes and damp meadows. Very common. All Divs.

First Record: T. Ordoyno, *Fl. Nott.* 1807.

SSP. *microcarpa* S. M. Walters.

Only Record: Thoresby Park, July 1958. Div. 2, Det. S. M. Walters.

Eleocharis multicaulis (Sm.) Sm. *Many stemmed Spike Rush*

Native. Bogs. Very rare. Divs. 1, 2.

First Record: G. Howitt, *Notts. Fl.* 1839.

1 Kirkby Hardwick, *G. Howitt*; Hills and Holes, Warsop.
2 Pool in Birklands, *Hopkinson.*

Eleocharis acicularis (L.) Roem. and Schult. *Slender Spike Rush*

Native. Muddy verges of still waters. Rather rare. All Divs.

First Record: North Leverton 1951.

1 Moor Green Reservoir.
2 Misson; Everton.
3 Trent Bank, North Leverton; Grantham Canal at Cropwell Butler and at Cropwell Bishop.
4 Grantham Canal, Colston Bassett.

(William's record for Rempstone probably was *E. pauciflora.*)

Eleocharis pauciflora (Lightf.) Link. *Few Flowered Spike Rush*

Native. Peaty places with base rich waters. Very rare. Divs. 1, 4.

First Record: Warsop, June 1953.

1 Hills and Holes, Warsop.
4 Rempstone Old Church Yard.

Scirpus sylvaticus L. *Wood Club Rush*

Native. Damp shady places. Frequent in the west, decreasing eastwards. Divs. 1, 2, 3.

First Record: C. Deering, *Cat. Stirp.* 1738.

1 Frequent.
2 Budby Carr, *Carr MS.*; Newstead; Wollaton Park; Clumber Lakeside.
3 Between Nottingham Meadows and Lenton, *Jowett*; Trentside, Newark, *Fisher*; Ballast Pits at Cottam and Rampton; Farndon Holt; Milton.

Scirpus maritimus L. *Sea Club Rush*

Native. Ponds and pits on the tidal reach of the Trent. Locally frequent. Divs. 2, 3.

First Record: J. W. Carr, *Tr. Nott. Nats.* 1904 "Warping Drain at Misson."

2 Misson, *Carr.*
3 Frequent in the Trent Valley below Newark; Adventive by the canal at Cotgrave.

Scirpus lacustris L. *Bulrush*

Native. Rivers, canals, ponds, etc. Very common, but absent from Div. 4. Divs. 1, 2, 3.

First Record: C. Deering, *Cat. Stirp.* 1738.

Scirpus Tabernaemontani Gmel. *Glaucous Bull Rush*

Native. Drains, ponds, etc. Locally frequent in the lower Trent and Idle Valleys. Divs. 1, 2, 3.

First Record: H. Fisher, *Rept. Brit. Ass.* 1893.

1 Nether Langwith, *Carr* (1904).
2 Misson; Everton; Cuckney.
3 Bottom Lock Newark, *Fisher*; Misterton; Bole; Besthorpe; Meering; Gringley.

Scirpus caespitosus L. *Deer Grass*

Native. Wet heaths. Probably extinct. Divs. 1, ?2.

First Record: T. Jowett, *Bot. Cals.* 1826.

1 Bulwell, Not uncommon about the rivulets to the West of the Leen, *Jowett*; On wet Heaths; common, *G. Howitt* (No division mentioned).

Scirpus setaceus L. *Bristle Scirpus*

Native. Damp sandy places. Frequent except in Div. 4. All Divs.

First Record: T. Jowett, *Bot. Cals.* 1826.

4 Thorney.

Scirpus fluitans L. *Floating Scirpus*

Native. Drains and pools on the Carrs. Rare. Divs. 2, 3.

First Record: J. W. Carr, *Tr. Nott. Nats.* 1905.

2 Park Drain Station, Misson†, *Carr*; and in other parts of the parish; Hesley; Gringley; Finningley; Everton.
3 Misterton.

Blysmus compressus (L.) Link. *Broad Blysmus*

Native. Marshy places, usually rich in bases. Very rare. Divs. 1, 2, 3.

First Record: T. Ordoyno, *Fl. Nott.* 1807.

1 Bulwell, *Jowett*; Sutton-in-Ashfield; Kirkby Harwick, *G. Howitt*; Annesley; Warsop: Teversal, *Carr* (1903); Lady Lee, Worksop, *Brown*; Hucknall; Langwith.
2 Fountain Dale, *G. Howitt*; Burns Green, Warsop, *Carr MS.*
3 Southwell Parks, *Ordoyno.*

Eriophorum latifolium Hoppe. *Broad Leafed Cotton Grass*

Native. Peaty Bogs. Probably extinct. Divs. 1, (4).

First Record: G. Howitt, *Notts. Fl.* 1839.

1 Newbound Mill, Mansfield; Between Newstead and Linby, *G. Howitt*; Bulwell Bogs, *Gilbert*; Two meadows near Newbound Mill, *Carr MS.*
4 Stapleford Moor, *G. Howitt* (probably in Lincolnshire).

Eriophorum angustifolium Honck. *Common Cotton Grass*

Native. Peaty Bogs. Now rare. Divs. 1, 2, 3.

First Record: C. Deering, *Cat. Stirp.* 1738. G. Howitt, *Notts. Fl.* 1839 "Frequent."

Modern Records:
1 Hills and Holes, Warsop; Gateford Fox Cover.
2 Rainworth; Misson; Hesley; Scaftworth; Clipstone; Hodsock; Harworth; Scrooby.

Eriophorum vaginatum L. *Hare's Tail Cotton Grass*

Native. Peat bogs. Very rare now. Div. 2.

First Record: T. Jowett, *Bot. Cals.* 1826. G. Howitt, 1839; "In turf bogs; common."

2 Sneinton; Lenton; Nottingham Park, *Jowett*; Bulwell Bog, *Gilbert*; Oxton Bogs, *Carr MS.*; Rainworth, near L. Lake.

Schoenus nigricans L. *Black Bog Rush*

Native. Base-rich peat bogs. Very rare. Divs. 1, 2, 3.

First Record: C. Deering, *Cat. Stirp.* 1738.

1 Basford Scottum, *Deering*; Pleasley, *G. Howitt*; Sookholme Moor†; Newbound Mill, Teversall, *Carr MS.*
2 Bulwell and Papplewick Forests, *Jowett*; Fountain Dale, *G. Howitt.*
3 Edingley Moor, *Ordoyno.*

Cladium mariscus (L.) Pohl. *Fen Sedge*

Native. Very rare. Div. 3.

Only Record: Ballast Pit near Misterton Soss, very little. June 1952.

Carex distans agg.

The old botanists did not differentiate *C. distans*, *C. binervis* and *C. Hostiana.*

1 Bulwell, *Jowett*; Derby Road and Bleak Hills, Mansfield, *G. Howitt.*
3 Clifton Pastures, *Jowett.*

Carex distans L. *Distant Sedge*

Native. Damp base-rich meadows. Very rare. Div. 1 only.

First Record: J. W. Carr, *Tr. Nott. Nats.* 1907.

1 Newbound Mill, Teversall, *Carr*; Scratta Wood, Shireoaks; Hills and Holes, Warsop.

Carex Hostiana DC. *Tawny Sedge*

Native. Base-rich grassland. Very rare. Div. 1 only.

First Record: J. W. Carr, *Tr. Nott. Nats.* 1904.

1 Church Warsop 1904; Sookholme Moor 1907; Teversal 1909, *Carr.*

Carex binervis Sm. *Moor Sedge*

Native. Acid Heaths. Locally frequent. All Divs.

First Record: T. Jowett's Herbarium, Bromley House, a specimen labelled "*C. distans* 1821, Papplewick Forest."

1 Bulwell Hall Wood; Gateford Fox Cover.
2 Papplewick Forest, *Jowett*; Coxmoor; Hesley; Harworth; Osberton.
3 West Drayton; Wigsley Wood.
4 Langford Moor†; Barnby, *H. Fisher*; Coddington; Brough.

Carex lepidocarpa Tausch.

Native. By base-rich streams and marshes. Rare. Divs. 1, 4.

First Record: Rempstone, June 1951, det. E. Nelmes.

1 Shireoaks; Sookholme; Hucknall; Church Warsop; Skegby; Langold.
4 Rempstone Old Church Yard.

Carex demissa Hornem. *Yellow Sedge*

Native. Damp grassland. Fairly common. Confined to lighter soils in 4. All Divs.

First Record: T. Ordoyno, *Fl. Nott.* 1807 (as *C. flava* L.)

Carex sylvatica Huds. *Wood Sedge*

Native. Damp strong woodland. Common, but absent from Div. 2. Divs. 1, 3. 4.

First Record: T. Ordoyno, *Fl. Nott.* 1807.

Carex Pseudocyperus L. *Cyperus Sedge*

Native. In marshes and by pools. Uncommon. Divs. 2, 3, 4.

First Record: T. Jowett, *Bot. Cals.* 1826, quoting Pulteney.

2 Finningley†, *Carr* (1903); Misson; Hesley; Everton.
3 Bank of R. Soar, *Pulteney*; Banks of Erewash; Toton, *G. Howitt*; Averham†, *Carr*; Balderton; Rufford.
4 Owthorpe, *Carr* (1903); Cropwell Bishop, *Carr MS.*; Colston Bassett; Kinoulton.

Carex rostrata Stokes. *Bottle Sedge*

Native. Marshes and pools. Not very common. All Divs.

First Record: T. Ordoyno, *Fl. Nott.* 1807.

1 Nether Langwith, *Carr MS.*; Scratta Wood, Shireoaks; Teversall; Nuthall.
2 Frequent.
3 Clifton (by Nottingham), *G. Howitt*; Calverton, *Carr MS.*; Kirklington; Balderton; Misterton; Oxton.
4 Rempstone.

Carex vesicaria L. *Bladder Sedge*

Native. Damp places. Uncommon. Divs. 1, 2, 3.

First Record: G. Howitt, *Notts. Fl.* 1839.

1 Banks of Erewash, *G. Howitt*; Bulwell, *Gilbert*; Moor Green Reservoir.
2 Haughton Decoy; Misson; Scaftworth; Mattersey.
3 Banks of River Trent, *Sidebotham*; Colwick, *Gilbert*; Attenborough; Old Trent Dyke, Newark; Walkeringham, *Carr MS.*; Girton; Collingham; Winkburn; Clifton by Nottingham.

Carex riparia Curt. *Great Pond Sedge*

Native. Lakes, canals, marshes, etc. Very common, but absent from 4. Divs. 1, 2, 3.

First Record: C. Deering, *Cat. Stirp.* 1738.

Carex acutiformis Ehrh. *Lesser Pond Sedge*

Native. Lakes, canals, marshes, etc. Very common. All Divs.

First Record: T. Ordoyno, *Fl. Nott.* 1807.

Carex pendula L. *Pendulous Sedge*

Native. Woods and "dumbles." Locally common. Divs. 1, 3.

First Record: T. Jowett, *Bot. Cals.* 1826.

1 Annesley†; Beauvale; Bagthorpe, *Jowett*; Felley Mill†, *G. Howitt*; Wollaton, *Mather*; Greasley; Watnall Coppice.
3 Roe and Dilliner Woods, Winkburn; Hockerton; Halloughton; Southwell; Thurgarton; Ossington; Epperstone.

Carex strigosa Huds.

Native. Damp strong woodland, often growing partly in water. Rare. Divs. 1, 3.

First Record: Park Wood, Caunton May 1952. det. E. Nelmes.

1 Dovedale Wood, Teversall; Skegby; Millington Springs.
3 Caunton; Bevercotes; Ossington; Grove; Winkburn; North Leverton; Weston; Wellow Park.

Carex pallescens L. *Pale Sedge*

Native. Woodland rides and grassy places. Formerly frequent, now rather rare. Divs. 1, 3, 4.

First Record: C. Deering, *Cat. Stirp.* 1738.

1 Bulwell.
3 Muskham Wood, *Fisher*; Roe Wood, Winkburn; Werner and Mather Woods, Caunton; Grassthorpe, in meadows; Clifton Pastures.
4 Stanton-on-Wolds.

Carex panicea L. *Carnation Grass*

Native. Damp meadows and marshes. Common. All Divs.

First Record: T. Ordoyno, *Fl. Nott.* 1807.

Carex flacca Schreb. *Glaucous Sedge*

Native. Grassland, particularly on clay and limestone. Very common. All Divs.

First Record: C. Deering, *Cat. Stirp.* 1738.

Carex hirta L. *Hairy Sedge*

Native. Waste ground, grassland and marshes. Very common. All Divs.

First Record: C. Deering, *Cat. Stirp.* 1738.

Carex pilulifera L. *Pill-headed Sedge*

Native. Dry heaths and woods. Common in Div. 2, less so elsewhere. All Divs.

First Record: T. Ordoyno, *Fl. Nott.* 1807.

1 Annesley; Teversall; Holbeck.
2 Common.
3 Frequent.
4 Langford Moor; Thorney.

Carex caryophyllea Latour *Spring Sedge*

Native. Grassy banks. Locally frequent. All Divs.

First Record: T. Ordoyno, *Fl. Nott.* 1807.

1 Frequent.
2 Nottingham Park, *Jowett*; Nottingham Church Cemetery, *Bohler* (1866); Thoresby Park; Carlton-in-Lindrick.
3 Frequent.
4 Gotham Hills; Stanton-on-Wolds.

Carex digitata L. *Fingered Sedge*

Native. Limestone Woods. Very rare or extinct. Div. 1.

Only Record: T. Jowett, *Bot. Cals.* 1826, "Pleasley Wood, Notts."

Carex elata All. *Tufted Sedge*

Native. Beside waters on light soils. Infrequent. Divs. 1, 2, 3.

First Record: G. Howitt, *Notts. Fl.* 1839, "Rather frequent."

1 Greasley; Styrrup, *Carr.*
2 Misson; Finningley; Ordsall; Scaftworth.
3 Banks of Trent, *Sidebotham*; Wigsley Wood; Besthorpe.

Carex acuta L. *Tufted Sedge*

Native. Beside waters and ponds. Frequent except in Div. 4. Divs. 1, 2, 3.

First Record: C. Deering, *Cat. Stirp.* 1738.

Carex nigra (L.) Reichard. *Black Sedge*

Native. Bogs and damp meadows. Common, but absent from Div. 4. Divs. 1, 2, 3.

First Record: T. Ordoyno, *Fl. Nott.* 1807.

Carex paniculata L. *Tussock Sedge*

Native. Black bogs, and by canals. Local. Divs. 1, 2, 3.

First Record: T. Ordoyno, *Fl. Nott.* 1807.

1 Frequent.
2 A frequent and characteristic plant of boggy woodland and of streamsides.
3 Haughton Decoy; Kirklington; Calverton; Chesterfield Canal at Everton and Gringley.

Carex diandra Schrank.

Native. Probably extinct.

Only Record: G. Howitt, *Notts. Fl.* 1839, "In bogs, rare; near the Bleak Hills, Mansfield."

Carex Otrubae Podp. *Fox Sedge*

Native. In damp places and by waters. Very common. All Divs.

First Record: C. Deering, *Cat. Stirp.* 1738.

Carex disticha Huds. *Brown Sedge*

Native. Marshes. Frequent except in Div. 4. All Divs.

First Record: T. Ordoyno, *Fl. Nott.* 1807.

4 Langford; Coddington; Rempstone.

Carex arenaria L. *Sand Sedge*

Native. Only on the blown sand, where it is often dominant. Div. 3.

First Record: Besthorpe 1950, det. E. Nelmes.

3 Besthorpe; Girton; Spalford; South Clifton; Sconce Hills, Newark; South Collingham, the last two localities are not considered to be blown sand by the geologists, but they carry the typical flora.

Carex divulsa Stokes. *Grey Sedge*

Native. Woods. Very rare. Divs. (2), 3.

First Record: J. Sidebotham, *Phyt. I* 1842.

3 Near Oxton (or 2); Colwick Park, *Sidebotham*; Frog Abbey, Averham, very little, det. E. Nelmes.

Carex spicata Huds. *Spiked Sedge*

Native. Hedges and grassy places on light land. Frequent, but absent from Div. 4. Divs. 1, 2, 3.

First Record: C. Deering, *Cat. Stirp.* 1738.

Carex Pairaei F. Schultz. *Prickly Sedge*

Native. Dry sandy grassland. Uncommon. Divs. 2, 3.

First Record: J. Brown in litt. 1952. Sandy roadside near Blyth, det. E. Nelmes.

2 Blyth, *Brown*; Carlton-in-Lindrick; Clumber; Manton Wood; Osberton.

3 Sconce Hills, Newark.

Carex echinata Murr. *Star headed Sedge*

Native. Marshy meadows. Formerly very common, now very rare. Not recorded from Div. 4. Divs. 1, 2, 3.

First Record: T. Ordoyno, *Fl. Nott.* 1807.

Modern Records:
2 Serlby; Scrooby; Osberton.
3 Calverton.

Carex remota L. *Remote Sedge*

Native. Damp woods. Common, but restricted to the sands in Div. 4.

First Record: T. Ordoyno, *Fl. Nott.* 1807.

4 Broadholme; Thorney; Harby.

Carex curta Good. *White Sedge*

Native. Bogs. Very rare. Div. 2.

First Record: J. W. Carr, *Tr. Nott. Nats.* 1905.

2 Lyndhurst, *Carr*; Ling's Wood, Scaftworth, a lot; Upper Flash Plantation, Carlton-in-Lindrick, several plants.

Carex ovalis L. *Oval Sedge*

Native. Damp meadows. Common except in Div. 4. All Divs.

First Record: C. Deering, *Cat. Stirp.* 1738.

4 Owthorpe; Langford; West Leake.

Carex pulicaris L. *Flea Sedge*

Native. Damp meadows. Formerly frequent, now rare. Not recorded for Div. 4. Divs. 1, 2, 3.

First Record; T. Ordoyno, *Fl. Nott.* 1807.

Modern Records:
3 Manser Gorse, Eakring; Meadow at North Leverton.

Carex dioica L. *Dioecious Sedge*

Native. Bogs. Very rare. Divs. 1, 2, 3.

First Record: T. Ordoyno, *Fl. Nott.* 1807.

1 Bulwell and Papplewick Bogs, *Jowett*; Sutton-in-Ashfield, *G. Howitt*; Hills and Holes, Warsop.
2 Oxton Bottoms, *Ordoyno*; "Frequent in the sand district," *G. Howitt*.
3 Edingley Moor, *Ordoyno*.

GRAMINACEAE

Panicum miliaceum L. *Millet*

Alien. Casual. Rubbish dumps. On all dumps. All Divs.

First Record: H. Fisher, *Proc. Brit. Ass.* 1893 "Newark."

Panicum colonum (L.) Link.

Alien. Casual. Rubbish dumps. Rare. Divs. 1, 3.

1 Bulwell 1958.
3 Nottingham 1958. Wilford 1958.

Panicum Crus-galli L. *Cock's Spur Panicum*

Alien. Casual. Carrot fields on the blown sands and gravels. Uncommon. Divs. 2, 3, 4.

First Record: *Victoria County History* 1906.

2 Frequent garden weed at Bramcote, *Butcher*.
3 North Clifton; Spalford; Girton.
4 South Scarle.

Setaria italica (L.) Beauv. *Italian Millet*

Alien. Casual. Rubbish dumps. On all dumps. All Divs.

First Record: Nottingham Dump 1953.

Setaria viridis (L.) Beauv.

Alien. Casual. Rubbish dumps and among carrots. Frequent. All Divs.

First Record: H. Fisher, *Proc. Brit. Ass.* 1893 "Newark."

Setaria glauca Beauv.

Alien. Casual. Rare. Div. 3.

Only Record: H. Fisher, *Rept. Brit. Ass.* 1893 "Newark."

Phalaris minor Retz.

Alien. Casual. Rubbish dumps. Uncommon. Divs. 2, 3.

First Record: Nottingham Dump 1958.

2 Cuckney Dump.
3 Nottingham Dump, 1958 et seq.

Phalaris canariensis L. *Canary Grass*

Alien. Casual. Dumps and waste ground. Frequent. All Divs.

First Record: Herb. T. Jowett 1824, "Wollaton, on a manure heap."

Phalaris arundinaceae L. *Small Reed*
Native. River sides and marshes. Very common. All Divs.
First Record: C. Deering, *Cat. Stirp.* 1738.

Anthoxanthum odoratum L. *Sweet Vernal Grass*
Native. Meadows. Very common. All Divs.
First Record: C. Deering, *Cat. Stirp.* 1738.

Alopecurus pratensis L. *Meadow Foxtail*
Native. Meadows. Very common. All Divs.
First Record: C. Deering, *Cat. Stirp.* 1738.

Alopecurus myosuriodes Huds. *Black Bent*
Native. Cornfields on heavy clay. Locally common. Divs. 2, 3, 4.
First Record: C. Deering, *Cat. Stirp.* 1738.
2 Welbeck.
3 and 4 Common.

Alopecurus geniculatus L. *Marsh Foxtail*
Native. Marshy meadows. Very common. All Divs.
First Record: C. Deering, *Cat. Stirp.* 1738.

Alopecurus x hybridus Wimm. *A. geniculatus x pratensis*
Only Record: J. W. Carr, *Trans. Nott. Nats.* 1905 "By Soar near Kegworth Bridge." Div. 3.

Milium effusum L. *Wood Millet*
Native. Damp woodland. Locally common. All Divs.
First Record: T. Jowett, *Bot. Cals.* 1826.
1 Common.
2 Newstead; Harworth; Rufford; Mattersey; Retford.
3 Common.
4 Bunny.

Phleum pratense L. *Timothy*
Native. Meadows, roadsides, etc. Very common. All Divs.
First Record: C. Deering, *Cat. Stirp.* 1738.

Phleum nodosum L.
Native. Dry banks and grassland. Common, less so on sand. All Divs.
First Record: C. Deering, *Cat. Stirp.* 1738.

Agrostis stolonifera L. *Fiorin*

Native. Damp grassland. Very common. All Divs.

First Record: C. Deering, *Cat. Stirp.* 1738.

Agrostis canina L. *Brown Bent*

Native. Dry sandy grassland. Distribution imperfectly known.

First Record: C. Deering, *Cat. Stirp.* 1738.

2 "Locally abundant in grass heath", *Hopkinson*; Budby Forest, *Brown*; Thoresby; Welbeck; Carlton-in-Lindrick; Osberton.
3 Girton.

Agrostis gigantea Roth. *Red Top*

Native. Arable fields. Distribution imperfectly known. Divs. 1, 2, 4.

First Record: J. W. Carr, *Tr. Nott. Nats.* 1903.

1 Kirkby-in-Ashfield, *Carr* 1903.
2 Frequent about Nottingham (or 3), *Carr* 1909
4 Stanton-on-Wolds; South Scarle; Rempstone (all on drift soils).

Calamagrostis epigeios (L.) Roth. *Bush Grass*

Native. Damp woods. Uncommon except in Div. 3. All Divs.

First Record: T. Ordoyno, *Fl. Nott.* 1807.

1 Bulwell, *Jowett*; Hodsock, *Mrs. Sandwith*; Owday Wood, Carlton, *Brown.*
2 Farnsfield; Styrrup.
3 Rather frequent.
4 West Leake, *Carr MS.*; Wigsley; Thorney; Harby; Langford Moor. All on sand or drift.

Calamagrostis canescens (Weber) Roth. *Purple Small Reed*

Native. Fen pastures and moist sandy woods. Local. Divs. 1, 2, 3.

First Record: T. Jowett, *Bot. Cals.* 1826.

1 Bulwell, *Jowett.*
2 Mowing meadows and woods at Misson; Styrrup; Ranskill; Scaftworth; Everton; Osberton Ash Holt, Hodsock.
3 Wigsley Wood; Roe Wood, Winkburn.

Apera Spica-venti (L.) Beauv. *Silky Bent*

Native. Sandy cornfields. Locally common especially on the edge of the Carrs.

First Record: J. Ray, *Phil. Letters* 1749 "Very plentifully among corn in the sandy grounds of this County." (Written from Wollaton 1607.)

1 Harworth Carr.
2 About Wollaton, *Ray*; Barrow Hills, Everton†, *Carr* 1904; Ordsall, *Carr* 1905; Blackcliff Hill, Ollerton, *Roffey*; Pusto Hill, Everton; Scaftworth; Misson; Styrrup; Harworth; Lound; Ranskill; Torworth; Finningley; Carlton-in-Lindrick; Osberton.
3 By footpath from Ordsall to Eaton Wood, *Carr MS.*; Collingham, *Leather*.

Apera interrupta (L.) Riechb.

Casual. Arable land. Very rare. Divs. 2, 3.

First Record: *Victoria County History*, 1906.

2 Bulb field at Welbeck 1960.
3 *Victoria County History*, 1906.

Aira caryophyllea L. *Silver Hair Grass*

Native. Sandy fields and commons. Also appears on well drained banks and path sides. Frequent. More widespread than the next but not occuring in such quantity. All Divs.

First Record: T. Ordoyno, *Fl. Nott.* 1807.

Aira praecox L. *Early Hair Grass*

Native. Sandy fields and commons. Locally common. All Divs.

First Record: T. Ordoyno, *Fl. Nott.* 1807.

1 Langwith; Strelley.
2 Very common.
3 Rolleston, *Fisher*; Common on the blown sand; Epperstone Park; Marnham.
4 Common on the sand and gravels.

(**Corynephorus canescens** (L.) Beauv.

Recorded by Deering, *Cat. Stirp.* 1738 with no locality.)

Deschampsia caespitosa (L.) Beauv. *Tufted Hair Grass*

Native. Damp meadows and woods. Very common. All Divs.

First Record: C. Deering, *Cat. Stirp.* 1738.

Deschampsia flexuosa (L.) Trin. *Wavy Hair Grass*

Native. Fields and heaths on sand. Locally abundant. All Divs.

First Record: C. Deering, *Cat. Stirp.* 1738.

1 Nether Langwith; Worksop, *Carr MS.*; Millington Springs, Bagthorpe.
2 Very common.
3 Langford; Eaton, *Carr MS.*; Walesby; Wigsley Wood; North Collingham; Girton; West Drayton; Spalford. (Confined to blown sand and to the river valleys near 2.)
4 Langford Moor; Thorney.

Holcus mollis L. *Wood Soft Grass*

Native. Sandy woods and pastures. Locally abundant, often dominant. All Divs.

First Record: T. Ordoyno, *Fl. Nott.* 1809.

Holcus lanatus L. *Yorkshire Fog*

Native. Poor pastures and waste ground. Very common. All Divs.

First Record: C. Deering, *Cat. Stirp.* 1738.

Trisetum flavescens Pers. *Yellow Oat Grass*

Native. Meadows and roadsides. Widespread. All Divs.

First Record: C. Deering, *Cat. Stirp.* 1738.

Avena fatua L. *False Oat*

Native. Cornfields on heavy soils. Very common in Divs. 3, 4. Scarce in 1, 2.

First Record: C. Deering, *Cat. Stirp.* 1738.

var *pilosa* Syme. Kersal 1952, det. C. E. Hubbard. Div. 3.

fatua x sativa Norwell 1952, det. C. E. Hubbard. Div. 3.

Avena strigosa Schreb.

Alien. Casual. Cornfields. Very rare. Divs. 2, 4.

First Record: G. Howitt, *Notts. Fl.* 1839.

2 Highfield House, Nottingham, *Lowe.*
4 Near West Leake, *G. Howitt.*

Avena pubescens Huds. *Hairy Oat Grass*

Native. Roadsides and rough grassland. Common. All Divs.

First Record: T. Ordoyno, *Fl. Nott.* 1807.

Avena pratensis L. *Meadow Oat Grass*

Native. Calcareous meadows. Rare. No recent records. All Divs.

First Record: T. Ordoyno, *Fl. Nott.* 1807.

1 Bulwell, *Ordoyno*; Mansfield Woodhouse; Grives Quarry, Kirkby, *G. Howitt*; Steetley, *Bohler* 1875.
2 Church Cemetery, Nottingham, *Bohler* 1866.
3 Beeston Meadows, *Mason.*
4 Crow Wood Hill, West Leake, *Carr MS.*

Arrhenatherum elatius (L.) J. C. Presl. *False Oat*

Native. Most grassy places. Very common. All Divs.

First Record: C. Deering, *Cat. Stirp.* 1738.

Sieglingia decumbens (L.) Bernh.

Native. Heaths and poor pastures. Uncommon except in Div. 2. Divs. 1, 2, 3.

First Record: T. Jowett, *Bot. Cals.* 1826.

1 Selston, *Jowett*; Teversall, *Carr MS.*; Moor Green; Harworth; Greasley.
2 Common.
3 Eakring; Milton.

Phragmites communis Trin. *Great Reed*

Native. River, pond, and canal sides, Willow holts, marshes. Common. All Divs.

First Record: C. Deering, *Cat. Stirp.* 1738.

Formerly cultivated for plastering.

Cynosurus echinatus L.

Alien. Casual. Waste places. Rare. Div. 3.

First Record: V. Leather, *Notts. W. F. S. Diary* 1934.

3 Fiskerton Wharf, *Leather*; Sugar Factory Sidings, Newark 1954.

Cynosurus cristatus L. *Dog's Tail*

Native. Meadows, road and path sides etc. Very common. All Divs.

First Record: C. Deering, *Cat. Stirp.* 1738.

Koeleria cristata (L.) Pers.

Native. Banks in calcareous meadows. Rare or overlooked (G. Howitt considered it frequent). Divs. 1, 2, 3.

First Record: T. Jowett's interleaved copy of Ordoyno 1821.

1 Nr. Bulwell, *Jowett*; Kirkby-in-Ashfield, *Carr MS.*; Hills and Holes, Warsop.
2 Edwinstowe, *Bohler* 1875; Church Cemetery, Nottingham, *Bohler* 1866; Bulwell Forest; Rufford; Barrow Hills, Everton, *Carr MS.*
3 Colwick Dumble, *Williams*; Trentside meadows at Farndon; Newark; Rolleston; Besthorpe; Girton.

Molinia caerulea (L.) Moench.

Native. Boggy meadows and heaths. Decreasing. All Divs.

First Record: T. Ordoyno, *Fl. Nott.* 1807.

1 Sutton-in-Ashfield; Teversall, *Carr MS.*; Sookholme; Church Warsop; Skegby; Annesley.
2 "Very common", *G. Howitt.* Still fairly widespread.
3 Edingley Moor, *Ordoyno*; Clifton (by Nottingham); Gamston Moor, *Jowett's Ordoyno*; Bothamsall, *Carr MS.*; Wigsley Wood; Spalford.
4 Langford Moor; Wigsley; Thorney.

Catabrosa aquatica (L.) Beauv. *Whorl Grass*

Native. Stream and canal sides. Widespread. All Divs.

First Record: C. Deering, *Cat. Stirp.* 1738.

1 Warsop, *Carr MS.*; Cossall; Trowell.
2 Nottingham Park, *G. Howitt*; Warsop; Harworth, *Carr MS.*; Papplewick; Clarborough; Scrooby; Scaftworth; Hodsock.
3 Nottingham Meadows, *Ordoyno*; Beeston, *Lowe*; Canal at Gamston, *Carr MS.*; Wiseton; Gringley; S. Collingham; Hayton; Clarborough; Everton; Calverton.
4 Rempstone.

Melica nutans L. *Mountain Melic*

Native. Limestone woodland. Very rare. Div. 1.

First Record: Mr. Stonehouse in How's *Phyt. Brit.* 1650.

1 In a hollow way betwixt Pleasley and Mansfield, *Stonehouse*; Pleasley Wood, *G. Howitt*; Scratta Wood, Shireoaks, *Brown.*

Melica uniflora Retz. *Wood Melic*

Native. Woodland. Locally frequent. Divs. 1, 2, 3.

First Record: C. Deering, *Cat. Stirp.* 1738.

1 Common.
2 Mattersey Wood.
3 In most woods and some hedges.

Dactylis glomerata L. *Cock's Foot Grass*

Native. Meadows, roadsides, etc. Very common. All Divs.

First Record: C. Deering, *Cat. Stirp.* 1738.

Briza media L. *Quaking Grass*

Native. Meadows on good soils. Common. All Divs.

First Record: C. Deering, *Cat. Stirp.* 1738.

Poa pratensis L. *Meadow Poa*

Native. Meadows, roadsides and all grassy places. Very common. All Divs.

First Record: C. Deering, *Cat. Stirp.* 1738.

Poa angustifolia L.

Native. Distribution incompletely known. Div. 1.

First Record: Pleasley Vale 1952.

1 Pleasley Vale: Mansfield Woodhouse, det. C. E. Hubbard.

Poa subcaerulea Sm.

Native. Dry meadows and banks. Distribution incompletely known. Divs. 2, 3.

First Record: Besthorpe 1953, det. C. E. Hubbard.

2 Finningley.
3 Besthorpe; Bunny Park.

Poa palustris L.

Alien. Wet places. Very rare. Div. 3.

Only Record: Ballast Pit at South Collingham 1951, det. C. E. Hubbard.

Poa trivialis L. *Rough Poa*

Native. Damp woods and meadows. Very common. All Divs.

First Record: T. Ordoyno, *Fl. Nott.* 1807.

Poa nemoralis L. *Wood Poa*

Native. Woods. Frequent except in Div. 4. All Divs.

First Record: G. Howitt, *Notts. Fl.* 1839.

4 Thorney; Cotgrave.

Poa compressa L. *Flattened Poa*

Native. Walls and dry places, especially on limestone. Uncommon, except in Div. 1. Divs. 1, 3, 4.

First Record: T. Ordoyno, *Fl. Nott.* 1807.

1 Frequent.
3 Southwell Parks, *Ordoyno*; Keyworth; Langford; Holme, *Carr MS.*; Arnold, *Williams*; Kersal; Nottingham; Farndon.
4 East Leake; Cotgrave, *Williams*; West Leake; Coddington; Bunny.

Poa annua L. *Annual Poa*

Native. Fields and disturbed ground. Very common. All Divs.

First Record: C. Deering, *Cat. Stirp.* 1738.

Poa distans L. *Distant Poa*

Native. Bare damp ground. Very restricted in range, though often occuring plentifully. Divs. 1, 2, 3.

First Record: T. Jowett, *Bot. Cals.* 1826, and see his interleaved copy of Ordoyno. "Near the Leen and its tributary rills from Nottingham to Bulwell in a course of at least six miles."

1 Bulwell; Aspley limekilns; Basford Town Street; Cinder Hill, *Jowett*; Quarry near Steetley Wood, *Brown*; Shireoaks Green, *Adams*; Bulwell Dump.

2 Lenton Town Street, *Jowett*.

3 Nottingham Meadows, *Jowett*; Nottingham Dump in quantity.

Glyceria maxima (Hartm.) Holmb. *Reed Grass*

Native. Wet meadows, river and canal sides, etc. Common. All Divs.

First Record: C. Deering, *Cat. Stirp.* 1738.

Glyceria fluitans agg. *Flote Grass*

Native. Marshy meadows. Very common. All Divs.

First Record: C. Deering, *Cat. Stirp.* 1738.

Very little work has been done on this group.

Glyceria fluitans (L.) R. Br.

Native. Marshy meadows. Probably common.

First Record: *Victoria County History* 1906.

Glyceria x pedicillata Townsend. *fluitans x plicata*

1 Wollaton, det. C. E. Hubbard.

Glyceria plicata Fr.

Native. Marshy meadows. Perhaps common. Divs. 1, 3.

First Record: Anne Gilbert, *Botany for Beginners* 1880.

1 Fields near Broxtowe, *Gilbert*; Bilborough, *Carr MS.*

3 Newark, *Fisher*; Nottingham; West Leake (or 4), *Carr* 1909. Sutton Bonington, *Carr MS.*; Tollerton Canal, *Williams*; Nottingham Sewage Farm.

Glyceria declinata Breb.

Native. Marshy meadows. Divs. 1, 2.

First Record: Cossall 1952, det. C. E. Hubbard.

1 Cossall.

2 Hesley, *Gibbons*.

Festuca rigida (L.) Kunth. *Hard Fescue*

Native. Dry bare places, mostly on calcareous soils. Fairly frequent except in 2. All Divs.

First Record: C. Deering, *Cat. Stirp.* 1738.

1 Frequent.
2 Nottingham Park upon the Rock; Wollaton Park Walls, *Deering*; Railway bank, Babworth.
3 Colwick Park Walls, *Jowett's Ordoyno*; Kingston-on-Soar, *Carr MS.*; Cropwell Bishop; Hawton; Clarborough; Granby.
4 Barnstone; Gotham; Normanton-on-Soar.

Festuca gigantea (L.) Vill. *Giant Fescue*

Native. Woods on strong soil. Common in 1 and 3, less so in 2 and 4. All Divs.

First Record: C. Deering, *Cat. Stirp.* 1738.

2 Elkesley; Hodsock, *Carr MS.*; Wiseton; Wollaton; Lound; Bothamsall.
4 Kinoulton; Thorney, *Carr MS.*; Thrumpton; Harby.

Festuca arundinacea Schreb. *Reed Fescue*

Native. Roadsides, damp rough grassland and disturbed ground. Common except in Div. 2. All Divs.

First Record: T. Ordoyno, *Fl. Nott.* 1807.

Festuca pratensis Huds. *Meadow Fescue*

F. elatior L.

Native. Fertile meadows and roadsides. Common. All Divs.

First Record: T. Ordoyno, *Fl. Nott.* 1807.

Festuca rubra L. *Red Fescue*

Native. Meadows on most soils, roadsides etc. Common. All Divs.

First Record: T. Ordoyno, *Fl. Nott.* 1807.

var *vulgaris* Gaud. Common.

var *fallax* Thuill.

Victoria County History. Div. 1.

var *megastachys* Gaud.

3 Lady Wood, Caunton.

var *glaucescens* Richt.

2 Farnsfield.
3 Garden weed at Farndon. ssp. *duriuscula* Syme.

var *duriuscula* Syme.

3 Farndon; Besthorpe.

var *dumetorum* (L.) Gaud.

3 Garden weed, Farndon; Clifton by Nottingham.

Festuca ovina L. *Sheep's Fescue*

Native. Meadows and banks on well drained soils both limestone and sand and gravel. Common. All Divs.

First Record: C. Deering, *Cat. Stirp.* 1738.

ssp. *eu-ovina* var. *glauca* Hack.

3 Gravelly meadows at South Collingham; Spalford Warrens.

Festuca longifolia Thuill.

Native. Meadows. Distribution imperfectly known. Divs. 1, 2.

1 Lady Lee, Worksop.
2 Nottingham Church Cemetery, *Bohler*; Ranby.

Festuca tenuifolia Sibth.

Native. Dry heaths and meadows. Locally plentiful. All Divs.

First Record: *Comital Flora* 1932.

1 Lady Lee, Worksop; Teversall; Greasley; East Kirkby.
2 Common.
3 Sconce Hills, Newark; Balderton; Eakring.
4 Langford Moor.

Festuca glauca var *caesia* Sm.

The Dillenian Edition of Ray's *Synposis* 1724 records a variety of (*F. ovina*) with glaucous leaves, being gathered on the 'backside of Nottingham Castle, by Mr. Sherard.' T. Jowett (1826) still found it there, and in Nottingham Park, and identified it as *F. caesia* (E. B. 246). It could however have been *F. ovina* ssp.*eu-ovina* var. *glauca* Hack. Div. 2.

Festuca Bromoides L. *Barren Fescue*

Native. Sandy heaths, dry banks and waste places. Common, especially in Div. 2. All Divs.

First Record: T. Ordoyno, *Fl. Nott.* 1807.

Festuca Myuros L. *Rat's tail Fescue*

Casual. Waste places. Rare. Divs. 2, 3, 4.

First Record: T. Ordoyno, *Fl. Nott.* 1807. "Walls and dry barren places". G. Howitt, *Notts. Fl.* 1389: "On walls and in sandy fields, rather frequent."

2 Nottingham Church Cemetery, *Bohler* 1866; Osberton and Babworth on the railway.
3 Hawton, *Fisher*; Railway line by Kelham sugar factory; Railway at Woodthorpe; Railway at Colwick.
4 Railway at Normanton-on-Soar.

x Festulolium Loliaceum (Huds.) P. Fourn.
Festuca pratensis x Lolium perenne

Native. With the parents. Common. All Divs.

First Record: T. Ordoyno, *Fl. Nott.* 1807.

Bromus sterilis L. *Barren Brome*

Native. Roadsides and waste ground. Very common. All Divs.

First Record: C. Deering, *Cat. Stirp.* 1738.

Bromus tectorum L.

Alien. Very rare.

Only Record: H. Fisher, *Rept. Brit. Ass.* 1893.

Bromus ramosus Huds. *Hairy Brome*

Native. Woods on strong land. Common, except in Div. 2.

First Record: C. Deering, *Cat. Stirp.* 1738.

Bromus erectus Huds. *Upright Brome*

Native. Grassland on calcareous soils. Widespread in rough ground in Divs. 1, 3 and 4.

First Record: A. Gilbert, *Botany for Beginners* 1880.

Bromus mollis L. *Soft Brome*

Native. Grassland. Very common. All Divs.

First Record: C. Deering, *Cat. Stirp.* 1738.

Bromus lepidus Holmb. *Slender Brome*

Denizen. Roadsides, edges of fields, etc. Widespread and frequent, but never in quantity. All Divs.

First Record: Mrs. Sandwith with J. P. M. Brennan, *B.E.C. Rept.* 1947, Misterton, Div. 3.

Bromus arvensis L.

Rare casual. Div. 3.

Only Record: T. Jowett, *Bot. Cals.* 1826, "Fields above Mapperley Place."

Bromus racemosus L. *Smooth Brome*

Native. Meadows. Distribution imperfectly known. Divs. 2, 3.

First Record: T. Jowett, *Bot. Cals.* 1826.

2 Bulwell Forest, *Gilbert.*
3 Nottingham Meadows; Between Bleasby and Morton, *Jowett*; Frequent in the Trent Vale, *G. Howitt*; Newark, *Fisher*; Caunton; Kersal; Cottam.

Bromus commutatus Schrad.

Native. Meadows. Distribution imperfectly known. Div. 3.

First Record: H. C. Watson, *Top. Bot.* 1873, Cooper's sp.

3 Newark, *Fisher*; Mapperley Plains, *Carr* 1904; Halloughton.
4 Crow Wood Hill, West Leake, *Carr MS.*

Bromus secalinus L. *Rye Brome*

Denizen. Cornfields. Formerly rather frequent, no modern records. Divs. 2, 3, 4.

First Record: C. Deering, *Cat. Stirp..* 1738, "Frequent among Corn."

2 Frequent among corn, *Bohler* 1875.
3 Nottingham, *Deering*; Southwell, *Ordoyno.*
4 West Leake, *G. Howitt.*

Bromus Thominii Hard.

Native. Grassland. Distribution imperfectly known. Divs. 1, 2, 3.

First Record: West Stockwith 1951.

1 Hills and Holes, Warsop.
2 Harworth; Oxton.
3 West Stockwith; Halloughton; Clifton by Nottingham.

Var *hirsutus* Holmb. Hills and Holes, Warsop. Div. 1.

All det. C. E. Hubbard.

Bromus carinatus Hook. and Arn.

Alien. Div. 3. Introduced by us to Farndon garden. Now doing well in the lane nearby.

Brachypodium sylvaticum (Huds.) Beauv. *Wood False Brome*

Native. Strong woodland and shady places. Common. Often dominant in woodland in Div. 1. All Divs.

First Record: C. Deering, *Cat. Stirp.* 1738.

Brachypodium pinnatum (L.) Beauv. *Heath False Brome*

Native. Banks and Pastures on basic soils. Frequent except in Div. 2. All Divs.

First Record: T. Jowett, *Bot. Cals.* 1826.

2 Rufford; Hesley; Wiseton; Harworth; Welbeck; Harlow Wood; Osberton.

Lolium perenne L. *Rye Grass*

Native. Meadows, roadsides and waste places. Very common. All Divs.

First Record: C. Deering, *Cat. Stirp.* 1738.

Lolium temulentum L. *Darnel*

Alien. Casual. Formerly a common weed, now a rare adventive on rubbish heaps. Divs. 1, 2, 3.

First Record: C. Deering, *Cat. Stirp.* 1738, "Common in Cornfields." G. Howitt (1839) already considered it rare.

1 Cornfields near Sutton; By the road to Bulwell, *Gilbert*; Dump at Sookholme.
2 Cuckney dump.
3 Ploughed lands, Southwell, *Ordoyno*; Nottingham Dump.

Lolium multiflorum Lam. *Italian Rye Grass*

Alien. Denizen. Commonly sown with seed mixtures and persisting for some years in meadows and around farm yards. All Divs.

First Record: E. J. Lowe, *British Grasses* 1872, Beeston.

Agropyron pungens (Pers.) Roem. and Schultz. *Sea Couch Grass*
Casual. Div. 3.

Only Record: Nottingham Meadows, 1958, persisting for many years.

Agropyron repens L. *Twitch*

Native. Arable land, roadsides and waste places. A common weed. All Divs.

First Record: T. Ordoyno, *Fl. Nott.* 1807.

Agropyron caninum Beauv. *Bearded Couch Grass*

Native. Woods and shady places on strong land. Frequent except in Div. 2. All Divs.

First Record: T. Ordoyno, *Fl. Nott.* 1807.

Nardus stricta L. *Mat Grass*

Native. Dry sandy heaths. Locally common. All Divs.

First Record: T. Ordoyno, *Fl. Nott.* 1807.

1 Frequent on the coal measures.
2 Common.
3 Edingley Moor, *Ordoyno*; Haughton; Cocking Moor, Wellow; Spalford.
4 Langford Moor; Rempstone.

Hordeum secalinum Schreb. *Meadow Barley*

Native. Meadows on most soils. Widespread, though never in great quantity, rare in Div. 2. All Divs.

First Record: C. Deering, *Cat. Stirp.* 1738.

Hordeum murinum L. *Wall Barley*

Native. Roadsides, and waste places. Common. All Divs.

First Record: C. Deering, *Cat. Stirp.* 1738.

Hordeum europaeum (L.) All. *Wood Barley*

Native. Limestone Woodland. Very Rare. Div. 1.

First Record: G. Howitt, *Notts. Flora* 1839.

1 Pleasley Park (Derbys.) and Wood; Woods near Felley Mill, *G. Howitt.*

Hordeum jubatum L.

Alien. Casual. Div. 1.

Only Record: Chicken run at Shireoaks. 1953.

Gymnospermae

PINACEAE

Juniperus communis L. *Juniper*

Native. Heaths. Extinct. Div. 3.

First Record: C. Deering, *Cat. Stirp.* 1738, "On a common going to Southwell about a mile beyond Oxton. I have also observed many pretty large Trees in Mr. Muster's Wilderness by Colwick Hall." T. Ordoyno: "Heaths and commons; but not frequent."

Taxus baccata L. *Yew Tree*

Denizen. Woods, hedges and Parkland. Formerly widely planted, now completely naturalised. All Divs.

First Record: C. Deering, *Cat. Stirp.* 1738.

Pinus sylvestris L. *Scotch Pine*

Possibly native in Div. 2 but nowhere else in the county. Widespread and completely naturalised. It is now very heavily planted for forestry, especially in Div. 2. Seven per cent of the Forestry Commission's plantations are of this species, and a higher proportion of those of some private owners. All Divs.

First Record: C. Deering, *Cat. Stirp.* 1738. "My Lord Middleton . . . and divers other Gentlemen have made considerable Plantations of it."

Pinus Larico Poiret. *Corsican Pine*

Alien. Very commonly planted for forestry, especially in Div. 2. Seventy five per cent of the Forestry Commission's plantations are of this species. It is beginning to regenerate naturally. All Divs.

Larix decidua Mill. *European Larch*

Alien. Planted for forestry (four per cent of the Forestry Commission's plantations). All Divs.

Larix leptolepis, *Tsuga heterophylla*, *Pseudotsuga Douglasii*, *Pinus contorta*, *Cupressus Lawsoniana*, *Thuya plicata*, *Picea Abies*, and *P. sitchensis* also occur in plantations.

Pteridophyta

EQUISETACEAE

Equisetum Telmateia Ehrh. *Great Horsetail*

Native. Wet woodland and meadows, often round springs. Locally frequent. All Divs.

First Record: C. Deering, *Cat. Stirp.* 1738.

1 Very frequent.
2 Nottingham Park, *Deering*; Stapleford; Annesley; Bothamsall; *Carr MS.*; Elkesley.
3 Between Lenton and Beeston, *Deering*; Laxton, *Carr* 1904; Bevercotes Park; Kersal; Grove.
4 Gotham.

Equisetum arvense L. *Common Horsetail, 'Toadpipe'*

Native. Arable land, wet meadows, waste ground. Very common. All Divs.

First Record: C. Deering, *Cat. Stirp.* 1738.

Equisetum sylvaticum L. *Wood Horsetail*

Native. Woods and shady places, chiefly on the coal measures. Often in large quantity. Divs. 1, 3.

First Record: C. Deering, *Cat. Stirp.* 1738.

1 Pinxton Dumble; Annesley Dumble; Fulwood; East Kirkby.
3 Colwick Wood; Nottingham Coppice, *Deering*; Newark; Southwell, *Ordoyno*.

Equisetum fluviatile L. *Water Horsetail*

Native. Rivers, canals and other still waters. Common. All Divs. First Record: T. Ordoyno, *Fl. Nott.* 1807.

Equisetum palustre L. *Marsh Horsetail*

Native. Marshes and bogs. Common. All Divs.

First Record: C. Deering, *Cat. Stirp.* 1738.

Equisetum hyemale L. *Dutch Rush*

Native. Bogs. Extinct or very rare. Divs. 1, 3.

First Record: C. Deering, *Cat. Stirp.* 1738.

1 Nettleworth Green . . . plentifully, *Deering*; Mr. Wyld's Bottoms, Nettleworth; Woodhouse Lees, *Bird's MS.* quoted by *G. Howitt.*
3 Between Edingley and Kirklington Moors, *G. Howitt.*

POLYPODIACEAE

Pteris aquilina L. *Bracken*

Native. Woods, heaths, roadsides, etc., on light soils. Very common. All Divs.

First Record: C. Deering, *Cat. Stirp.* 1738.

Blechnum spicant (L.) With. *Hard Fern*

Native. Damp acid heathland and woods. Rare and decreasing. Divs. 2, 3, 4.

First Record: C. Deering, *Cat. Stirp.* 1738.

2 Bury Hills, Mansfield, *Deering*; Bulwell; Oxton; Linby, *Lowe* 1866; Manor Woods, Worksop, *Bohler* 1875; Bothamsall, *Carr MS.*; Annesley; Rainworth; Hesley; Coxmoor; Scaftworth.
3 Spalford; Besthorpe; Wigsley Wood.
4 Langford Moor†, *Ordoyno.*

Phyllitis Scolopendrium (L.) Newn. *Hart's tongue*

Native. Limestone woods, clay dumbles, and walls.

First Record: C. Deering, *Cat. Stirp.* 1738.

Widespread but never abundant, except in Div. 1. All Divs.

1 Frequent.
2 Oxton Bottoms, *Ordoyno*; Newstead; Wollaton; Clipstone; Welbeck; Retford; These last five records from walls.
3 Fairly frequent on walls. Wooded Dumbles at Gonalston and at Burton Joyce.
4 On walls at Sutton Bonington and at Barnstone.

Asplenium Trichomanes L. *Maidenhair Spleenwort*

Native. Old walls and railway bridges. Local. Divs. 1, 2, 3.

First Record: C. Deering, *Cat. Stirp.* 1738.

1 Fairly frequent.
2 Annesley Hall, *Deering*; Wollaton Park Walls, *Ordoyno*; Nottingham Park, *Jowett*; Welbeck.
3 Colwick Park Wall, *Jowett*; Sturton Church, *Miller*; Newark Castle; Stanford and Normanton-on-Soar; Farndon; North Clifton.

Asplenium Adiantum-nigrum L. *Black Spleenwort*

Native. Walls, rocks. Less common than the last. All Divs.

First Record: C. Deering, *Cat. Stirp.* 1738.

1 Stone quarries near Mansfield, *G. Howitt*; Steetley, *Bohler* 1875; Cresswell Crags.
2 About the Rock Holes in Nottingham Park, *Deering*, *Lowe* 1866; Wollaton; Highfield House, Nottingham, *Lowe* 1866; Welbeck.
3 Southwell Church, *Bird* (see *Jowett*); Caunton Church, *Reynolds*; River Wall, Littleborough, *Carr MS.*; Newark, Canal bridge; Stanford-on-Soar; Bingham; Laxton.
4 Colston Basset.

Asplenium Ruta-muraria L. *Wall Rue*

Native. Walls, railway bridges, rocks. The commonest of these three ferns. All Divs.

First Record: C. Deering, *Cat. Stirp.* 1738.

1 Common.
2 and 3 Frequent.
4 Sutton Bonington; Barnstone.

Athyrium Filix-foemina (L.) Roth. *Lady Fern*

Native. Damp woods, particularly round springs and streams. Common. All Divs.

First Record: T. Ordoyno, *Fl. Nott.* 1738.

Polystichum setiferum (Forsk.) Woynar. *Soft Shield Fern*

Native. Damp woodland, especially on the waterstones. Rather rare. Divs. 1, 2, 3.

First Record: E. J. Lowe's list in R. Allen's *Nottingham and its Environs* 1866.

1 *Victoria County History.*
2 In a wood near Stapleford, *Lowe.*
3 Cross Lane Osiers, Elston; Eakring Brail; Wellow Park, common; Margaret Springs, Oxton.

Polystichum aculeatum (L.) Roth. *Hard Shield Fern*

Native. Banks in woods, hedgebanks, dumbles. Widespread, but seldom occuring in quantity. All Divs.

First Record: C. Deering, *Cat. Stirp.* 1738.

1 Kimberley Toll Bar, *G. Howitt*; Mansfield, *Lowe*; Cresswell Crags; Pleasley Vale; Watnall.
2 Bleak Hills, Mansfield, *G. Howitt*; Wollaton; Bulwell (or 1); Papplewick, *Lowe* 1866.
3 Frequent.
4 Stanton-on-Wolds, *Lowe.*

Dryopteris Filix-mas (L.) Schott. *Male Fern*

Native. Woods, hedges, walls. Very common. All Divs.

First Record: C. Deering, *Cat. Stirp.* 1738.

var *incisa* Moore; Not uncommon, *Lowe* 1866.

Dryopteris Borreri Newn.

Native. Woods. In most woods in Divs. 1, 2 and 3 but not very abundant.

First Record: Margaret Springs, Oxton 1954, det. A. H. G. Alston.

Dryopteris cristata (L.) A. Gray. *Crested Buckler Fern*

Native. Woodland Bogs. Probably extinct. Div 2.

First Record: T. Jowett, *Bot. Cals.* 1826.

2 Oxton Bogs, *Jowett*, *Lowe* 1866, and was known from here until about the turn of the century; Bulwell Bog, *Lowe* 1866, and *Sidebotham* in *Newman's British Ferns.*

Dryopteris x uliginosa Kuntze. *D. cristata x spinulosa.*

2 Oxton Bogs, *Lowe* 1866.

Dryopteris spinulosa (Mull.) Watt. *Narrow Buckler Fern*

Native. Wet woods. Frequent except in 4. All Divs.

First Record: G. Howitt, *Notts. Fl.* 1839.

4 Frequent on the sand; West Leake.

Dryopteris dilatata (Hoffm.) A. Gray. *Broad Buckler Fern*

Native. Woods, hedges, walls. Very common. All Divs.

First Record: C. Deering, *Cat. Stirp.* 1738.

var *dumetorum* Moore: Rocks in Nottingham Park; Near Mansfield, *G. Howitt*; Mansfield, *Lowe* 1866. Div. 2.

var *tanacetifolia* Moore: Wollaton, *Lowe* 1866.

var *collina* Moore. Wollaton; Stanton-on-Wolds, *Lowe* 1866.

Thelypteris Oreopteris (Ehrh.) C.Chr. *Sweet Mountain Fern*

Native. Moist woods on sand and waterstones. Rare. Divs. 2, 3.

First Record: T. Jowett, *Bot. Cals.* 1826.

2 Oxton Bogs, *Jowett*; Bulwell, *Lowe*; Coxmoor, Kirkby; Drain-side at Misson.

3 Hartswell near Farnsfield, *G. Howitt*; Margaret Springs, Oxton; New Park Rufford; Wigsley Wood; Spalford.

Thelypteris palustris Schott. *Marsh Fern*

Native. Shady Bogs. Probably extinct. Div. 2.

First Record: T. Jowett, *Bot. Cals.* 1826.

2 Oxton Bogs, *Jowett*. It was seen here by Mr. R. M. Payne in 1944, but the Bogs have dried out a lot recently and we have been unable to find the fern in his locality; (Coxmoor, Kirkby, *Hopkinson*, probably in error for *T. Oreopteris*.)

(**Thelypteris Dryopteris** (L.) Slosson. *Oak Fern*

This is recorded for Pleasley Forges in Turner and Dillwyn's *Botanist's Guide* 1805 and Ordoyno's *Flora Nottinghamiensis* 1807, on the authority of Deering's *Filix ramosa minor* Syn. 125. The locality is doubtfully in Nottinghamshire, and we agree with G. Howitt that the plant was probably *Cystopteris fragilis*.)

Cystopteris fragilis (L.) Bernh. *Brittle Bladder Fern*

Native. Limestone rocks and old walls. Very rare. Divs. 1, 2.

First Record: T. Ordoyno, *Fl. Nott.* 1807.

1 Pleasley Wood, *G. Howitt*; Basford Old Church, *Lowe*; Walls in Pleasley Vale; Near Newbound Mill by Mansfield; Lock Walls, Eastwood.

2 Oxton Church, *Ordoyno* per *Miss Piggott*; Wall near Nottingham Forest, *Gilbert*; Railway Bridge, Manton Wood.

Polypodium vulgare L. *Common Polypody*

Native. Rocks, walls and sandy hedgebanks. Uncommon. All Divs.

First Record: C. Deering, *Cat. Stirp.* 1738.

1 Cresswell Crags; Wall at Mansfield Woodhouse.
2 Nottingham Park and Nottingham Sandhills, *Deering*; Sparken Hill, Worksop; Hundred Acre Wood, Carlton-in-Lindrick, *Bohler* 1875; Walls of Blyth Church, *Carr MS.*; Derby Road, Nottingham; Bulwell, *Gilbert*; Wall at Cuckney.
3 Walls of the Palace at Southwell, *Ordoyno*; Wall at Epperstone; By Egmanton Wood; Spalford, *Carr MS.*; Wigsley Wood.
4 Hedge at Wigsley; Hedge at Barnby; Coddington Golf Course.

Ceterach officinarum DC. *Rustyback*

Native. Walls. Rare. Divs. 2, 3.

First Record: T. Jowett, *Bot. Cals.* 1826.

2 One plant on Nottingham Castle, *Lowe* 1866; Wall by Welbeck Lake.
3 Colwick Park Wall, *Jowett, Lowe* 1866; Walls at Normanton-on-Soar; Railway Bridge at Stanford-on-Soar, a lot.

OSMUNDACEAE

Osmunda regalis L. *Royal Fern*

Native. Bogs. Very rare. All Divs.

First Record: C. Deering, *Cat. Stirp.* 1738.

1 Leaver's Close, Mansfield, *Deering*; Hedge near Bulwell Hall, *Jowett.*
2 Old Gravel pits at Finningley, about twenty small plants 1956, flourishing in 1961.
3 Wigsley Wood, *Cole.*
4 Stapleford (i.e. Langford) Moor; The Hollow near Potter's Hill, Collingham; Mr. Jacob Ordoyno's Carr Closes at Coddington, *Ordoyno.*

OPHIOGLOSSACEAE

Botrychium Lunaria (L.) Sw. *Moonwort*

Native. Meadows and heaths. Rare. Divs. 1, 2, 3.

1 Eastwood, *Deering*; Mansfield Race Course, *G. Howitt.*
2 Stapleford Cloud, *Tutin* (see *Jowett*); Edwinstowe Forest, *Ordoyno*; Near Newstead; Mansfield Forest, *G. Howitt*; Ranskill; Barrow Hills, Everton.
3 Sutton-on-Trent, *Ordoyno*; Clifton Cow Pasture (by Nottingham), *Jowett*; Laxton Pastures; East Markham; Meadow by the Lincoln Road, *Carr MS.*

Ophioglossum vulgatum L. *Adder's Tongue*

Native. Moist meadows and woodland rides. Still fairly frequent, less so in Div. 4. All Divs.

First Record: C. Deering, *Cat. Stirp.* 1738.

LYCOPODIACEAE

Lycopodium clavatum L. *Stag's Horn Club Moss*

Native. Heaths. Now very rare. Div. 2.

First Record: T. Ordoyno, *Fl. Nott.* 1807.

2 Mansfield Forest, *Ordoyno*, *G. Howitt*; Frequent on Sherwood Forest, *Bohler* 1875; Welbeck, *Friend* 1900; Finningley Gravel Pit; Ride side, Clipstone Forest.

Lycopodium inundatum L. *Marsh Club Moss*

Native. Acid Bogs. Probably extinct. Div. 2.

Only Record: G. Howitt, *Notts. Fl.* 1839. Bogs on the Rainworth Water.

Lycopodium Selago L. *Fir Tree Club Moss*

Native. Heaths. Probably extinct. Div. 2.

Only Record: G. Howitt, *Notts. Fl.* 1839, "Rare; Mansfield Forest near the gate leading to Blidworth."

CHARACEAE

Nitella opaca Ag.

Native. Drains and ponds. Local. Divs. 1, 2, 3.

First Record: Mrs. Sandwith in J. W. Carr's MS. 1916.

1 or 2 Harworth, *Mrs. Sandwith.*
2 Annesley Lake; Wollaton Park Lake.
3 In the canal near Misterton, *Mrs. Sandwith.*

Nitella flexilis Ag.

Native. Streams and drains, chiefly on peat. Rare. Divs. 1, 2, 4.

First Record: T. Jowett, *Bot. Cals.* 1826.

1 Spring at Kirkby Hardwick, *Jowett*; Spring on Sutton Forest by the railway, *G. Howitt*; Near Worksop, *Searle.*
2 Spring on Bulwell Forest, *G. Howitt*; Finningley.
4 Langford Moor.

Tolypella prolifera Leonh.

Native. Canals. Rare. Div. 1.

Only Records: Nottingham Canal at Wollaton 1953, and Awsworth 1961.

Tolypella glomerata Leonh.

Native. Lakes. Very rare. Div. 1.

Only Record: Langold Lake in fair quantity 1959.

Chara vulgaris L.

Native. Ponds, drains, canals. Rather frequent. All Divs.

First Record: C. Deering, *Cat. Stirp.* 1738.

var *longbracteata* Kuetz.

1 Nottingham Canal between Newthorpe and Awsworth, *Carr MS.*
2 Warping Drain, Misson, *Mrs. Sandwith.*
3 Canal at Misterton, *Mrs. Sandwith*; Brook in the Park, Kingston-on-Soar, *Carr MS.*

var *papillata* Wallr. is as common as the type.

var *refracta* Kuetz.

2 New Ballast Pits, Misson.
3 Canal at Misterton, *Mrs. Sandwith.*

Chara hispida L.

Native. Streams, ponds, drains and canals, especially on limestone. Frequent. All Divs.

First Record: C. Deering, *Cat. Stirp.* 1738.

Chara contraria Kuetz.

Native. Very rare. Div. 1.

Only Record: Pond in the brickyard, Sutton-in-Ashfield 1895, *Carr MS.*

Chara aspera Willd.

Native. Lakes and ponds. Rare. Divs. 1, 3.

First Record: Mrs. Sandwith in J. W. Carr's MS., *c.*1916.

1 Lake at Langold, *Mrs. Sandwith.*
3 Ballast Pits at Misterton.

Chara globularis Thuill.

Native. Canals and streams. Rare. Divs. 2, 3.

First Record: Mrs. Sandwith in J. W. Carr's MS. 1918.

2 In the R. Poulter at Hardwick Grange, Clumber, *Mrs. Sandwith.*
3 Canal near Misterton, *Mrs. Sandwith.*

var *capillacea* (Thuill) Zanev.

Native. Canals and ponds. Widespread. Divs. 1, 2, 3.

First Record: J. W. Carr MS. as *C. fragilis* Desv.

1 Nottingham Canal between Awsworth and Newthorpe; Sutton-in-Ashfield Brickyard; Shireoaks Park; Hills and Holes, Warsop, *Carr MS.*
2 Pond near Idle Stop, Misson, *Mrs. Sandwith*; Bestwood Duck-ponds.
3 Chesterfield Canal, Misterton, *Carr MS.*; R. Idle, Misterton Soss; Attenborough gravel pits.

Chara delicatula Ag.

Native. Drains and ponds, chiefly on peat. Very local. Divs. 1, 2.

First Record: Drain on the Bombing Range, Misson 1954.

1 Brick pit at Awsworth.
2 Misson; Drains at Finningley; Ballast Pits at Barnby Moor.

We would like to record our thanks to Mr. G. O. Allen who has been most kind in determining specimens in this family.

Musci

SPHAGNACEAE

We are not competent to write on the mosses of Notts., but since the bogs of the county are rapidly drying out it seems a pity not to include the following records of *Sphagnum*. We should like to thank Miss Ursula Duncan who has named our own specimens.

Sphagnum palustre L.

Native. Divs. 2, 3.

2 J. W. Carr in *Victoria County History*; Vicar Water, Clipstone.
3 Calverton Moor.

Sphagnum papillosum Lindb.

2 J. W. Carr in *Victoria County History* 1906.

Sphagnum compactum DC.

2 Oxton Forest, *G. Howitt.*

Sphagnum squarrosum Pers. ex Crome.

2 Oxton Bogs, *G. Howitt*, per *W. Valentine*; Annesley Lake; Ling's Wood, Scaftworth.

Sphagnum recurvum P. Beauv.

1 Balloon Houses Wood, Trowell.
2 J. W. Carr in *Victoria County History* 1906.

Sphagnum cuspidatum Ehrh.

2 J. Bohler in White's *Worksop*, 'wet places by the rivers' sides.'

Sphagnum subsecundum Nees. var. *auriculatum* (Schp.) Lindb.

2 Osberton Flash Wood.
4 J. W. Carr in *Victoria County History*.

Sphagnum acutifolium Ehrh.

2 In bogs, very common, *G. Howitt*; In wet places by the rivers' sides, *Bohler* in White's *Worksop*.

Sphagnum fimbriatum Wils.

2 Vicar Water, Clipstone; Coxmoor, East Kirkby; Hesley; Harworth in two places; Ling's Wood, Scaftworth; Hundred Acre Wood, Carlton-in-Lindrick.

Sphagnum Girgensohnii Russ.

2 Osberton Flash Wood.

Sphagnum plumulosum Roell.

1 Stanley.
2 J. W. Carr in *Victoria County History*; By Annesley Lake; Railway cutting at Rainworth; Hesley; Finningley.

Sphagnum fallax Kling.

2 J. W. Carr in *Victoria County History* 1906.

INDEX